8

CLAMP

TRANSLATED AND ADAPTED BY
William Flanagan

LETTERED BY
Dana Hayward

BALLANTINE BOOKS · NEW YORK

A Del Rey Trade Paperback Original

xxxHOLiC vol. 8 copyright © 2006 by CLAMP
English translation copyright © 2006 by CLAMP

Published in the United States by Del Rey Books, an imprint of The Random House Publishing Group, a division of Random House, Inc., New York.

DEL REY is a registered trademark and the Del Rey colophon is a trademark of Random House, Inc.

Publication rights arranged through Kodansha Ltd.

First published in Japan in 2006 by Kodansha Ltd., Tokyo.

ISBN-10: 0-345-48336-7
ISBN-13: 978-0-345-48336-2

Printed in the United States of America

www.delreymanga.com

9   8   7   6   5

Translator and Adaptor—William Flanagan
Lettering—Dana Hayward

xxxHOLiC crosses over with *Tsubasa*. Although it isn't necessary to read *Tsubasa* to understand the events in *xxxHOLiC*, you'll get to see the same events from different perspectives if you read both series!

Contents

Honorifics Explained

Throughout the Del Rey Manga books, you will find Japanese honorifics left intact in the translations. For those not familiar with how the Japanese use honorifics and, more important, how they differ from American honorifics, we present this brief overview.

Politeness has always been a critical facet of Japanese culture. Ever since the feudal era, when Japan was a highly stratified society, use of honorifics—which can be defined as polite speech that indicates relationship or status—has played an essential role in the Japanese language. When addressing someone in Japanese, an honorific usually takes the form of a suffix attached to one's name (example: "Asuna-san"), or as a title at the end of one's name, or in place of the name itself (example: "Negi-sensei," or simply "Sensei!").

Honorifics can be expressions of respect or endearment. In the context of manga and anime, honorifics give insight into the nature of the relationship between characters. Many English translations leave out these important honorifics, and therefore distort the feel of the original Japanese. Because Japanese honorifics contain nuances that English honorifics lack, it is our policy at Del Rey not to translate them. Here, instead, is a guide to some of the honorifics you may encounter in Del Rey Manga.

-san: This is the most common honorific, and is equivalent to Mr., Miss, Ms., Mrs. It is the all-purpose honorific and can be used in any situation where politeness is required.

-sama: This is one level higher than "-san." It is used to confer great respect.

-dono: This comes from the word "tono," which means "lord." It is an even higher level than "-sama" and confers utmost respect.

-kun: This suffix is used at the end of boys' names to express familiarity or endearment. It is also sometimes used by men amongst friends, or when addressing someone younger or of a lower station.

-chan: This is used to express endearment, mostly toward girls. It is also used for little boys, pets, and even among lovers. It gives a sense of childish cuteness.

Bozu: This is an informal way to refer to a boy, similar to the English term "kid" or "squirt."

Sempai/Senpai: This title suggests that the addressee is one's senior in a group or organization. It is most often used in a school setting, where underclassmen refer to their upperclassmen as "sempai." It can also be used in the workplace, such as when a newer employee addresses an employee who has seniority in the company.

Kohai: This is the opposite of "sempai," and is used toward underclassmen in school or newcomers in the workplace. It connotes that the addressee is of a lower station.

Sensei: Literally meaning "one who has come before," this title is used for teachers, doctors, or masters of any profession or art.

-[blank]: This is usually forgotten in these lists, but it is perhaps the most significant difference between Japanese and English. The lack of honorific means that the speaker has permission to address the person in a very intimate way. Usually, only family, spouses, or very close friends have this kind of permission. Known as *yobisute*, it can be gratifying when someone who has earned the intimacy starts to call one by one's name without an honorific. But when that intimacy hasn't been earned, it can be very insulting.

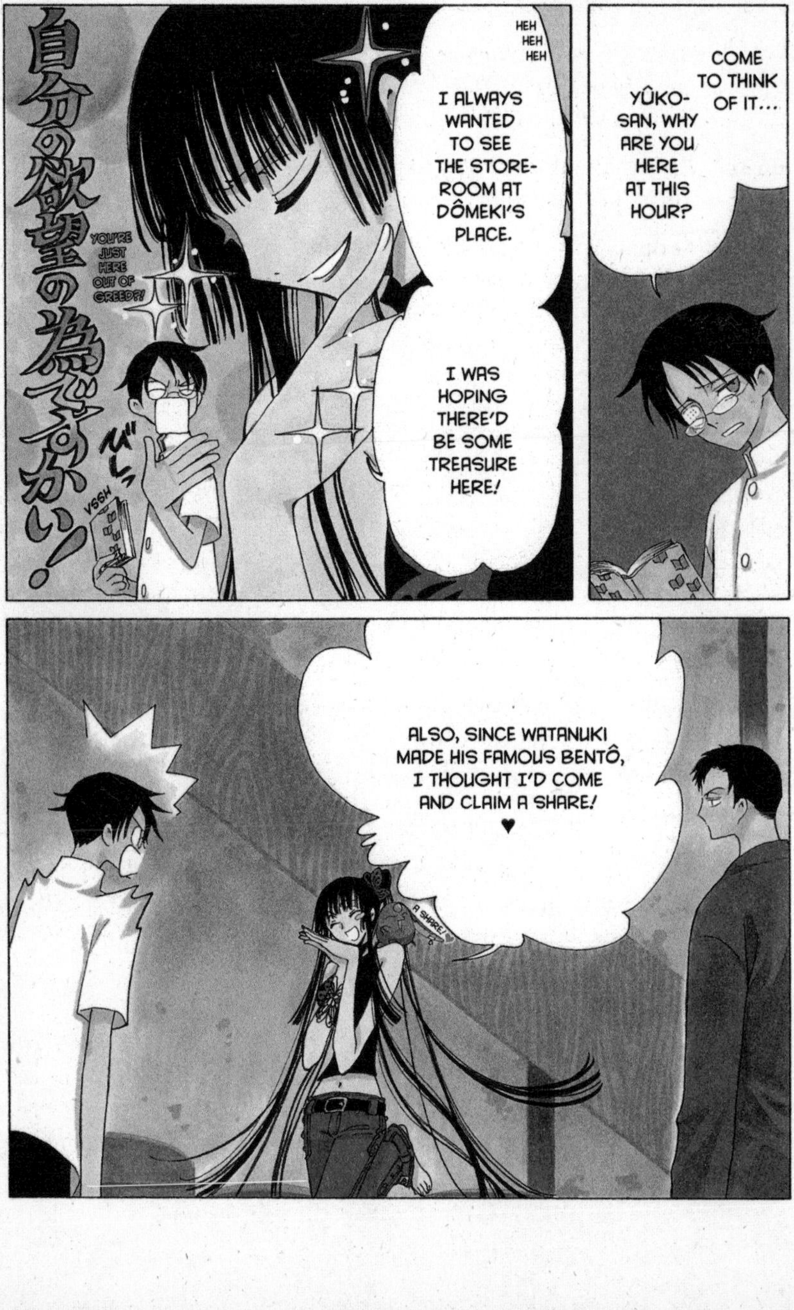
COME TO THINK OF IT...
YÛKO-SAN, WHY ARE YOU HERE AT THIS HOUR?
HEH HEH HEH
I ALWAYS WANTED TO SEE THE STORE-ROOM AT DÔMEKI'S PLACE.
I WAS HOPING THERE'D BE SOME TREASURE HERE!
自分の欲望の為ですかい!
YOU'RE JUST HERE OUT OF GREED?!
びしっ
VSSH
ALSO, SINCE WATANUKI MADE HIS FAMOUS BENTÔ, I THOUGHT I'D COME AND CLAIM A SHARE! ♥
A SHARE! ♥

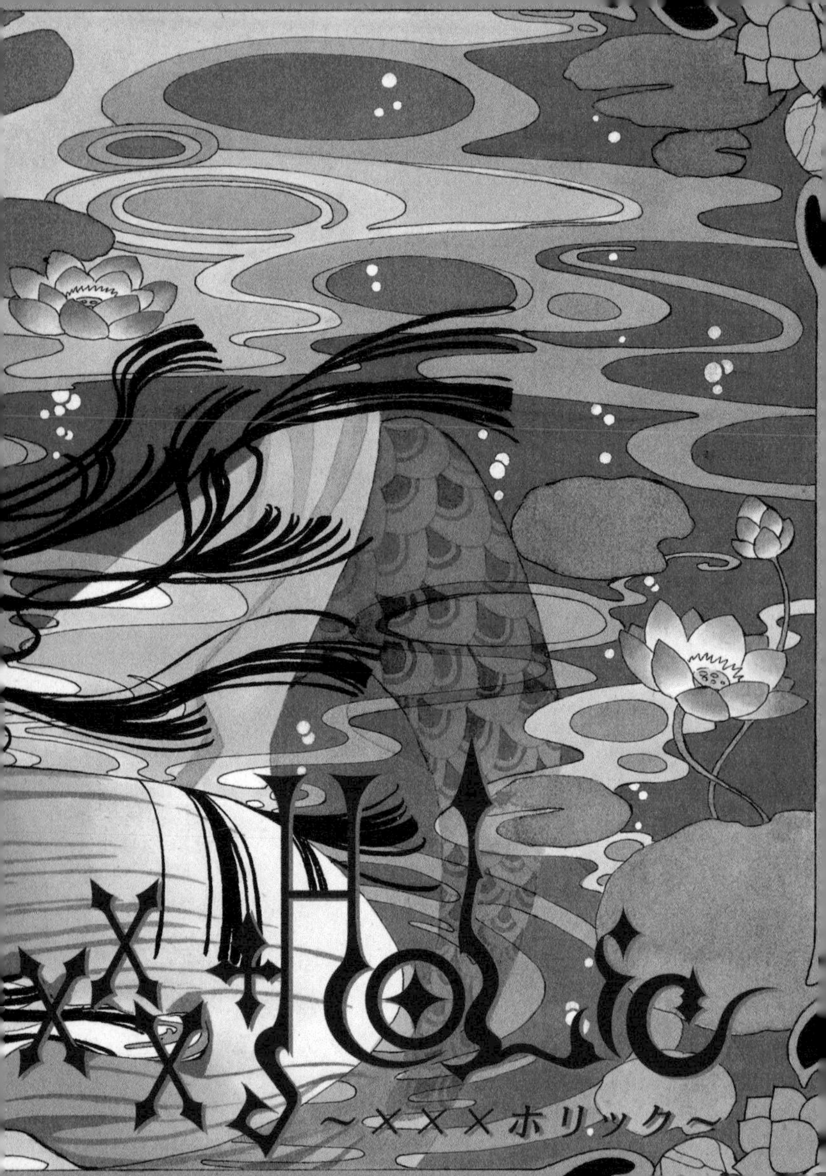
xxxHOLiC
~×××ホリック~

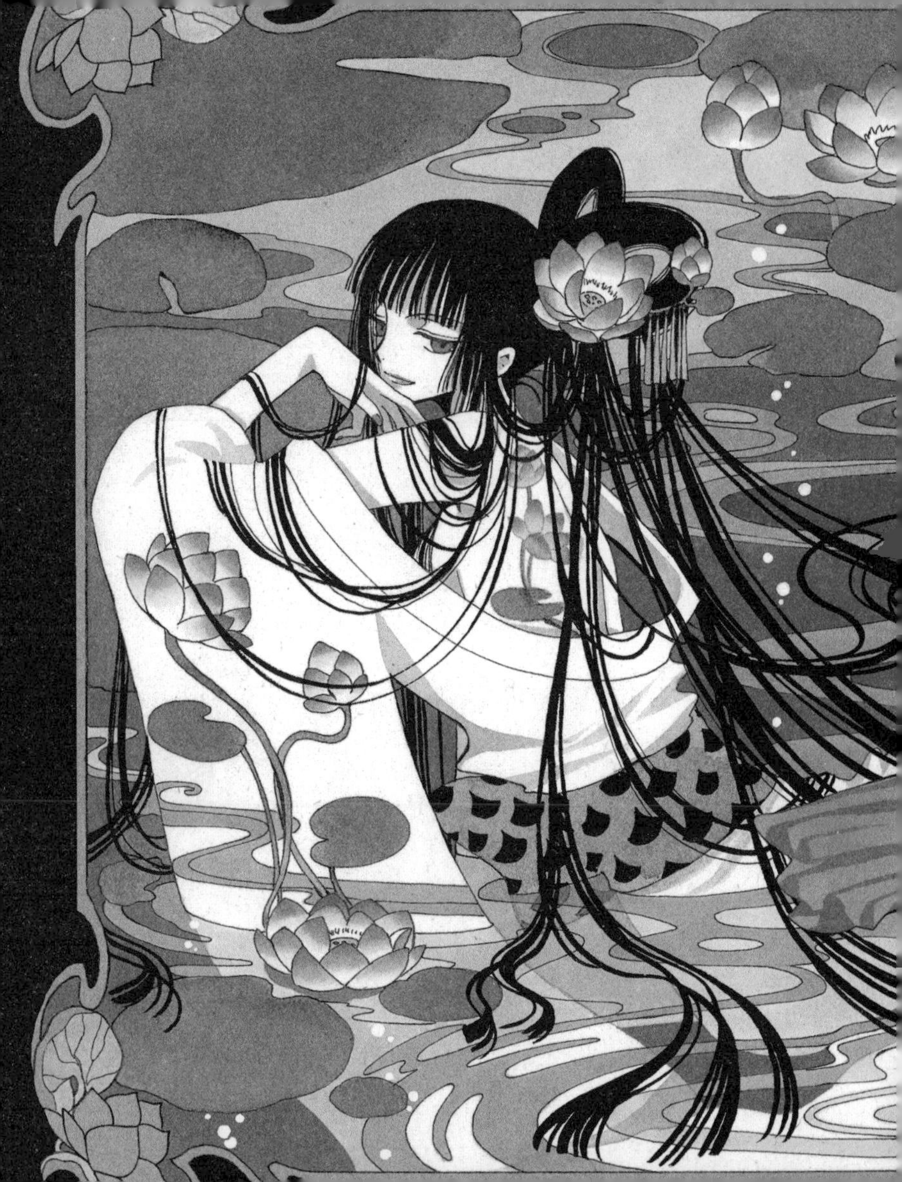

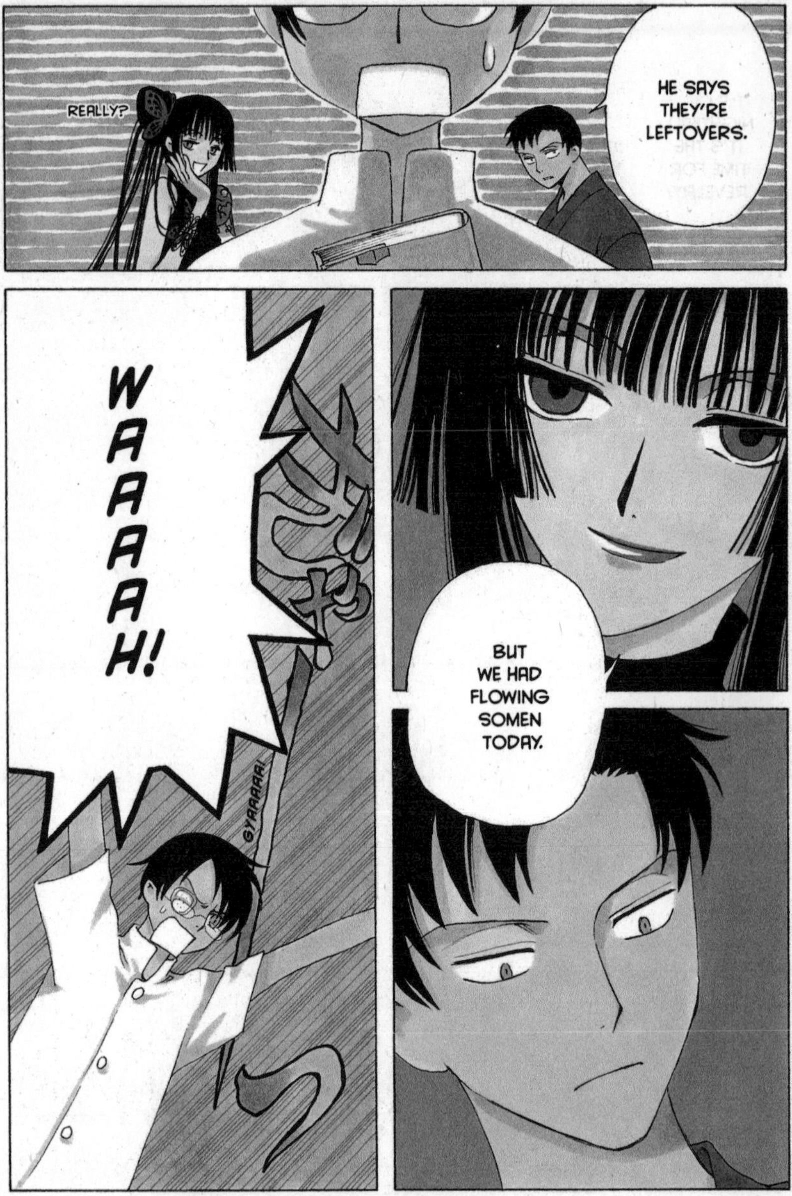
HE SAYS THEY'RE LEFTOVERS.
REALLY?
BUT WE HAD FLOWING SOMEN TODAY.
WAAAAAH!
GYAAAAA!

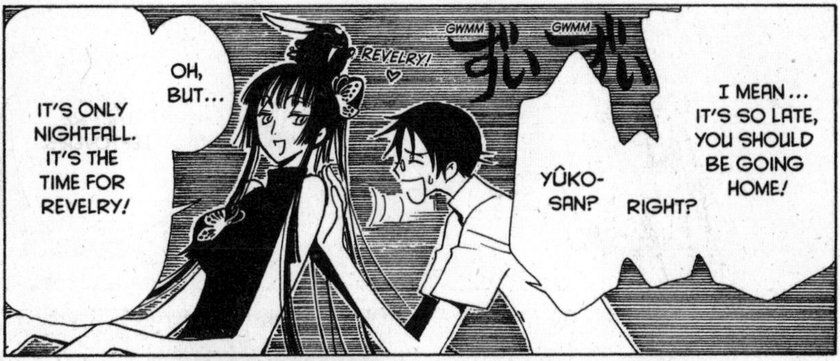
I MEAN... IT'S SO LATE, YOU SHOULD BE GOING HOME!
RIGHT?
YÛKO-SAN?
GWMM
GWMM
REVELRY!
OH, BUT...
IT'S ONLY NIGHTFALL. IT'S THE TIME FOR REVELRY!
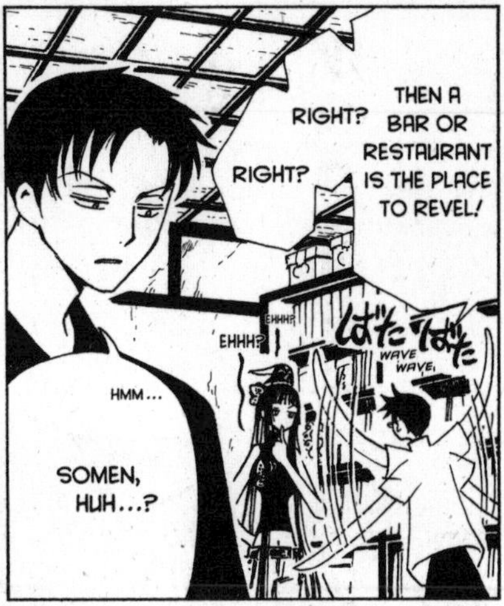
THEN A BAR OR RESTAURANT IS THE PLACE TO REVEL!
RIGHT?
RIGHT?
WAVE WAVE
EHHH?
EHHH?
HMM...
SOMEN, HUH...?
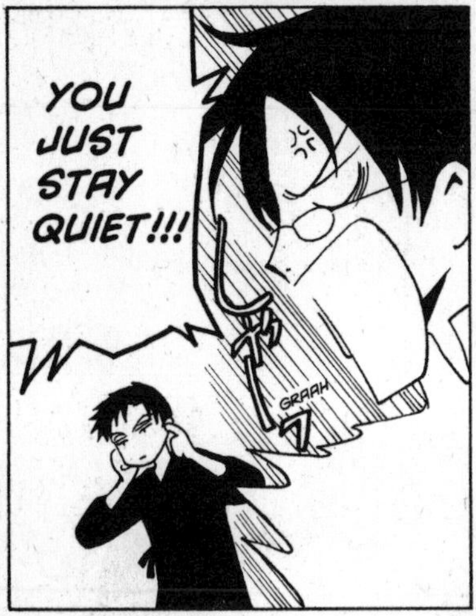
YOU JUST STAY QUIET!!!
GRAAH
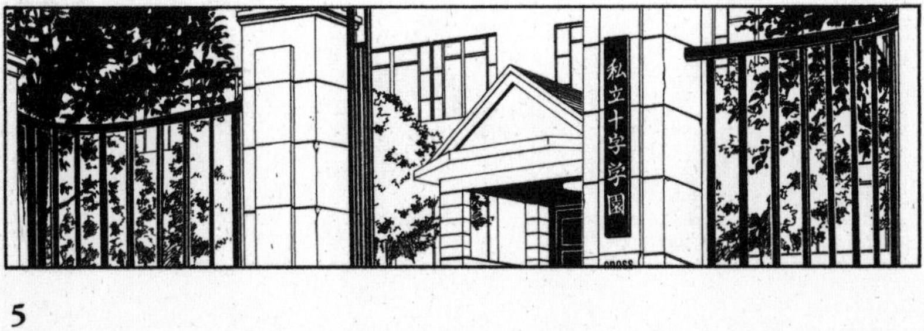
私立十字学園
CROSS

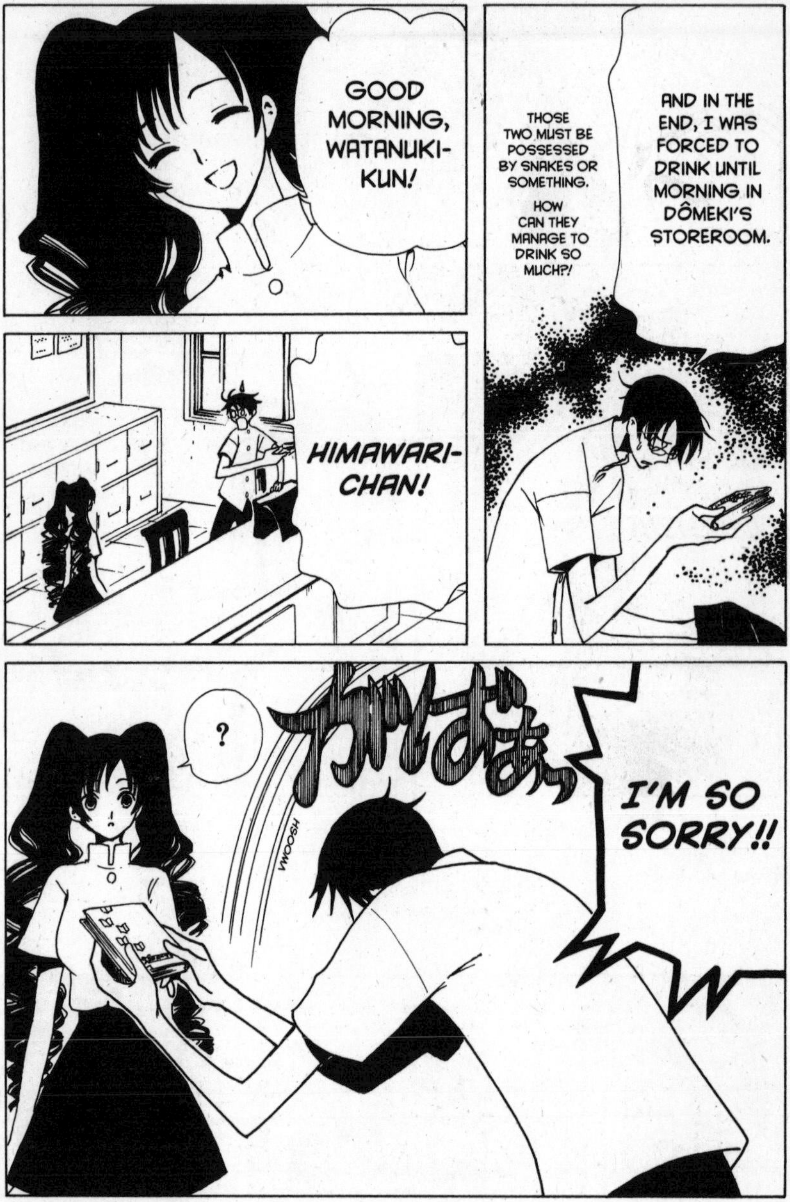
AND IN THE END, I WAS FORCED TO DRINK UNTIL MORNING IN DÔMEKI'S STOREROOM.
THOSE TWO MUST BE POSSESSED BY SNAKES OR SOMETHING.
HOW CAN THEY MANAGE TO DRINK SO MUCH?!
GOOD MORNING, WATANUKI-KUN!
HIMAWARI-CHAN!
I'M SO SORRY!!
?
VWOOSH

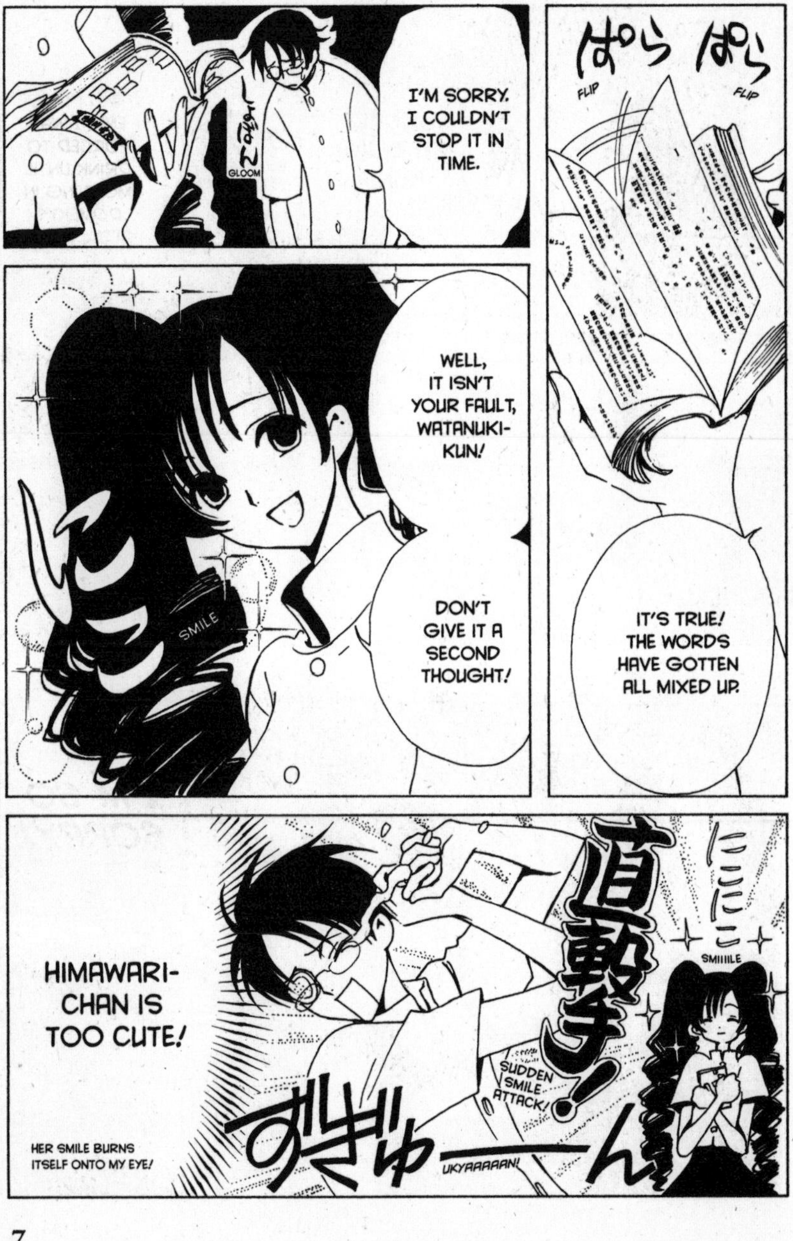
ぱら ぱら
FLIP
FLIP
IT'S TRUE! THE WORDS HAVE GOTTEN ALL MIXED UP.
GLOOM
I'M SORRY. I COULDN'T STOP IT IN TIME.
WELL, IT ISN'T YOUR FAULT, WATANUKI-KUN!
DON'T GIVE IT A SECOND THOUGHT!
SMILE
SMIIIILE
SUDDEN SMILE ATTACK!
UKYAAAAAN!
HIMAWARI-CHAN IS TOO CUTE!
HER SMILE BURNS ITSELF ONTO MY EYE!

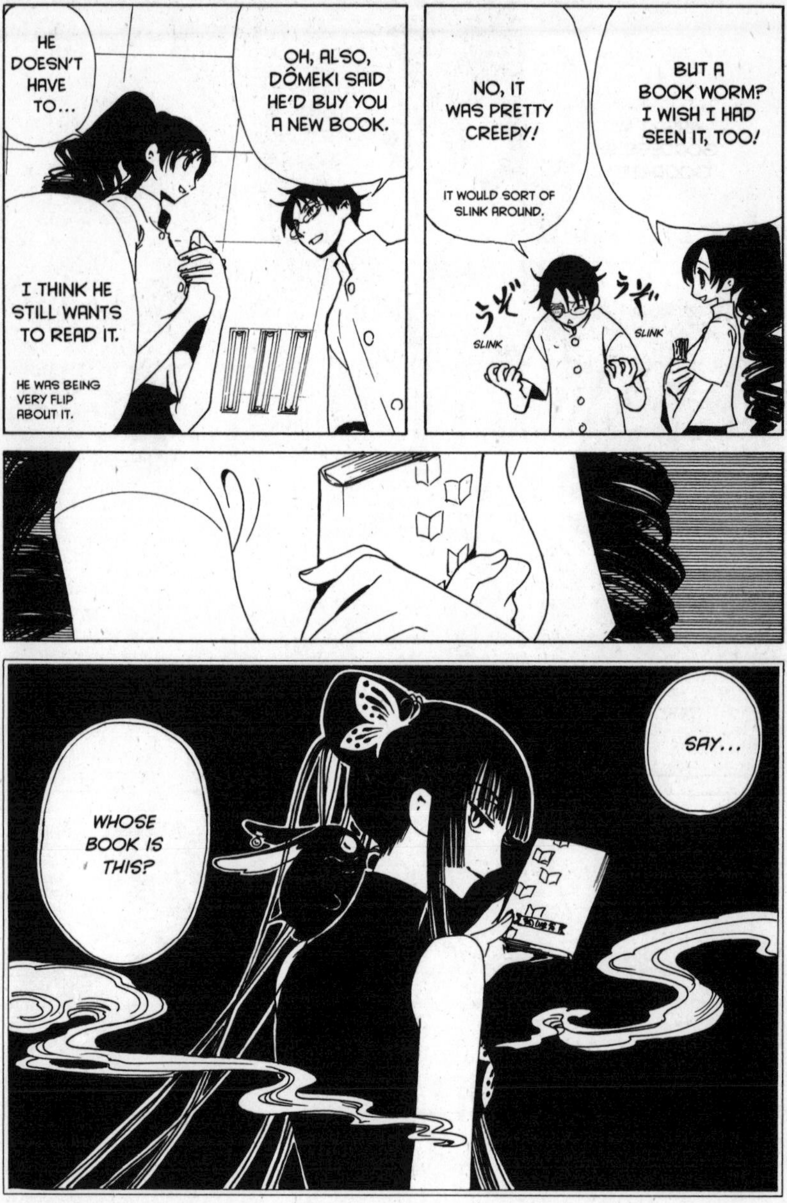
BUT A BOOK WORM? I WISH I HAD SEEN IT, TOO!
NO, IT WAS PRETTY CREEPY!
IT WOULD SORT OF SLINK AROUND.
うぞ
SLINK
うぞ
SLINK
OH, ALSO, DÔMEKI SAID HE'D BUY YOU A NEW BOOK.
HE DOESN'T HAVE TO...
I THINK HE STILL WANTS TO READ IT.
HE WAS BEING VERY FLIP ABOUT IT.
SAY...
WHOSE BOOK IS THIS?

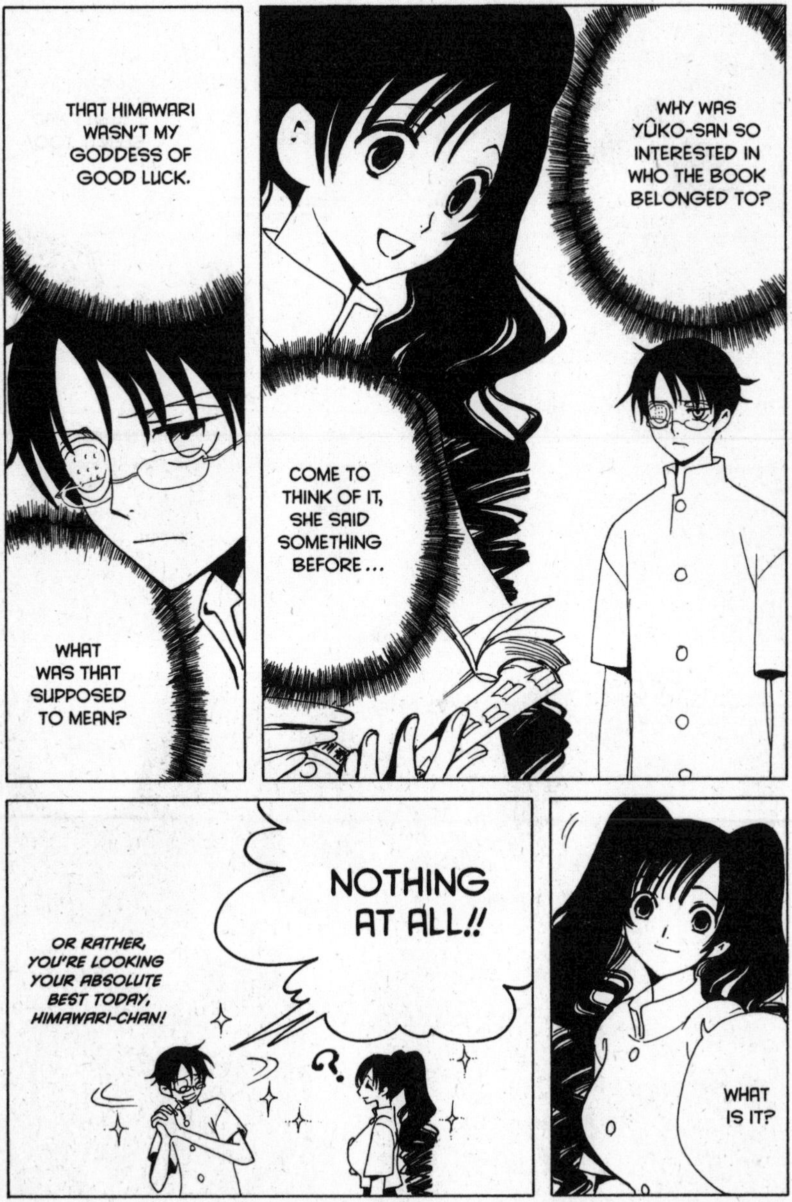
WHY WAS YÛKO-SAN SO INTERESTED IN WHO THE BOOK BELONGED TO?
COME TO THINK OF IT, SHE SAID SOMETHING BEFORE...
THAT HIMAWARI WASN'T MY GODDESS OF GOOD LUCK.
WHAT WAS THAT SUPPOSED TO MEAN?
WHAT IS IT?
NOTHING AT ALL!!
OR RATHER, YOU'RE LOOKING YOUR ABSOLUTE BEST TODAY, HIMAWARI-CHAN!

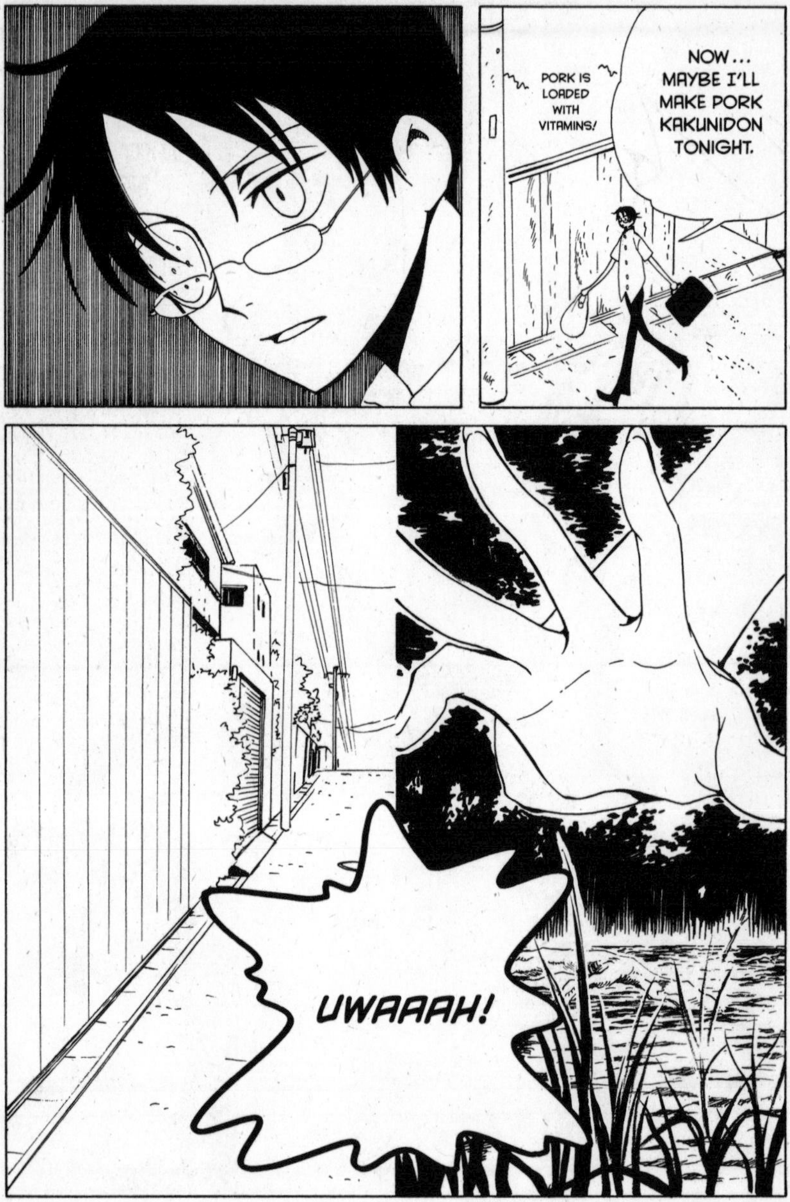
NOW... MAYBE I'LL MAKE PORK KAKUNIDON TONIGHT.
PORK IS LOADED WITH VITAMINS!
UWAAAH!

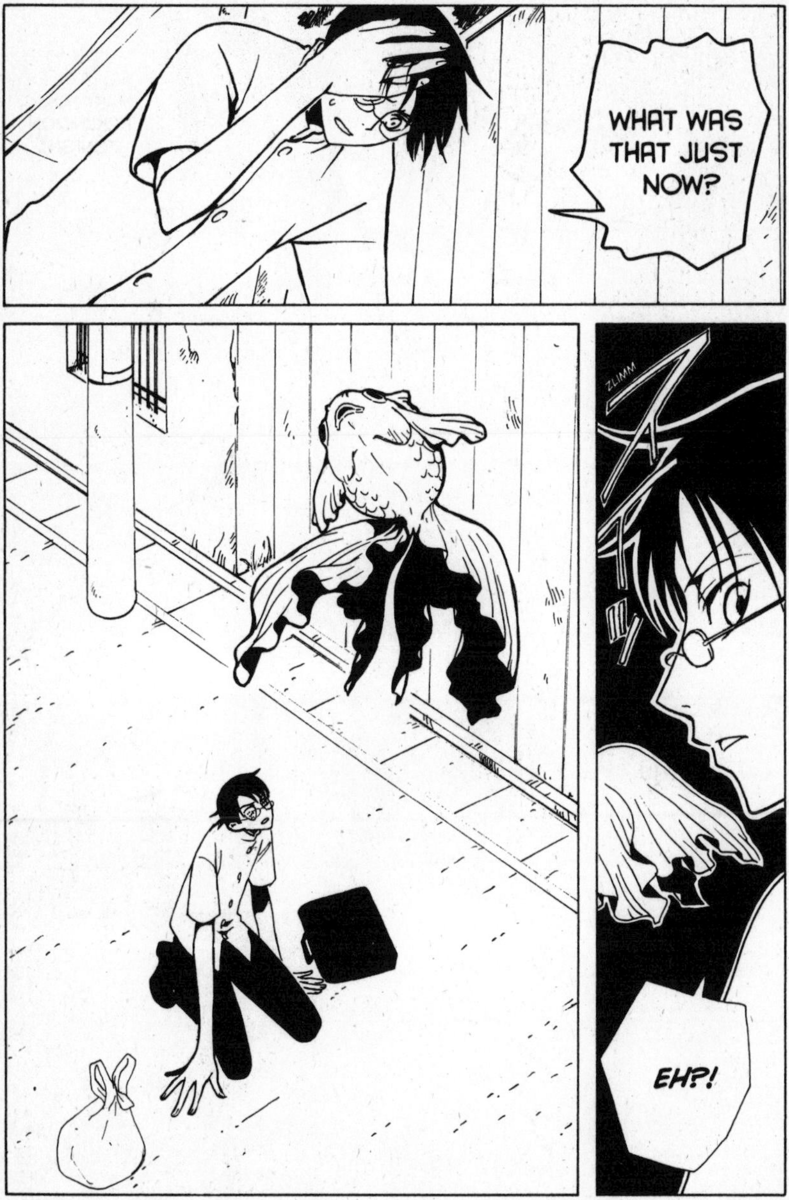
WHAT WAS THAT JUST NOW?
ZLIMM
EH?!

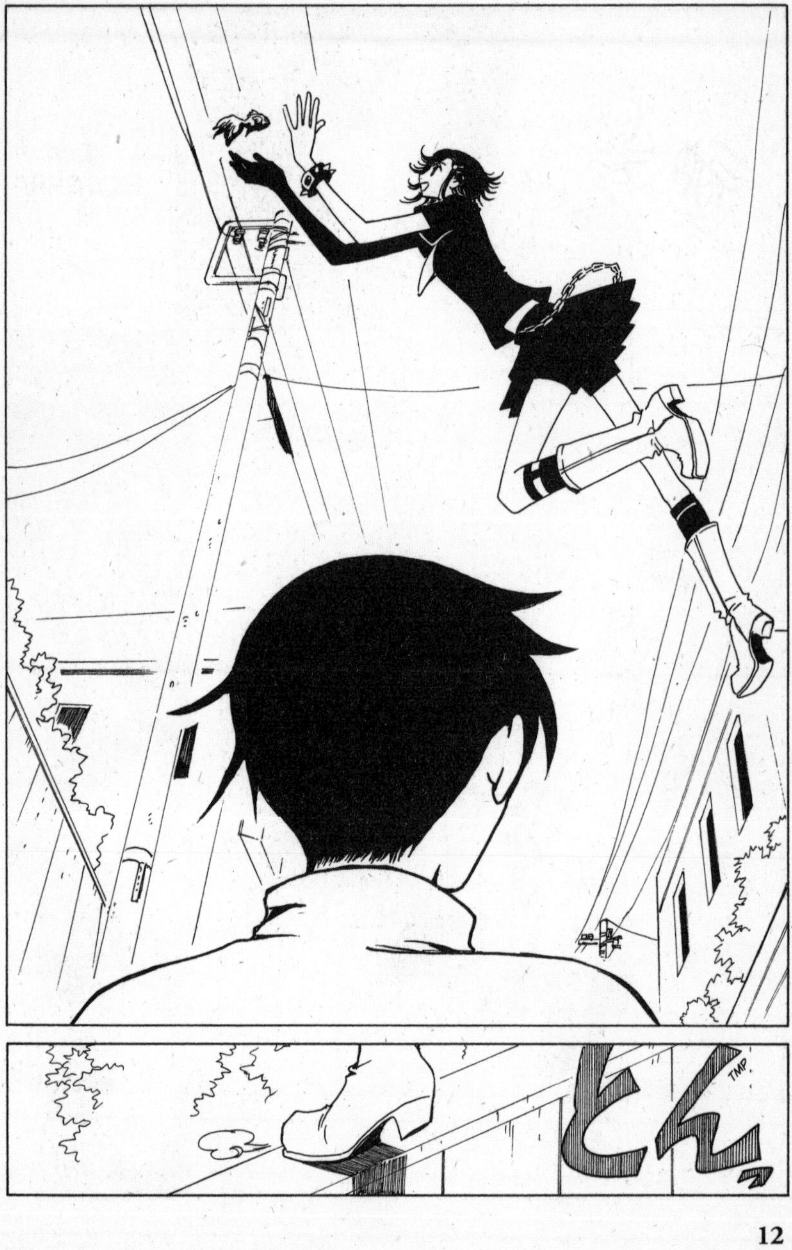
とん
TMP.

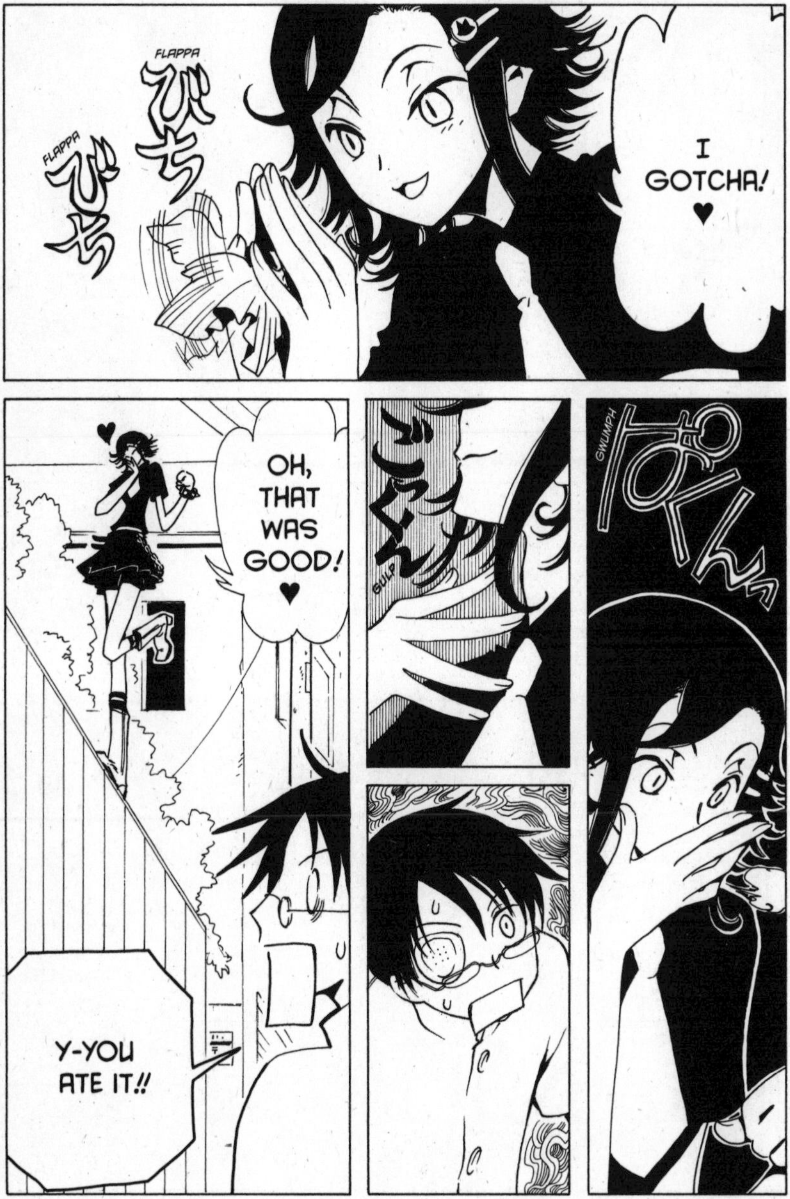

I GOTCHA! ♥
FLAPPA
びち
FLAPPA
びち
GWUMPH
ぱくん
GULP
ごっくん
OH, THAT WAS GOOD! ♥
Y-YOU ATE IT!!

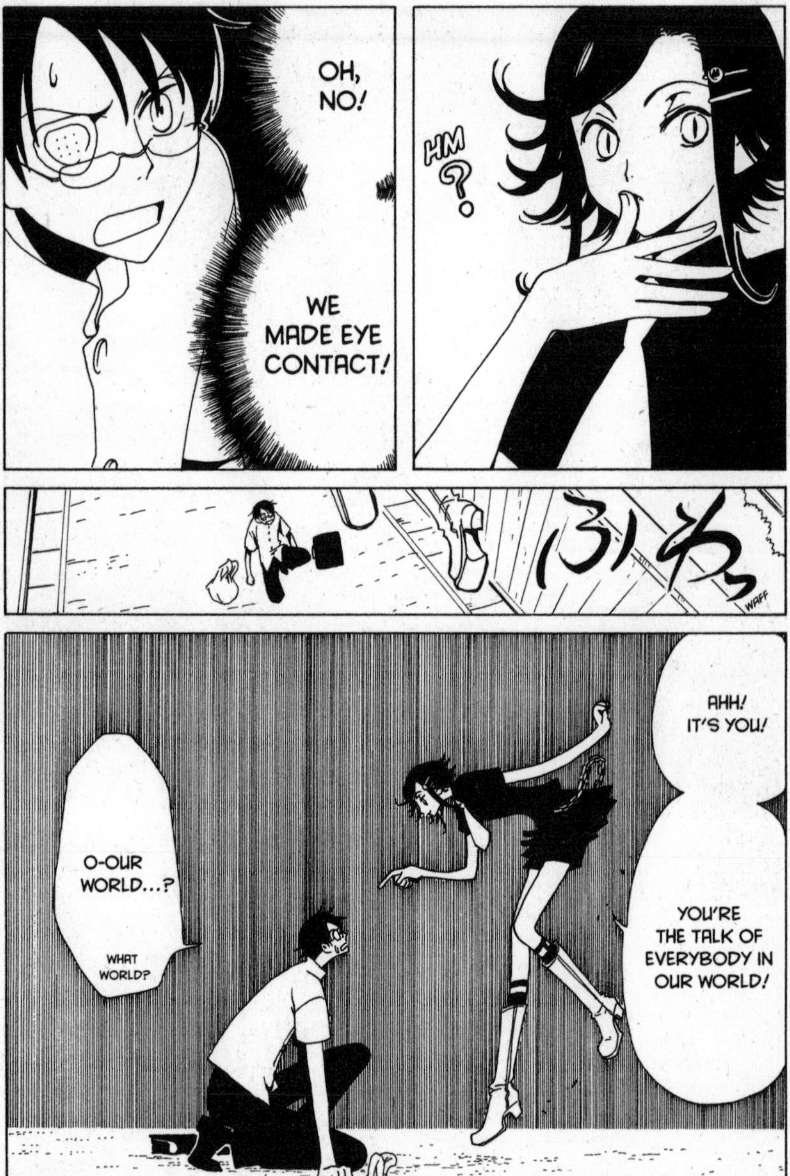
HM?
OH, NO!
WE MADE EYE CONTACT!
ふわっ
WAFF
AHH! IT'S YOU!
YOU'RE THE TALK OF EVERYBODY IN OUR WORLD!
O-OUR WORLD...?
WHAT WORLD?

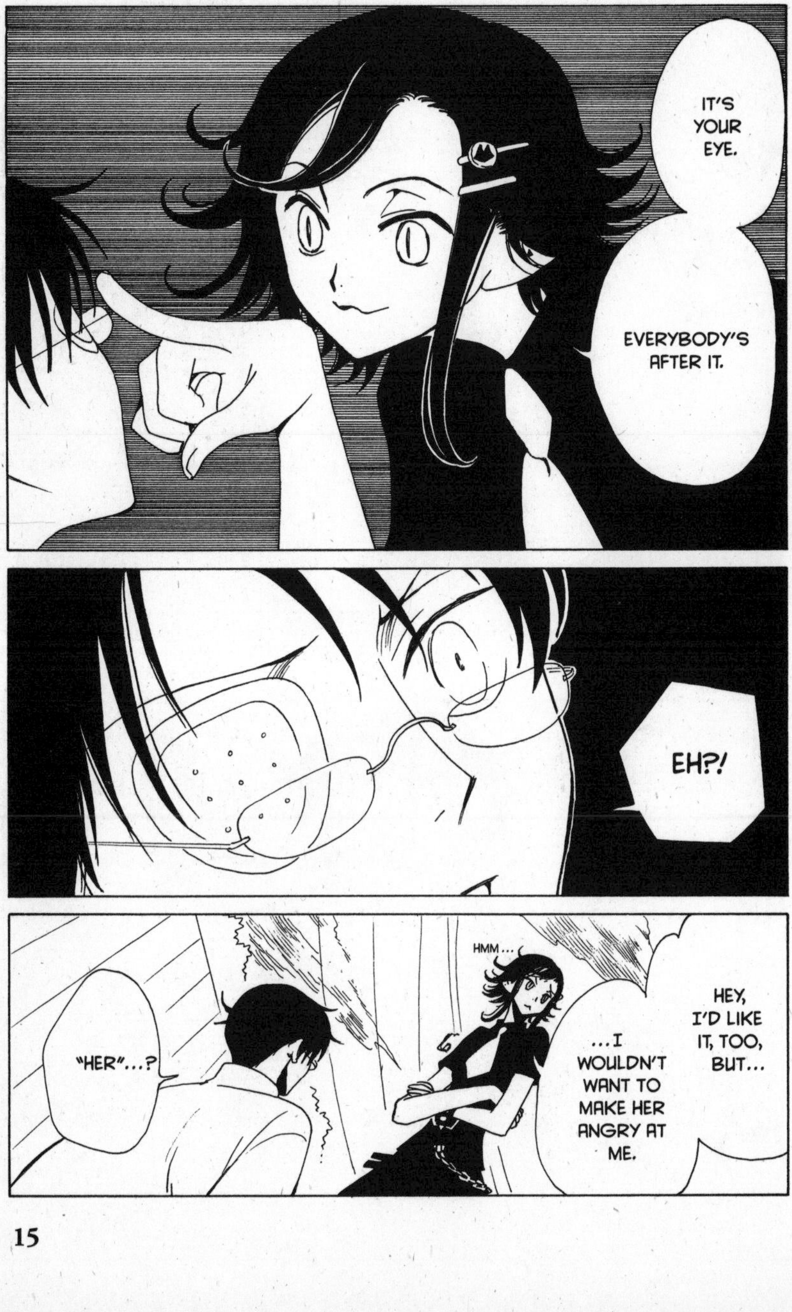
IT'S YOUR EYE.
EVERYBODY'S AFTER IT.
EH?!
HEY, I'D LIKE IT, TOO, BUT...
...I WOULDN'T WANT TO MAKE HER ANGRY AT ME.
HMM...
"HER"...?

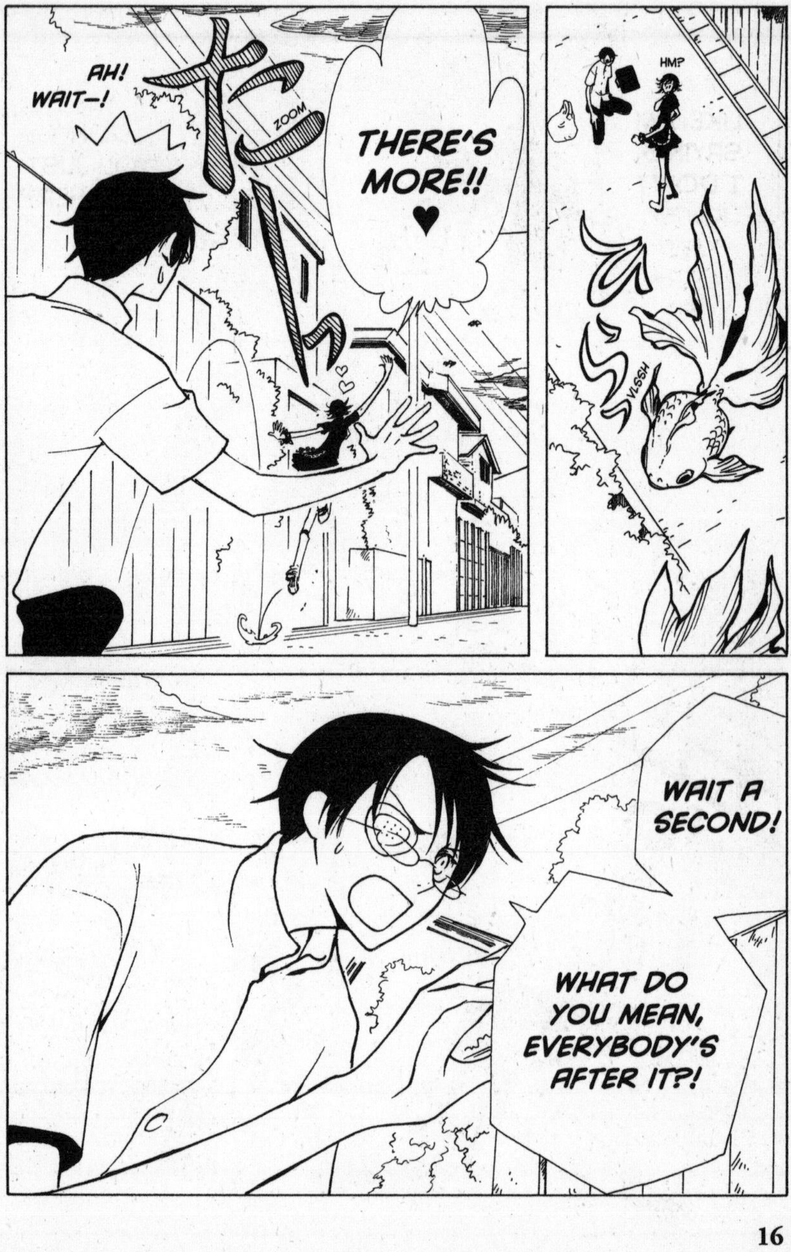
HM?
VLSSH
THERE'S MORE!! ♥
ZOOM
AH! WAIT–!
WAIT A SECOND!
WHAT DO YOU MEAN, EVERYBODY'S AFTER IT?!

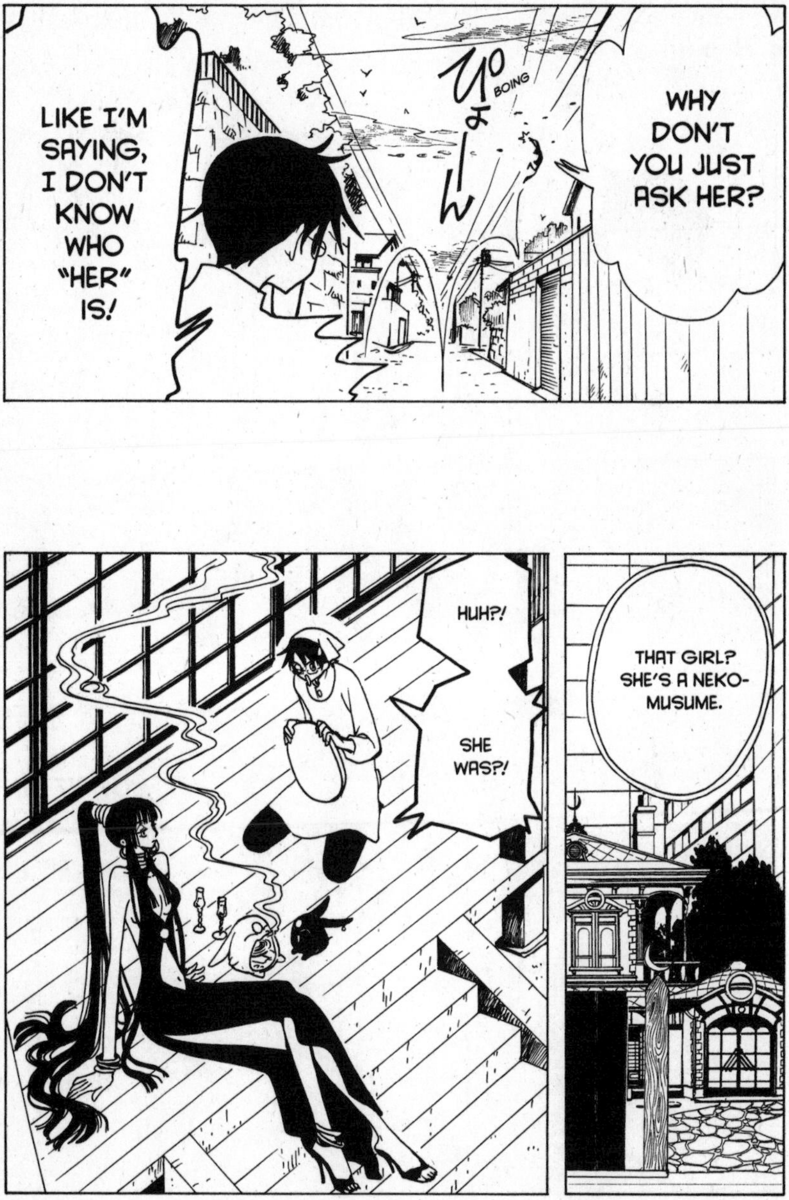
WHY DON'T YOU JUST ASK HER?
BOING
LIKE I'M SAYING, I DON'T KNOW WHO "HER" IS!
THAT GIRL? SHE'S A NEKO-MUSUME.
HUH?!
SHE WAS?!

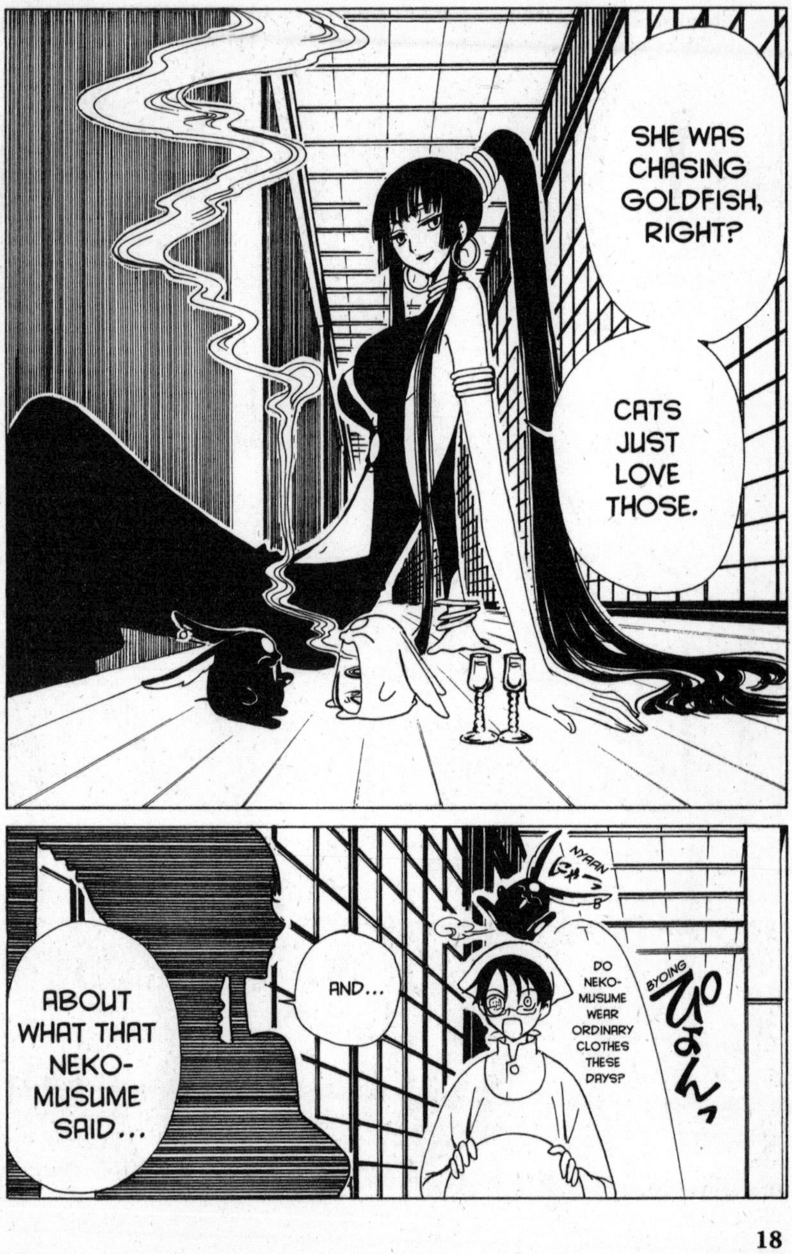
SHE WAS CHASING GOLDFISH, RIGHT?
CATS JUST LOVE THOSE.
NYAAN
にゃーっ
BYOING
ぴょんっ
DO NEKO-MUSUME WEAR ORDINARY CLOTHES THESE DAYS?
AND...
ABOUT WHAT THAT NEKO-MUSUME SAID...

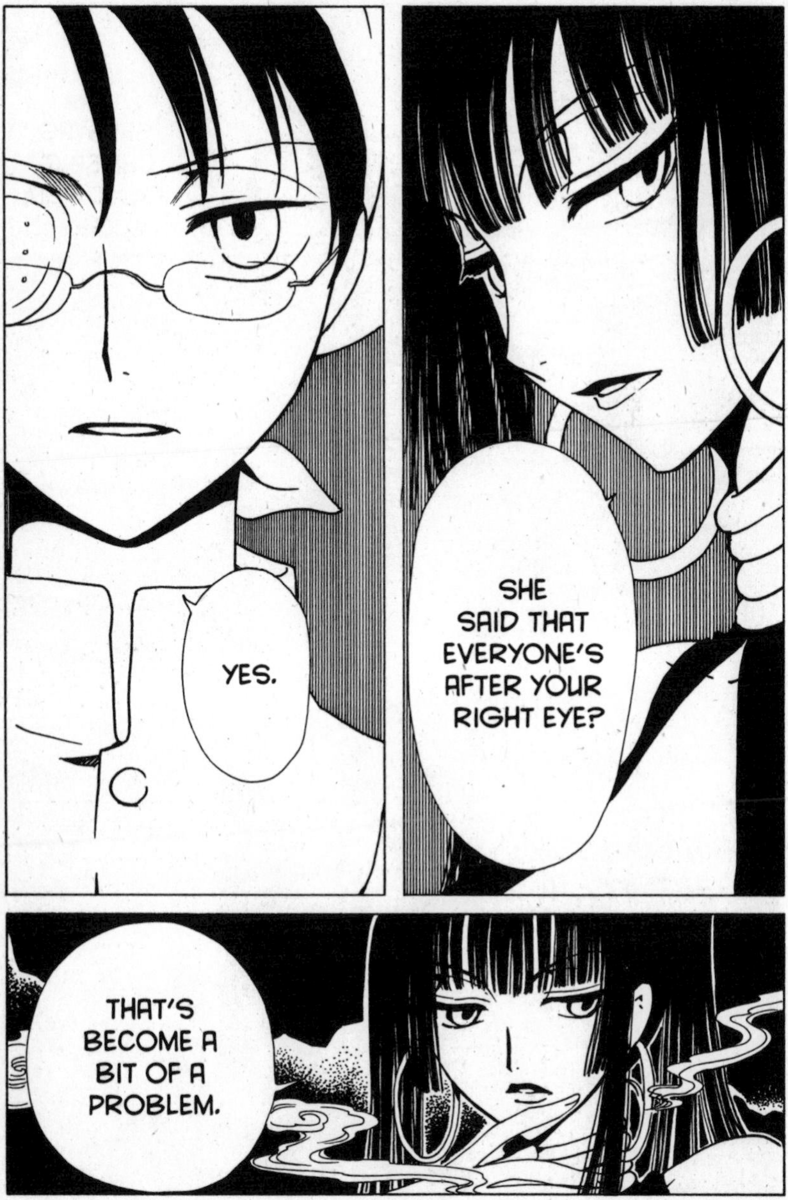
SHE SAID THAT EVERYONE'S AFTER YOUR RIGHT EYE?
YES.
THAT'S BECOME A BIT OF A PROBLEM.

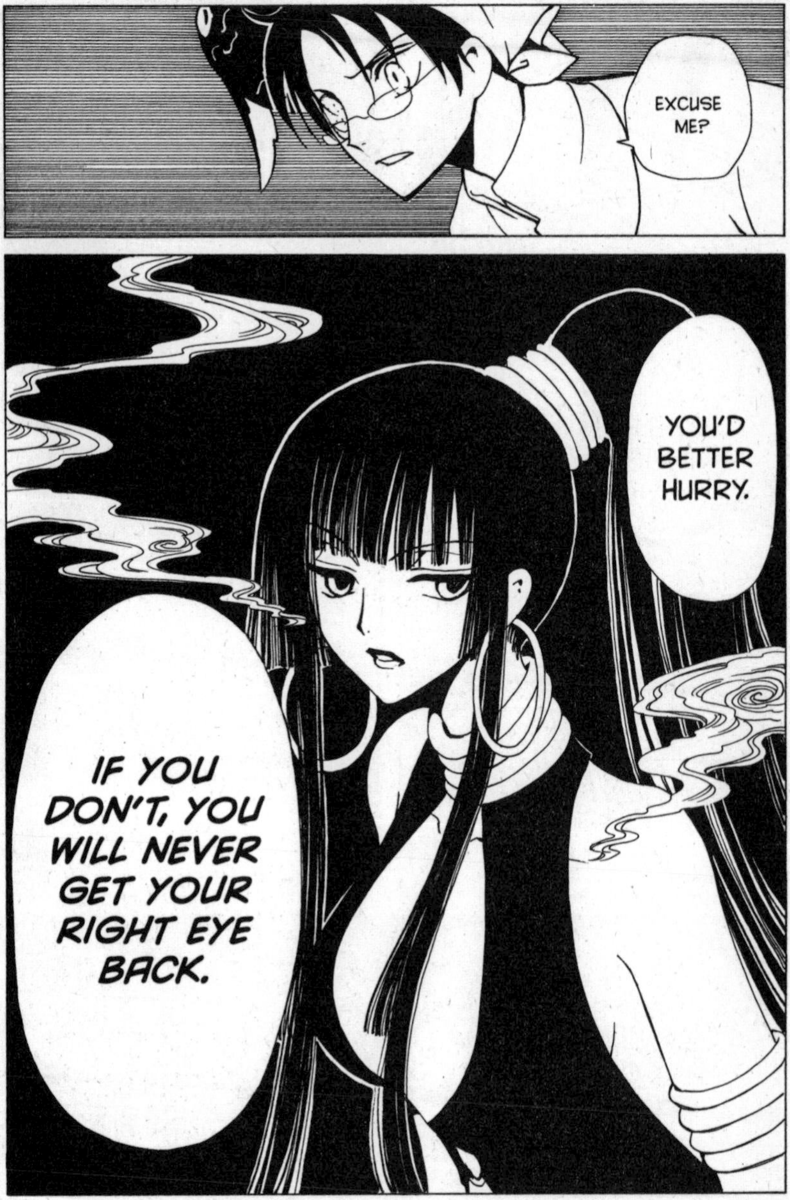
EXCUSE ME?
YOU'D BETTER HURRY.
IF YOU DON'T, YOU WILL NEVER GET YOUR RIGHT EYE BACK.

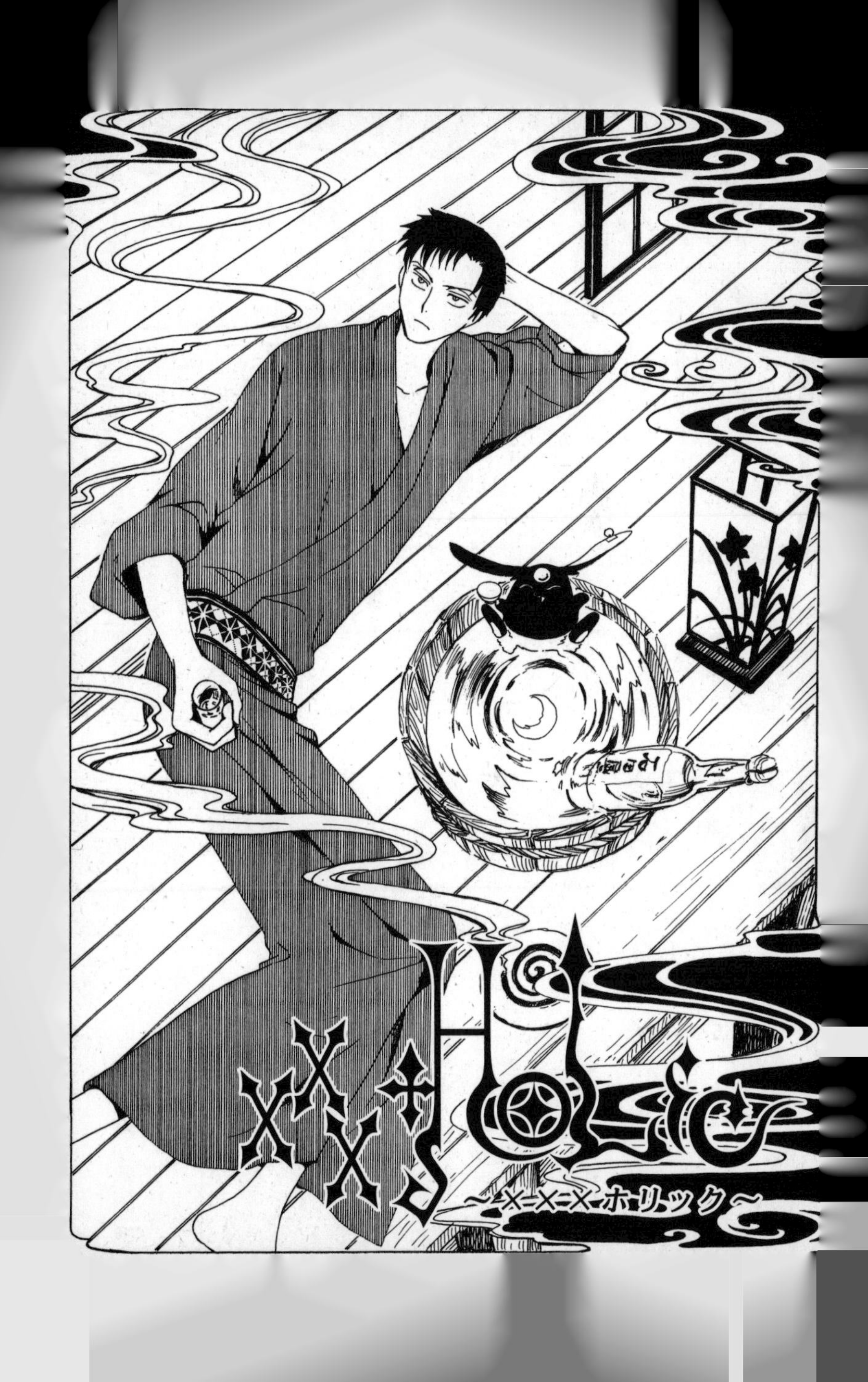
xxxHOLiC
~×××ホリック~

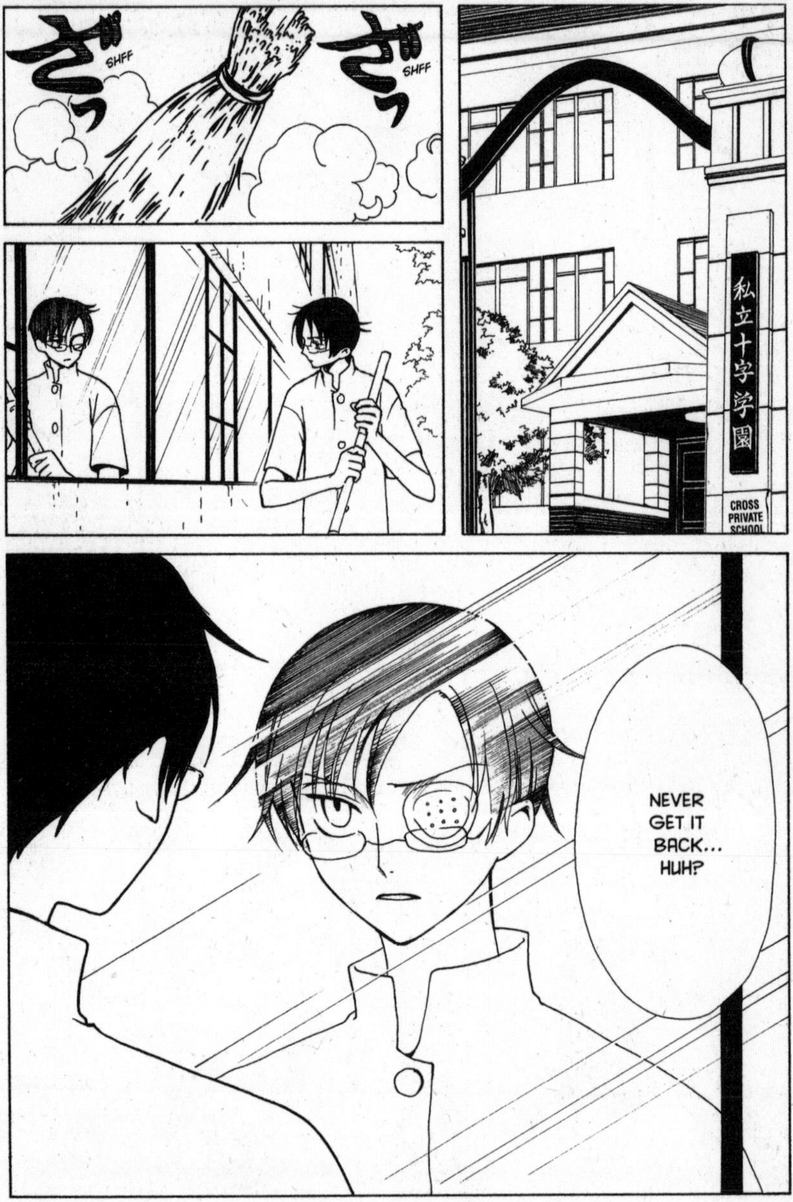
私立十字学園
CROSS PRIVATE SCHOOL
ざっ
SHFF
ざっ
SHFF
NEVER GET IT BACK... HUH?

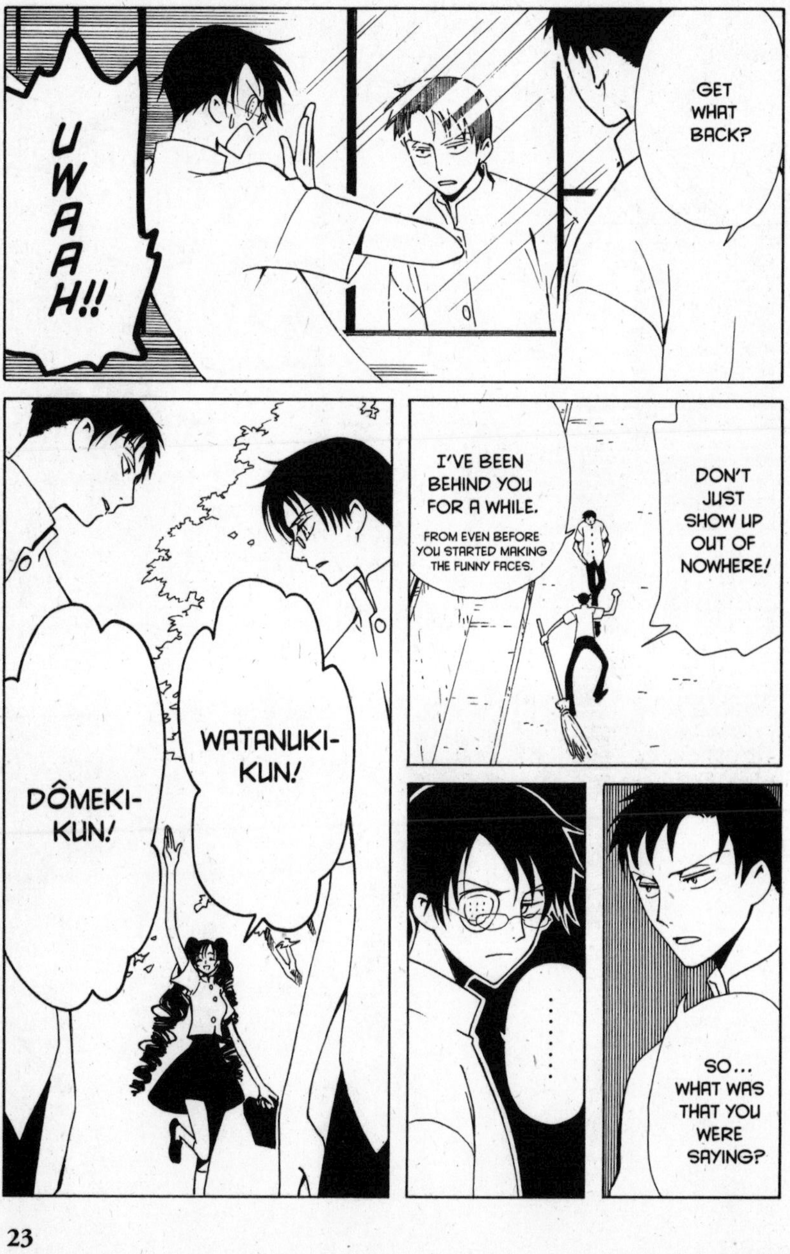
GET WHAT BACK?
UWAAAH!!
DON'T JUST SHOW UP OUT OF NOWHERE!
I'VE BEEN BEHIND YOU FOR A WHILE.
FROM EVEN BEFORE YOU STARTED MAKING THE FUNNY FACES.
SO... WHAT WAS THAT YOU WERE SAYING?
......
WATANUKI-KUN!
DÔMEKI-KUN!

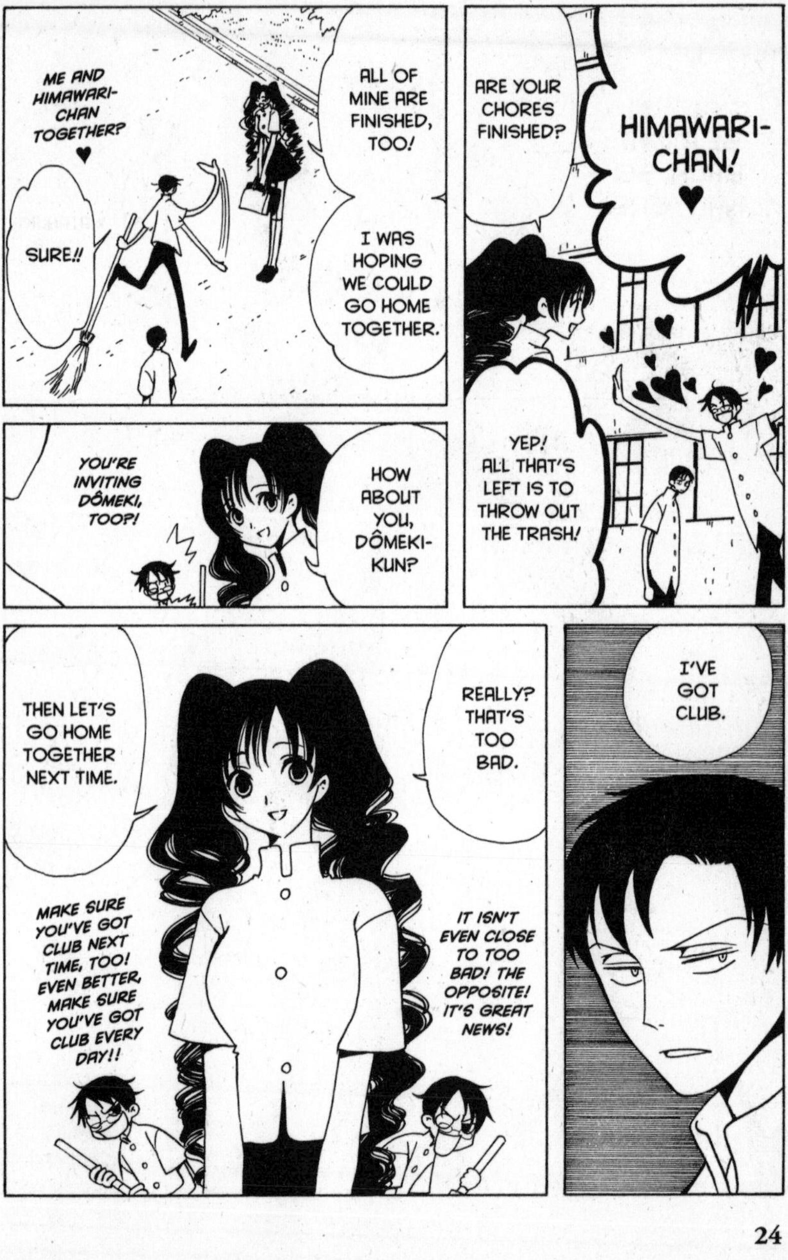
HIMAWARI-CHAN! ♥
ARE YOUR CHORES FINISHED?
YEP! ALL THAT'S LEFT IS TO THROW OUT THE TRASH!
ALL OF MINE ARE FINISHED, TOO!
I WAS HOPING WE COULD GO HOME TOGETHER.
ME AND HIMAWARI-CHAN TOGETHER? ♥
SURE!!
HOW ABOUT YOU, DÔMEKI-KUN?
YOU'RE INVITING DÔMEKI, TOO?!
I'VE GOT CLUB.
REALLY? THAT'S TOO BAD.
THEN LET'S GO HOME TOGETHER NEXT TIME.
IT ISN'T EVEN CLOSE TO TOO BAD! THE OPPOSITE! IT'S GREAT NEWS!
MAKE SURE YOU'VE GOT CLUB NEXT TIME, TOO! EVEN BETTER, MAKE SURE YOU'VE GOT CLUB EVERY DAY!!

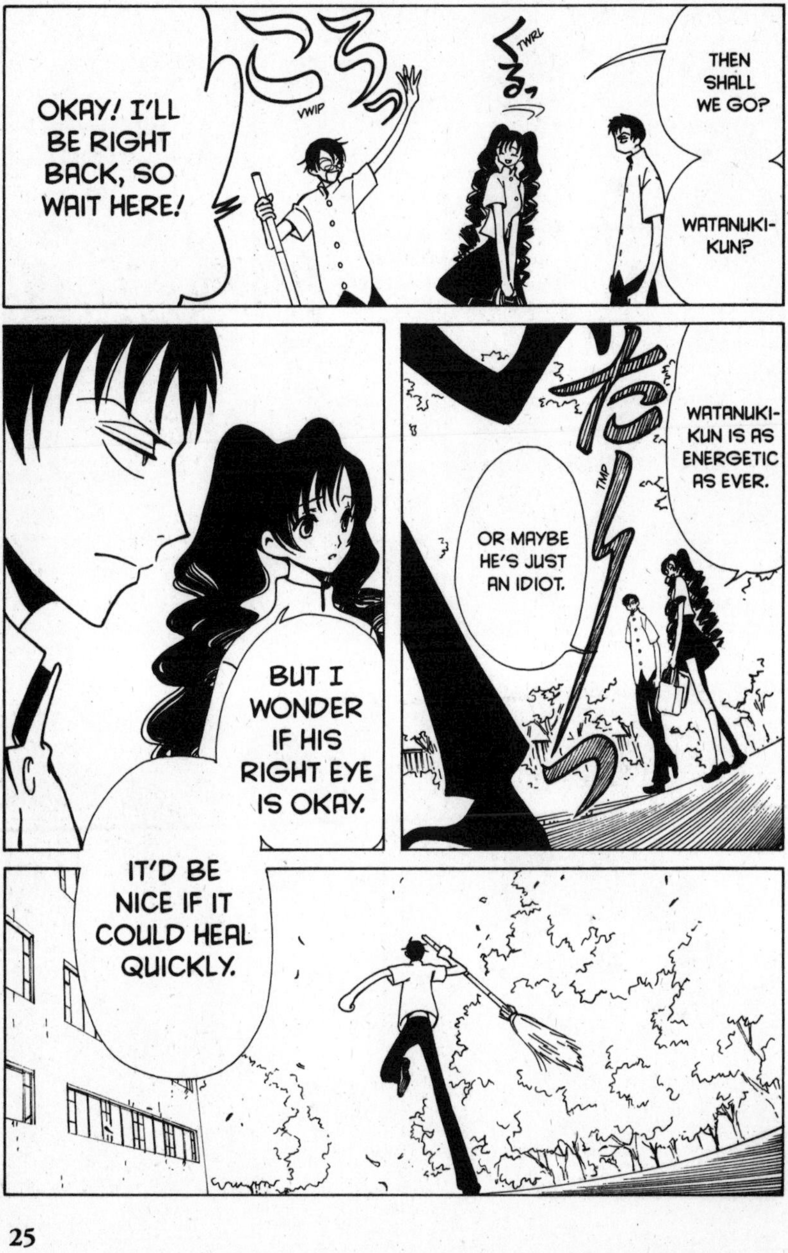
THEN SHALL WE GO?
WATANUKI-KUN?
TWRL
VWIP
OKAY! I'LL BE RIGHT BACK, SO WAIT HERE!
WATANUKI-KUN IS AS ENERGETIC AS EVER.
TMP
OR MAYBE HE'S JUST AN IDIOT.
BUT I WONDER IF HIS RIGHT EYE IS OKAY.
IT'D BE NICE IF IT COULD HEAL QUICKLY.

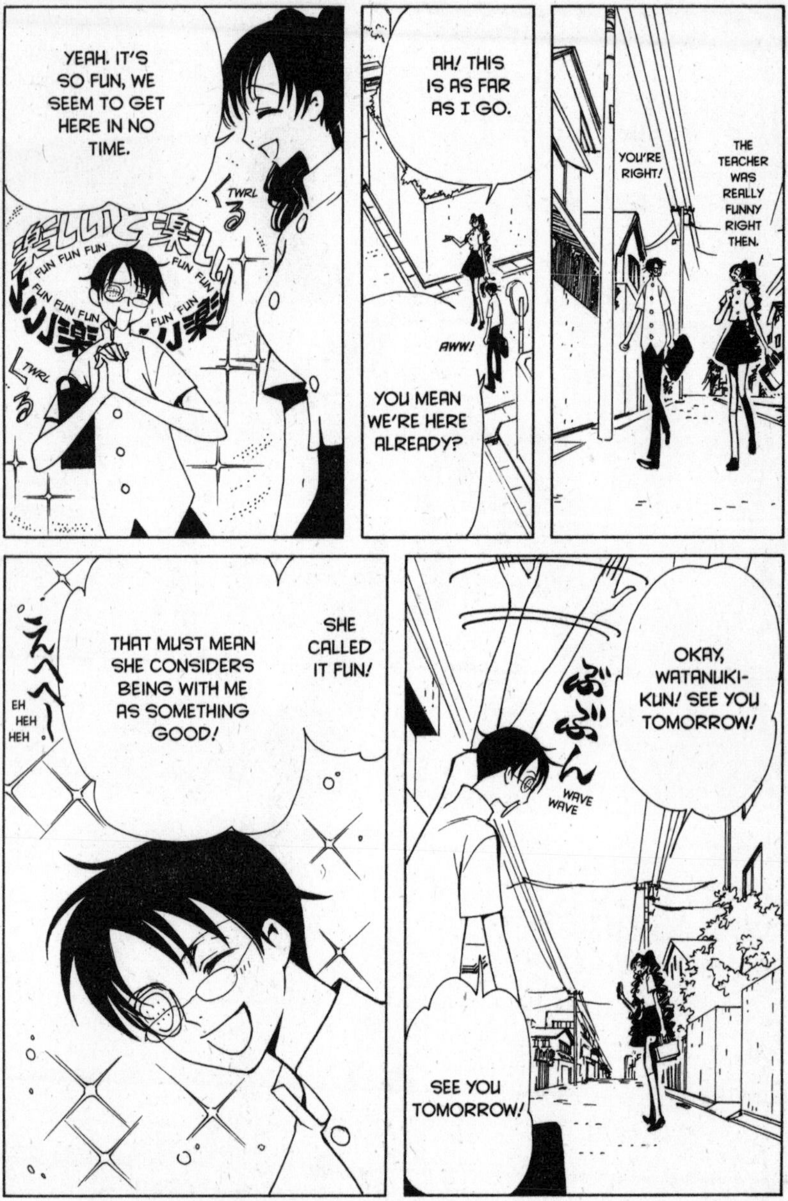
THE TEACHER WAS REALLY FUNNY RIGHT THEN.
YOU'RE RIGHT!
AH! THIS IS AS FAR AS I GO.
AWW!
YOU MEAN WE'RE HERE ALREADY?
YEAH. IT'S SO FUN, WE SEEM TO GET HERE IN NO TIME.
くる TWRL
FUN FUN FUN FUN FUN
FUN FUN FUN FUN FUN
くる TWRL
OKAY, WATANUKI-KUN! SEE YOU TOMORROW!
ぶんぶん WAVE WAVE
SEE YOU TOMORROW!
SHE CALLED IT FUN!
THAT MUST MEAN SHE CONSIDERS BEING WITH ME AS SOMETHING GOOD!
えへへ~ EH HEH HEH

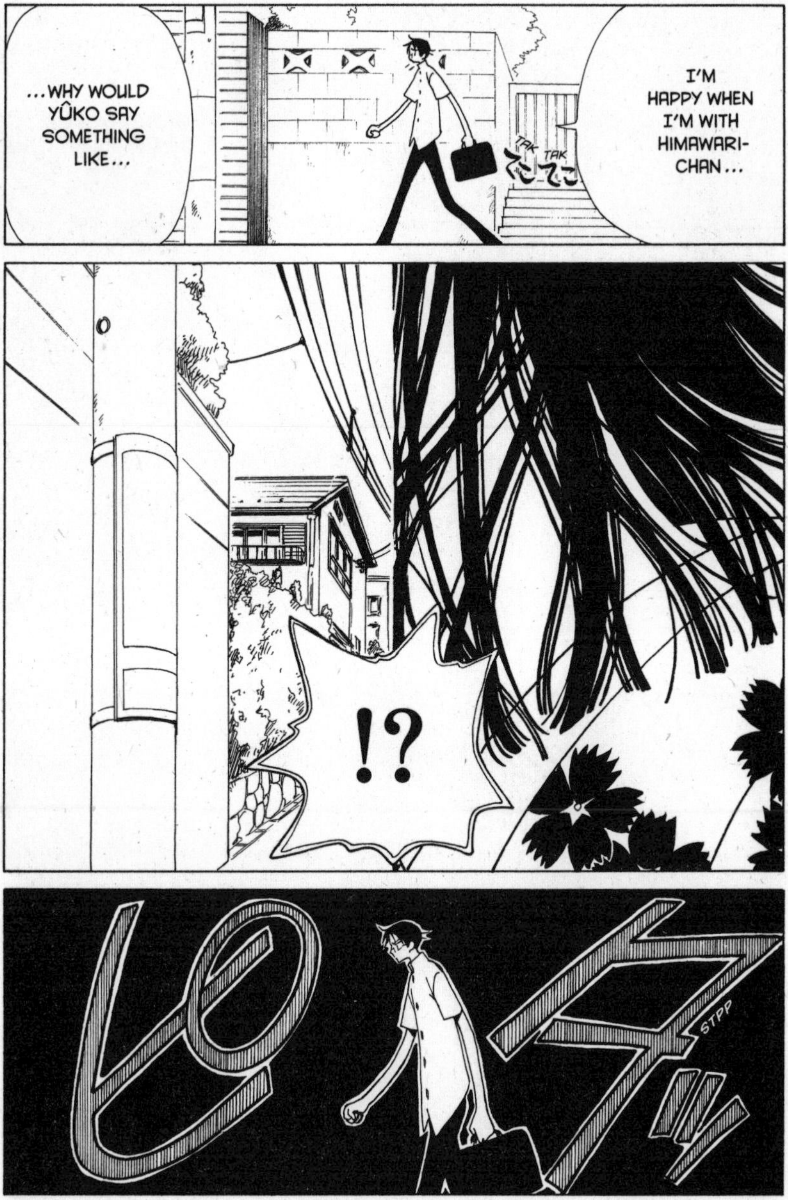
I'M HAPPY WHEN I'M WITH HIMAWARI-CHAN...
TAK TAK
...WHY WOULD YÛKO SAY SOMETHING LIKE...
!?
STPP

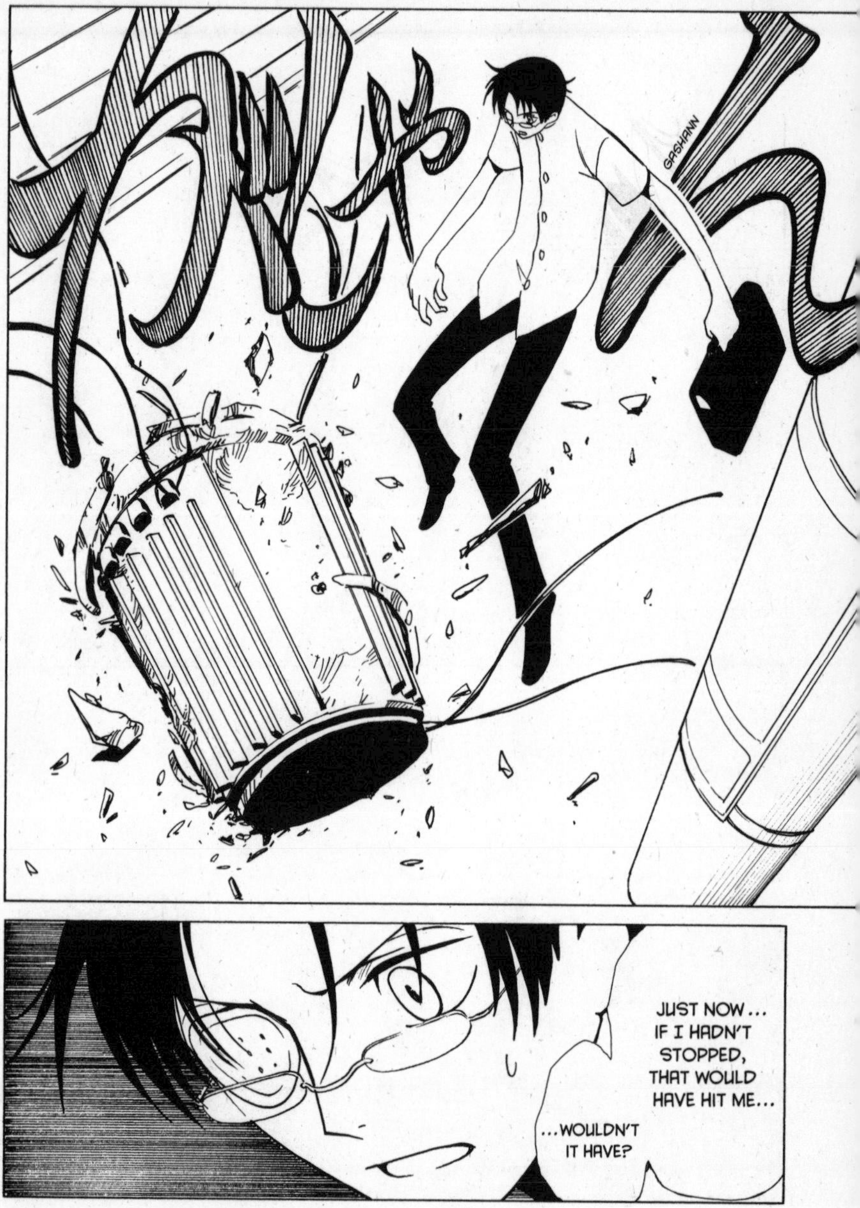
GASHANN
JUST NOW... IF I HADN'T STOPPED, THAT WOULD HAVE HIT ME...
...WOULDN'T IT HAVE?

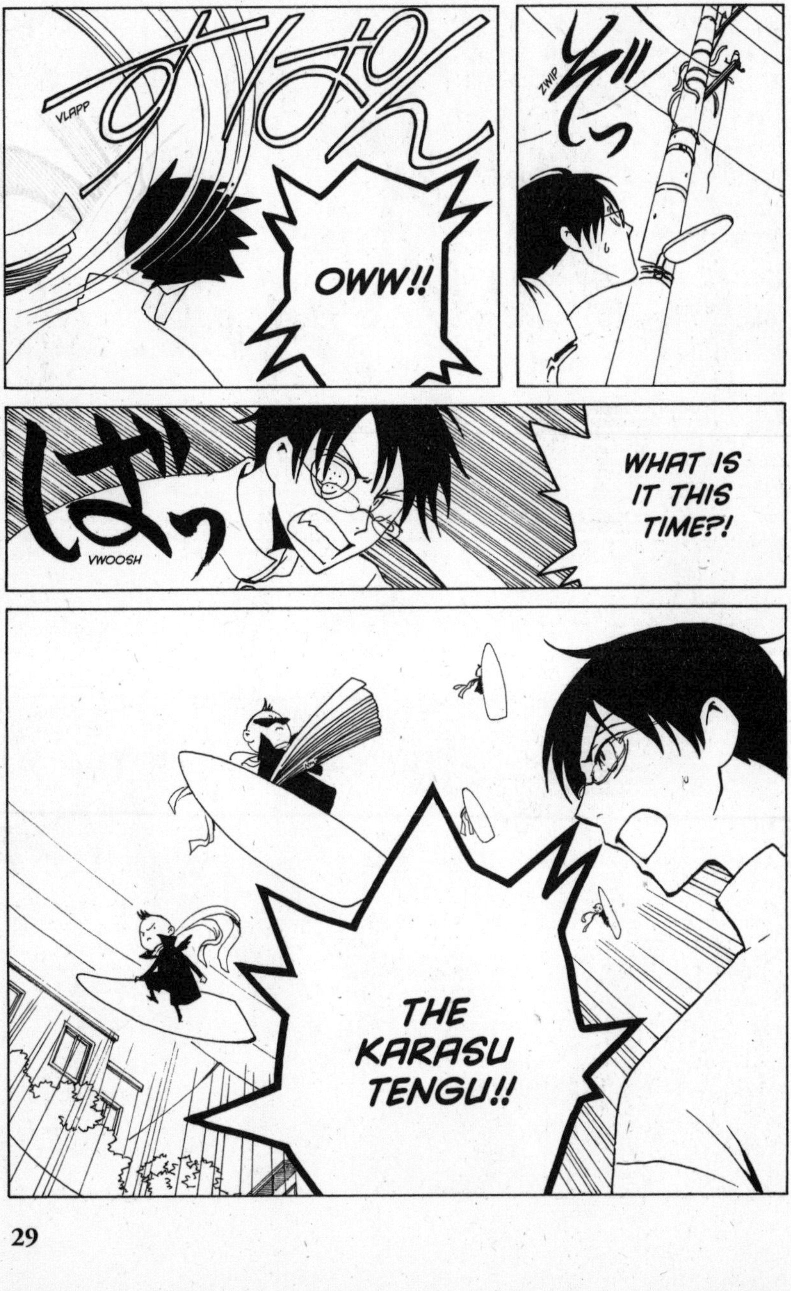
ぞっ
ZWIP
すぱん
VLAPP
OWW!!
WHAT IS IT THIS TIME?!
ばっ
VWOOSH
THE KARASU TENGU!!

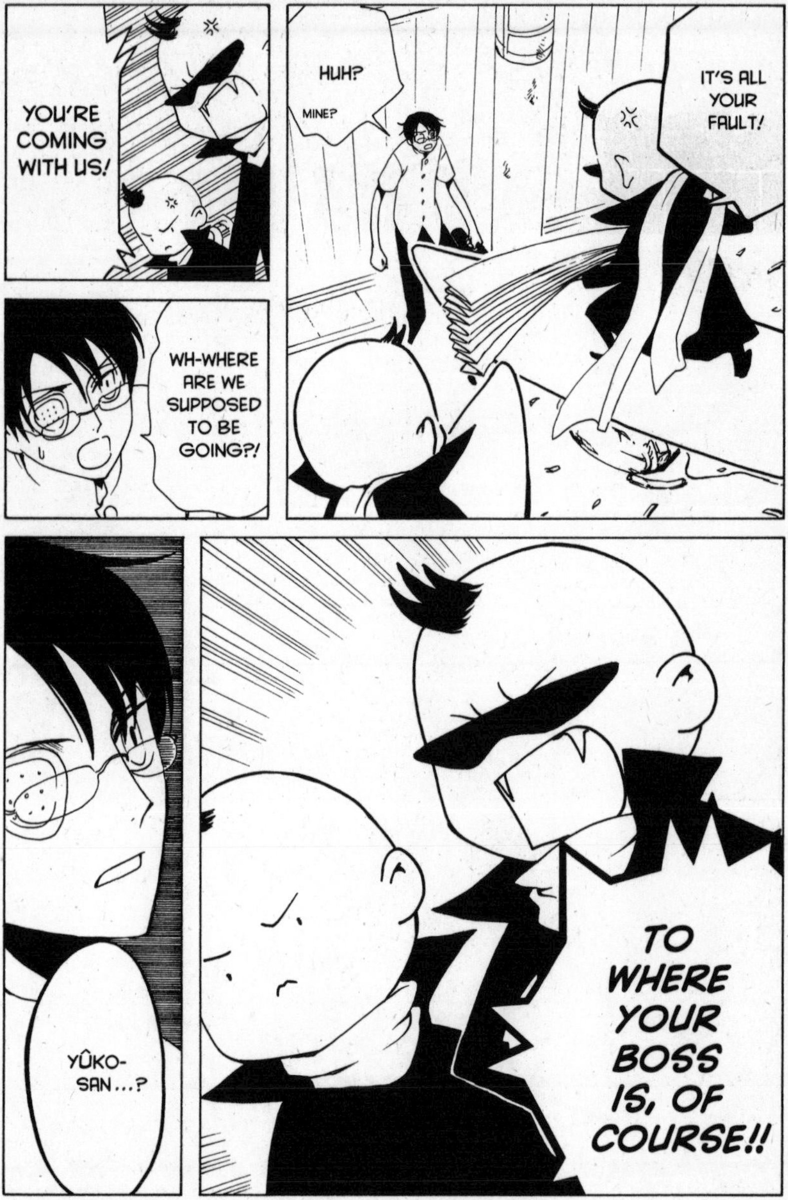
IT'S ALL YOUR FAULT!
HUH?
MINE?
YOU'RE COMING WITH US!
WH-WHERE ARE WE SUPPOSED TO BE GOING?!
TO WHERE YOUR BOSS IS, OF COURSE!!
YÛKO-SAN...?

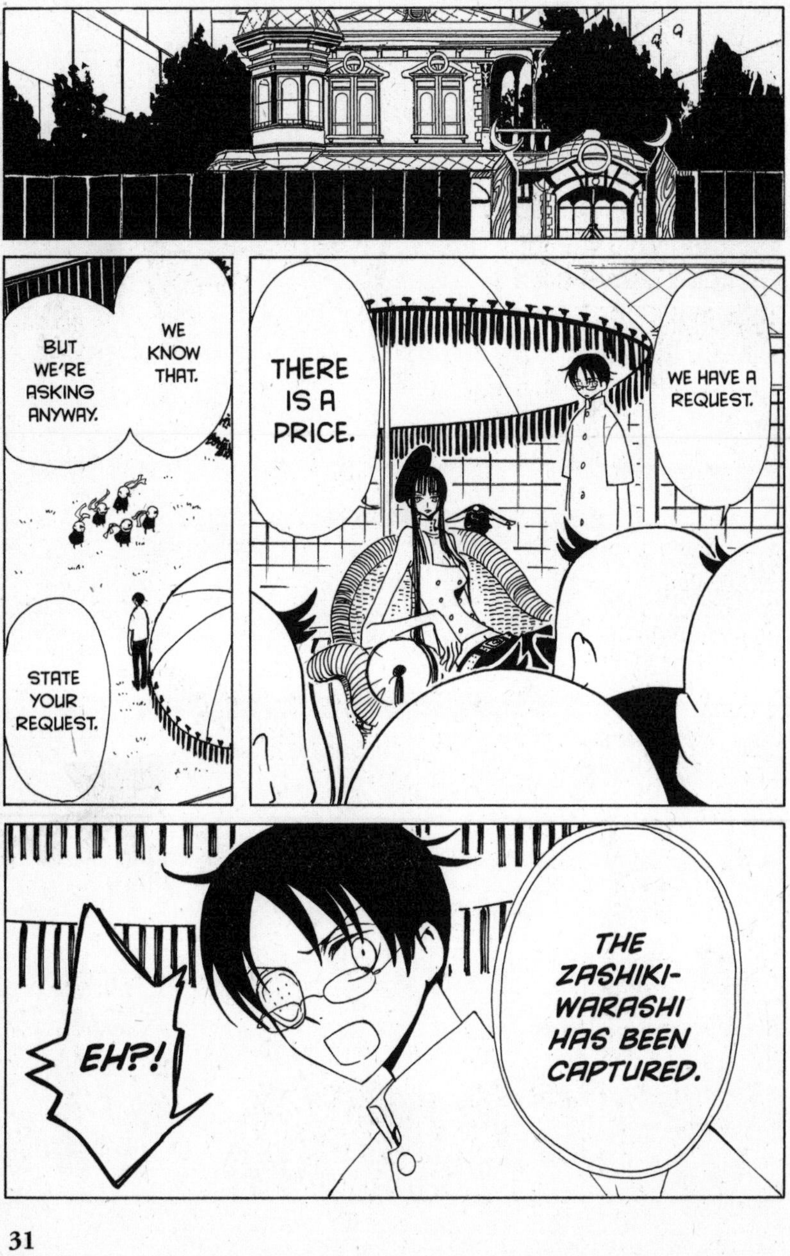
WE HAVE A REQUEST.
THERE IS A PRICE.
WE KNOW THAT.
BUT WE'RE ASKING ANYWAY.
STATE YOUR REQUEST.
THE ZASHIKI-WARASHI HAS BEEN CAPTURED.
EH?!

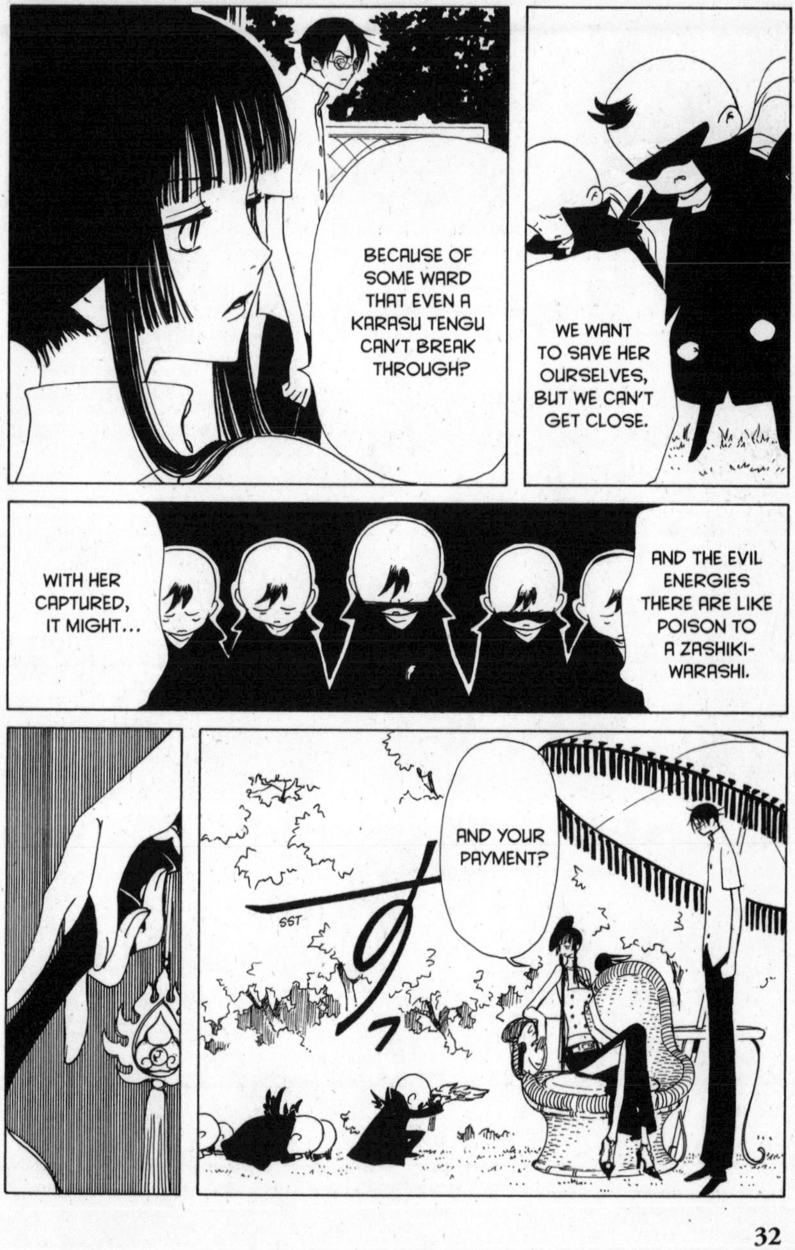
WE WANT TO SAVE HER OURSELVES, BUT WE CAN'T GET CLOSE.
BECAUSE OF SOME WARD THAT EVEN A KARASU TENGU CAN'T BREAK THROUGH?
AND THE EVIL ENERGIES THERE ARE LIKE POISON TO A ZASHIKI-WARASHI.
WITH HER CAPTURED, IT MIGHT...
AND YOUR PAYMENT?
SST

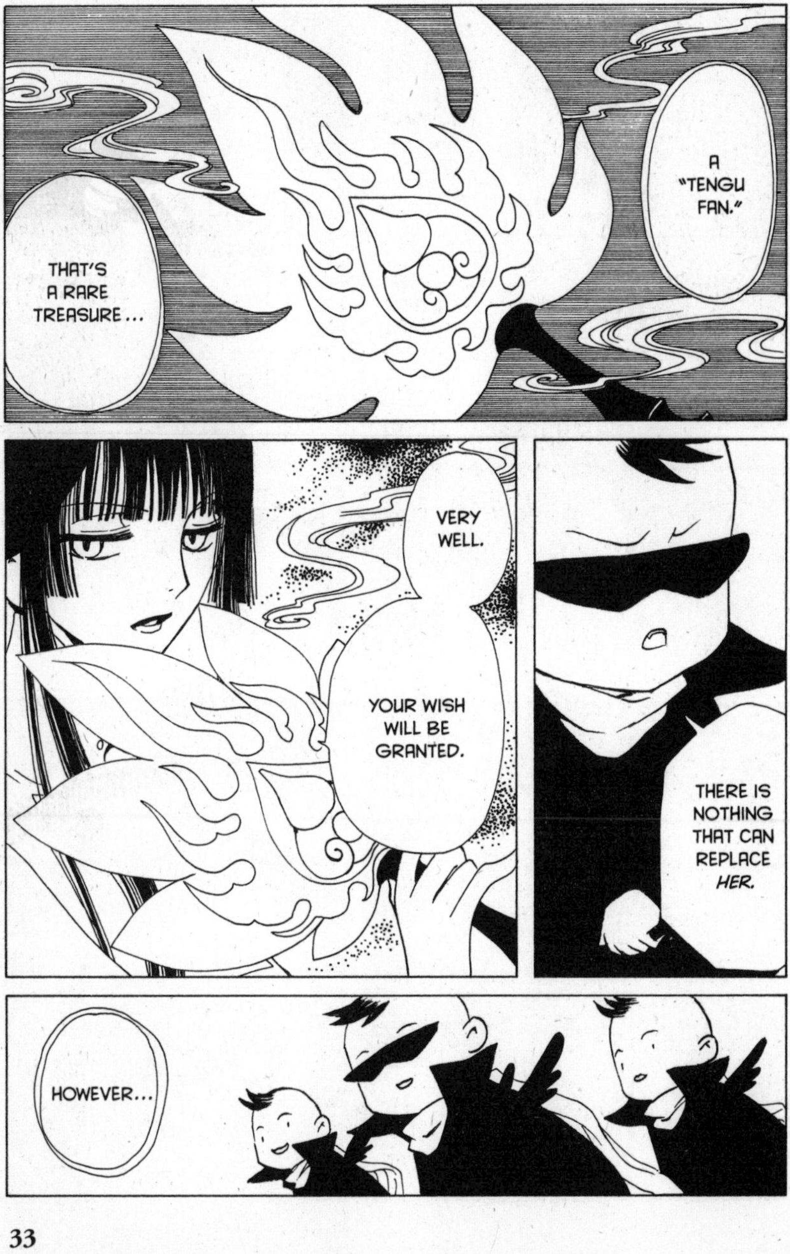
A "TENGU FAN."
THAT'S A RARE TREASURE...
THERE IS NOTHING THAT CAN REPLACE *HER.*
VERY WELL.
YOUR WISH WILL BE GRANTED.
HOWEVER...

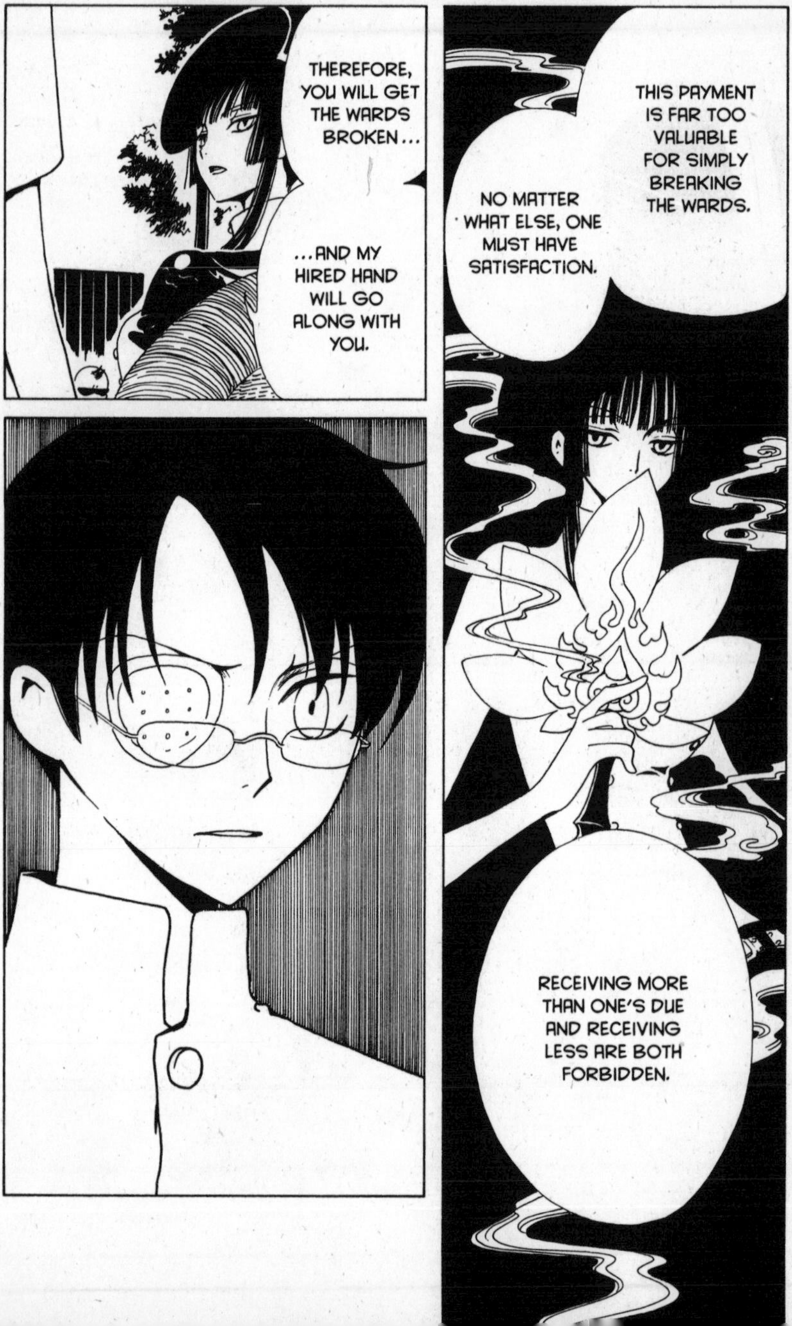
THIS PAYMENT IS FAR TOO VALUABLE FOR SIMPLY BREAKING THE WARDS.
NO MATTER WHAT ELSE, ONE MUST HAVE SATISFACTION.
RECEIVING MORE THAN ONE'S DUE AND RECEIVING LESS ARE BOTH FORBIDDEN.
THEREFORE, YOU WILL GET THE WARDS BROKEN...
...AND MY HIRED HAND WILL GO ALONG WITH YOU.

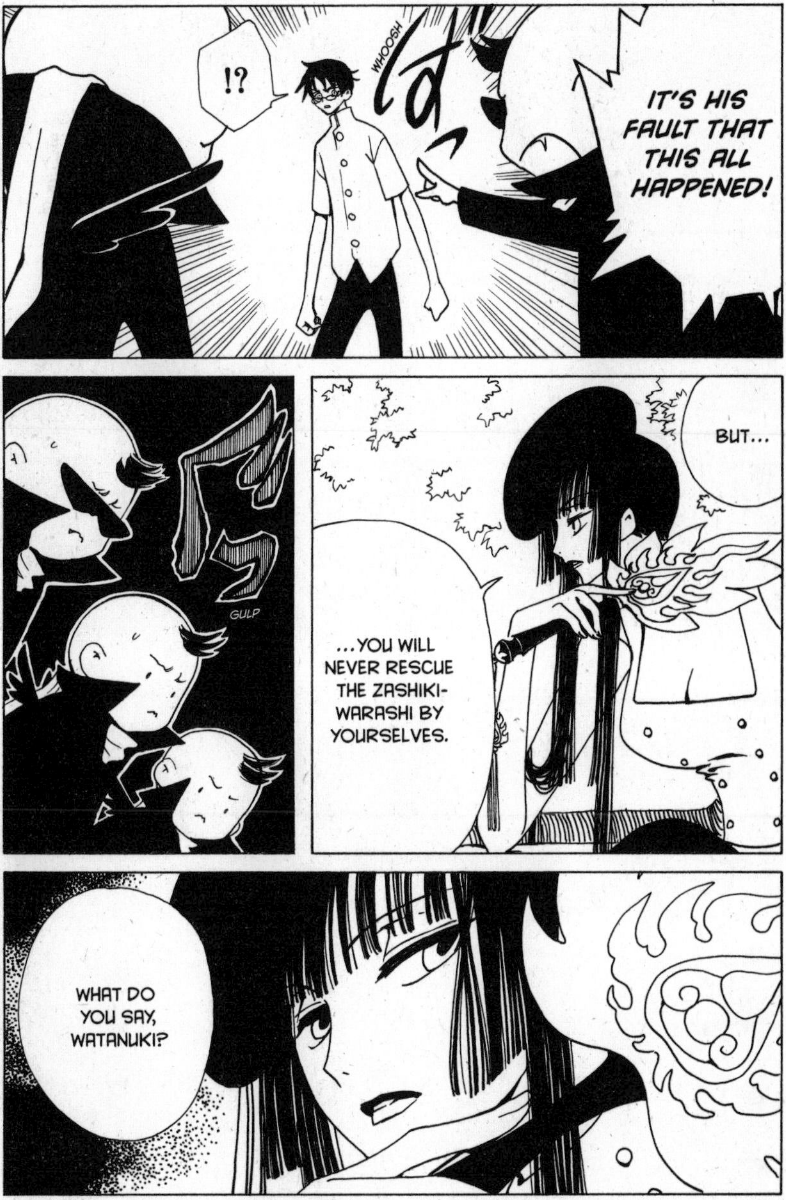
IT'S HIS FAULT THAT THIS ALL HAPPENED!
WHOOSH
!?
BUT...
...YOU WILL NEVER RESCUE THE ZASHIKI-WARASHI BY YOURSELVES.
GULP
WHAT DO YOU SAY, WATANUKI?

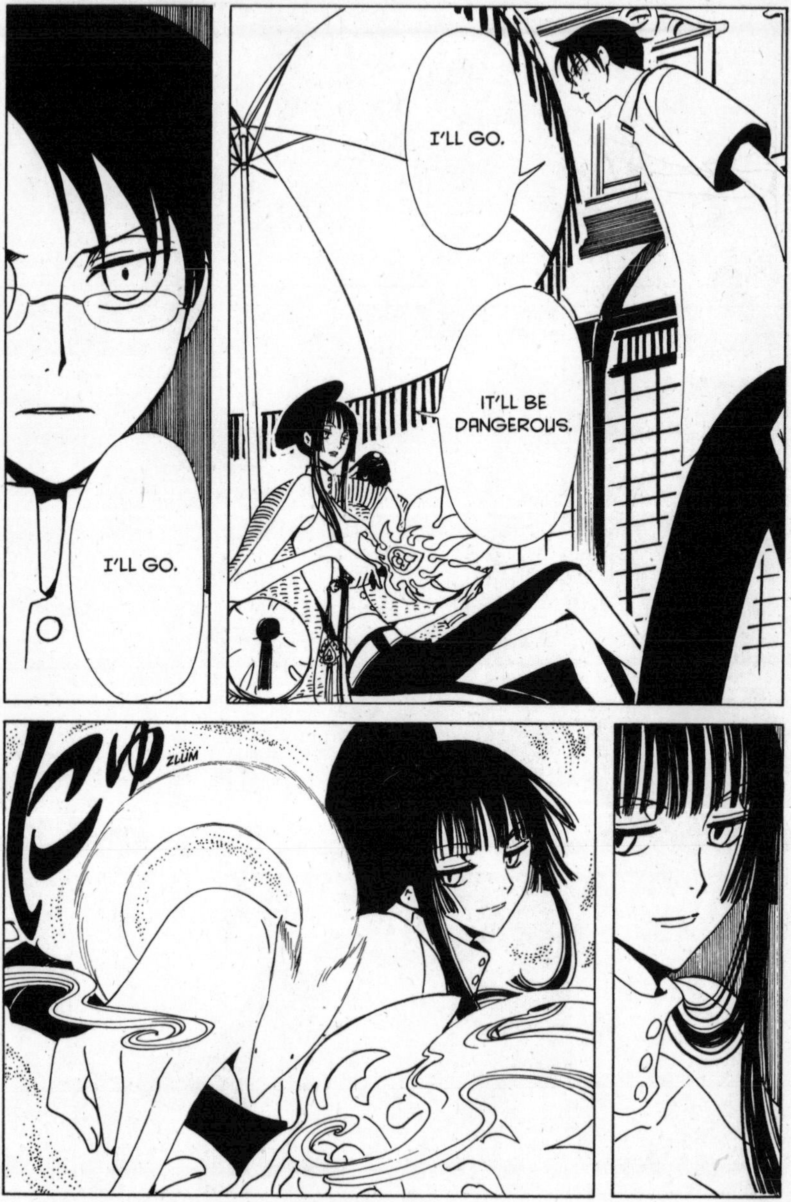
I'LL GO.
IT'LL BE DANGEROUS.
I'LL GO.
にゅ
ZLUM

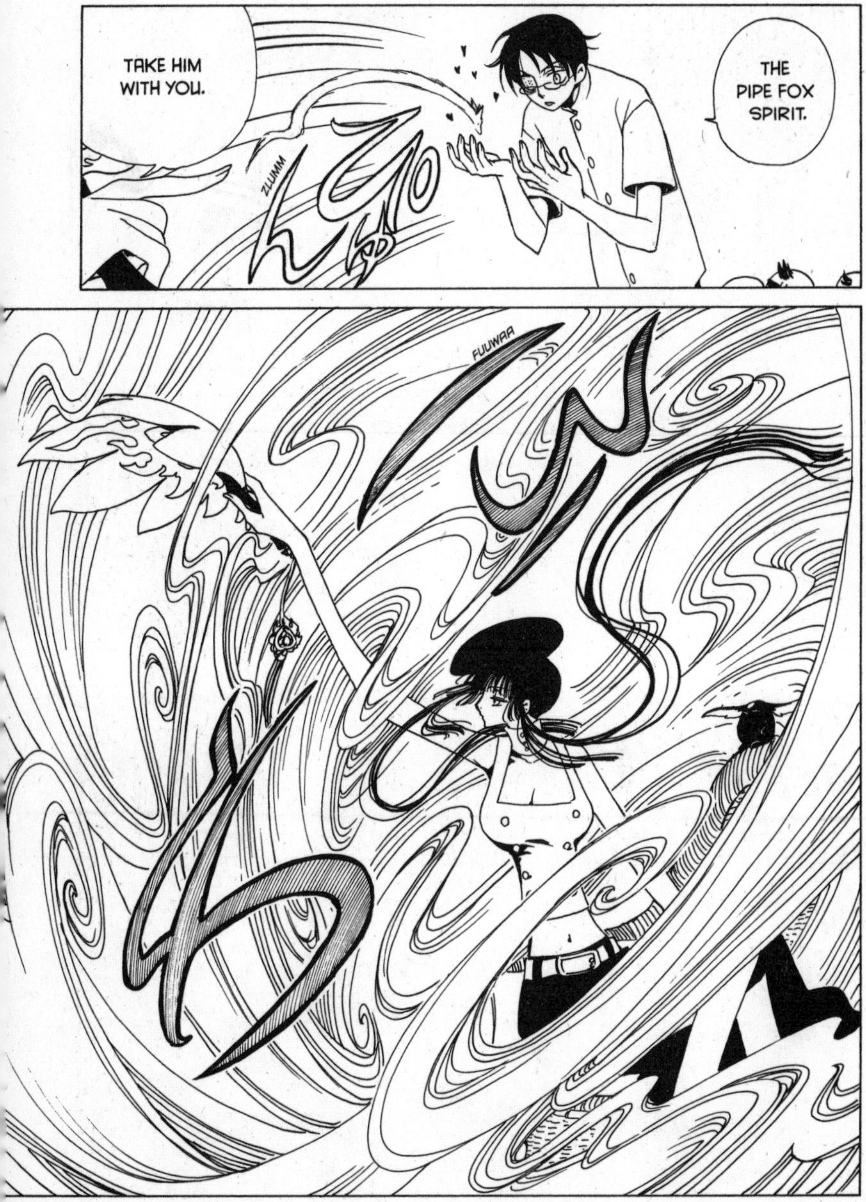
THE PIPE FOX SPIRIT.
TAKE HIM WITH YOU.
ZLUMM
FUUWAA

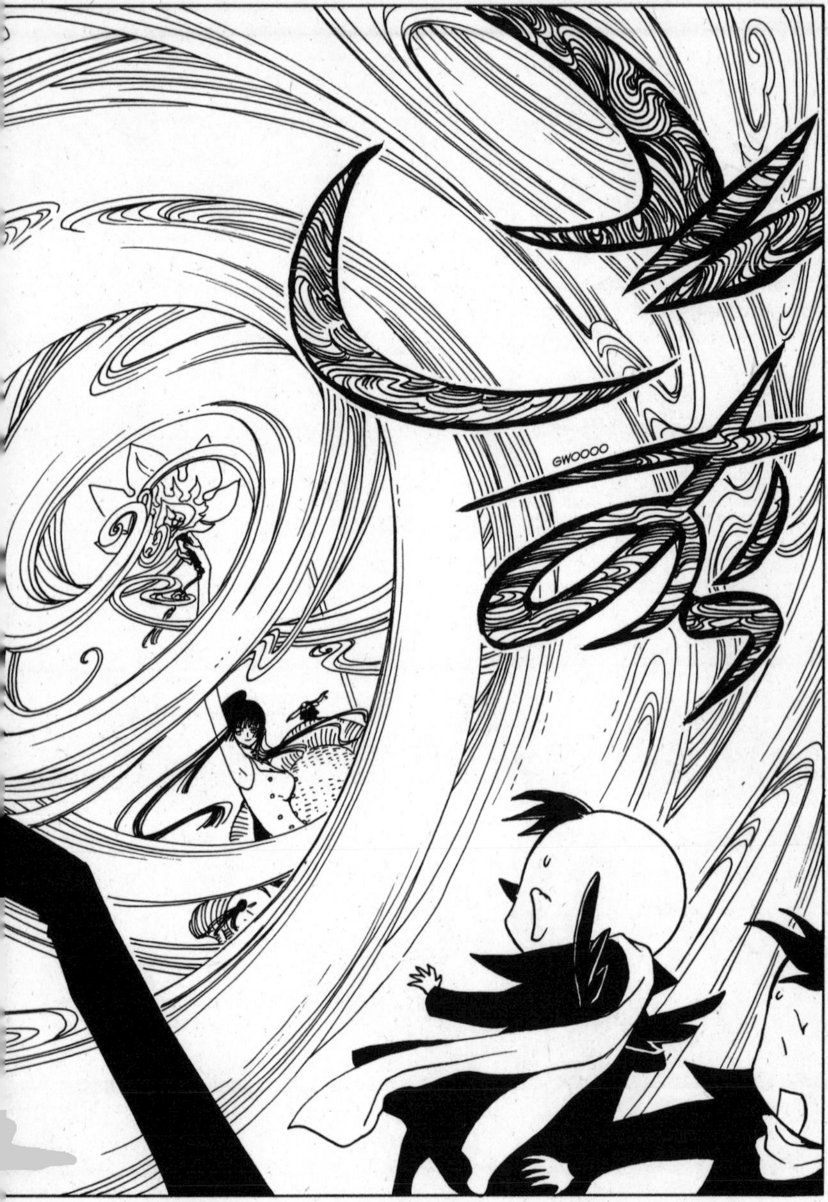
GWOOOO

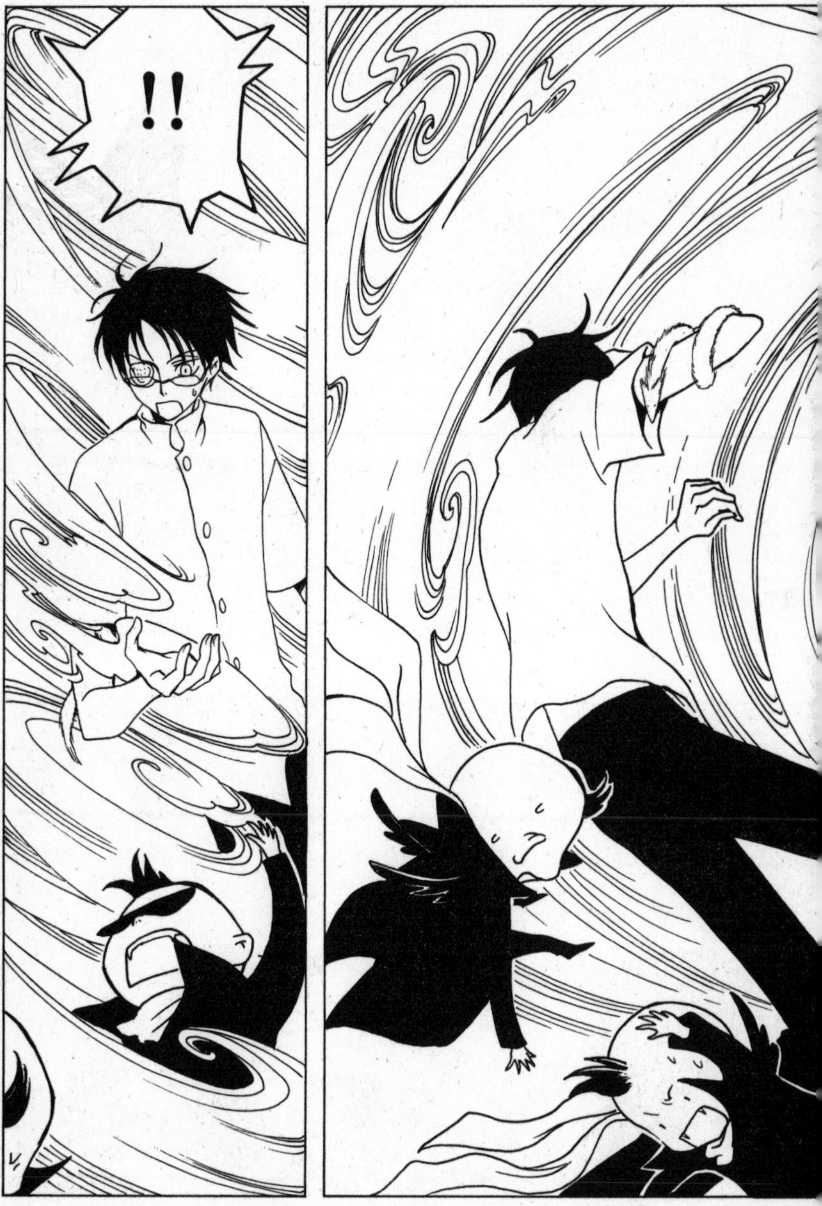
!!

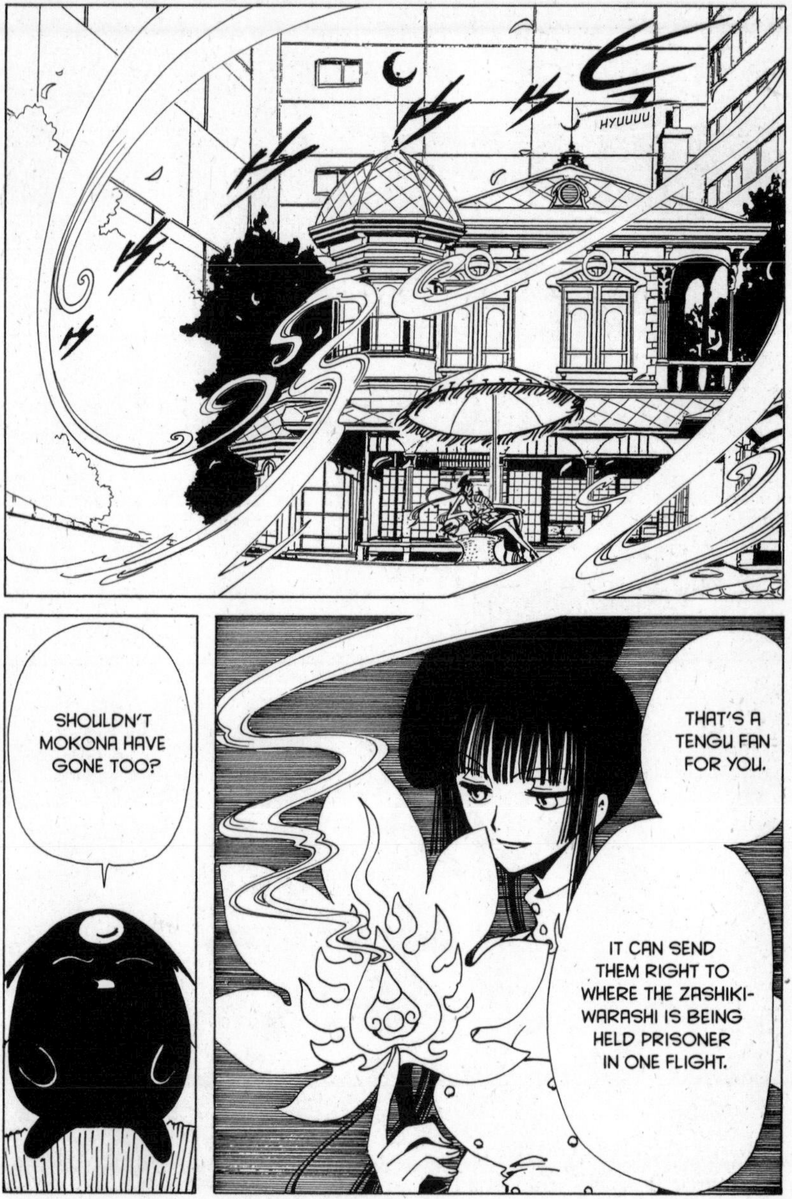
HYUUUU
THAT'S A TENGU FAN FOR YOU.
IT CAN SEND THEM RIGHT TO WHERE THE ZASHIKI-WARASHI IS BEING HELD PRISONER IN ONE FLIGHT.
SHOULDN'T MOKONA HAVE GONE TOO?

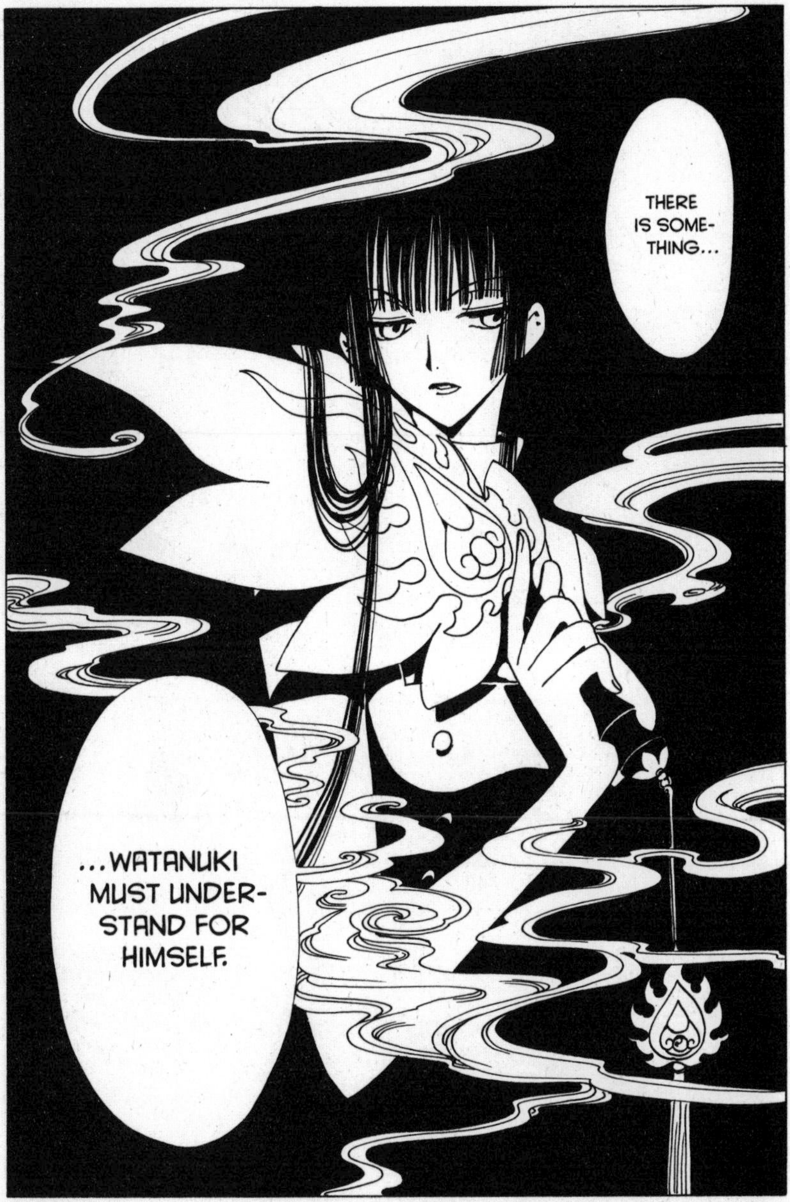
THERE IS SOME-THING...
...WATANUKI MUST UNDER-STAND FOR HIMSELF.

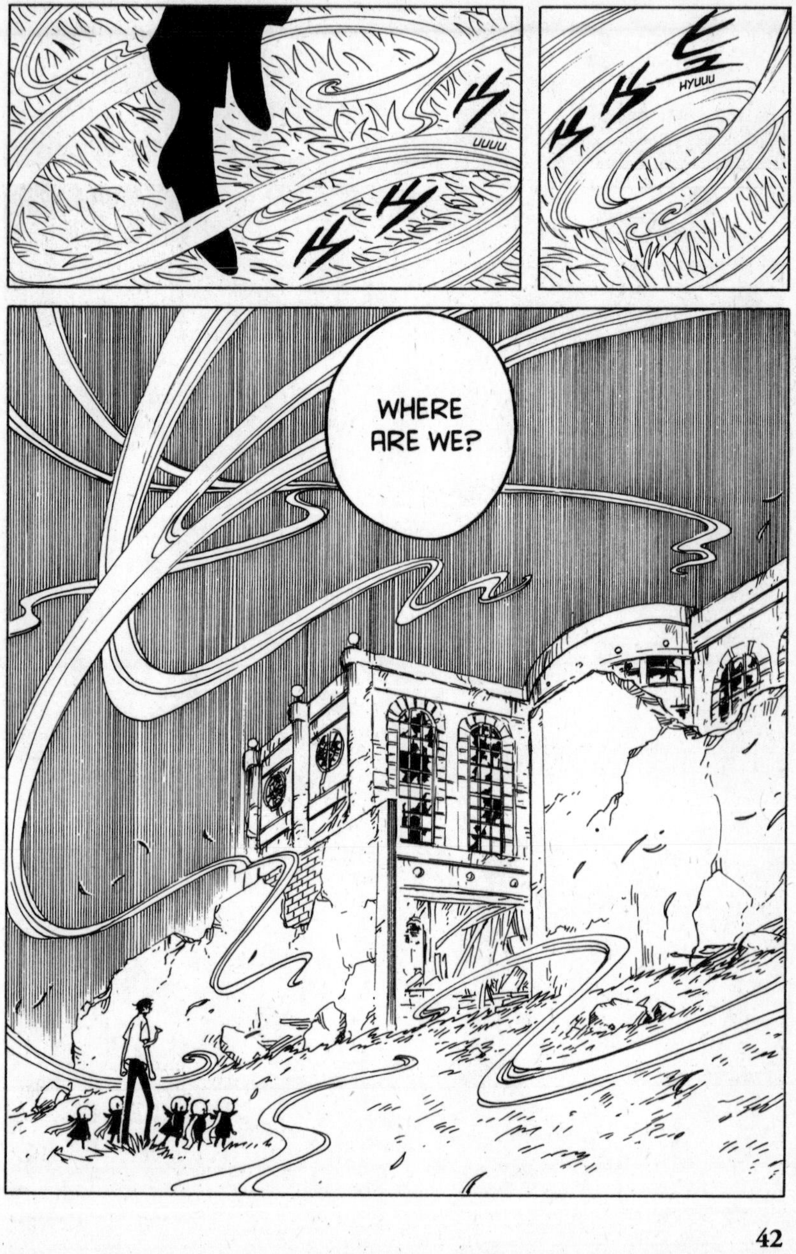
HYUUU
UUUU
WHERE ARE WE?

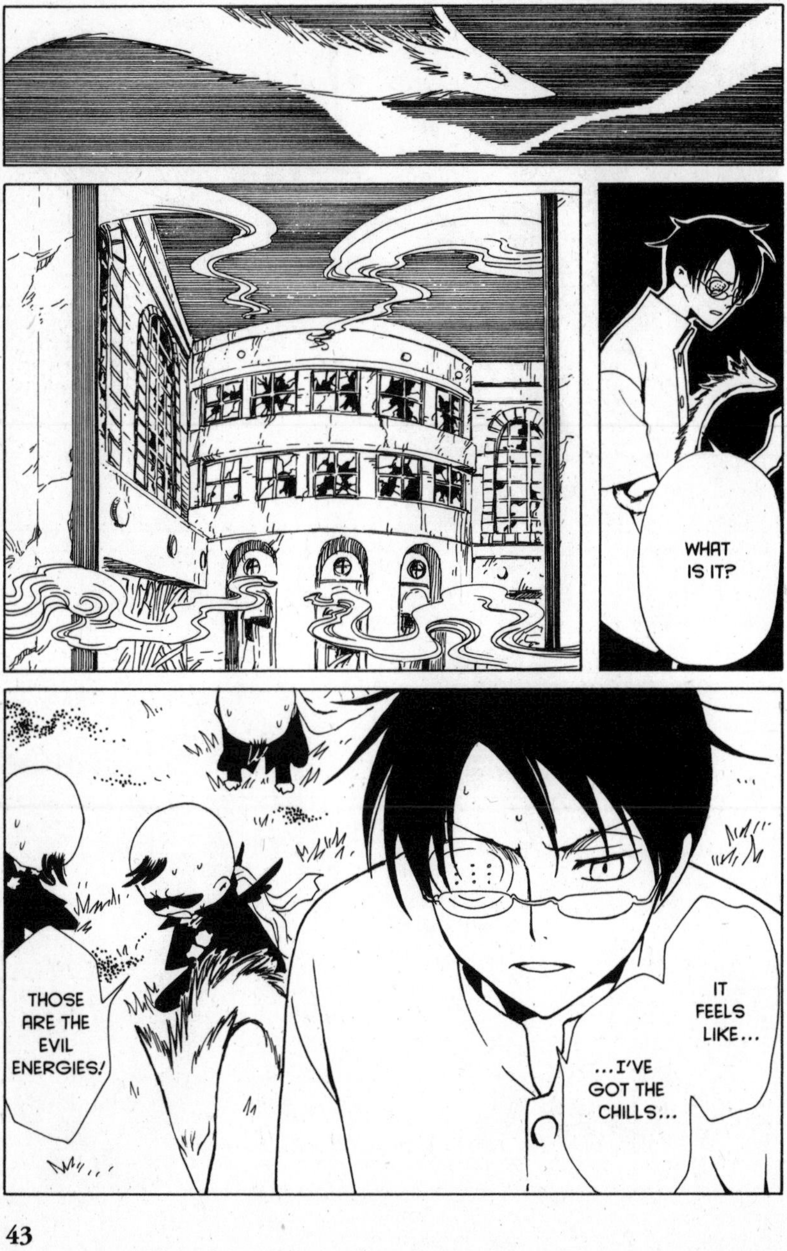
WHAT IS IT?
IT FEELS LIKE...
...I'VE GOT THE CHILLS...
THOSE ARE THE EVIL ENERGIES!

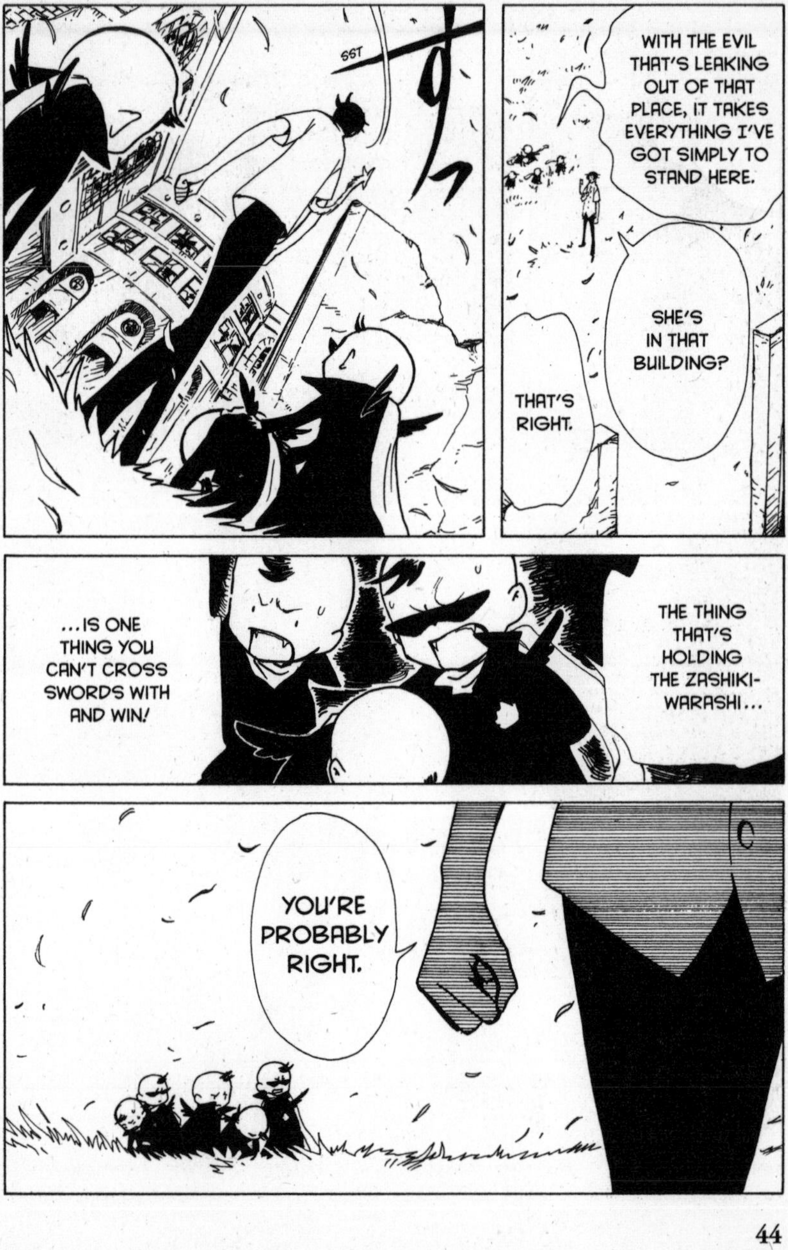
WITH THE EVIL THAT'S LEAKING OUT OF THAT PLACE, IT TAKES EVERYTHING I'VE GOT SIMPLY TO STAND HERE.
SHE'S IN THAT BUILDING?
THAT'S RIGHT.
SST
THE THING THAT'S HOLDING THE ZASHIKI-WARASHI...
...IS ONE THING YOU CAN'T CROSS SWORDS WITH AND WIN!
YOU'RE PROBABLY RIGHT.

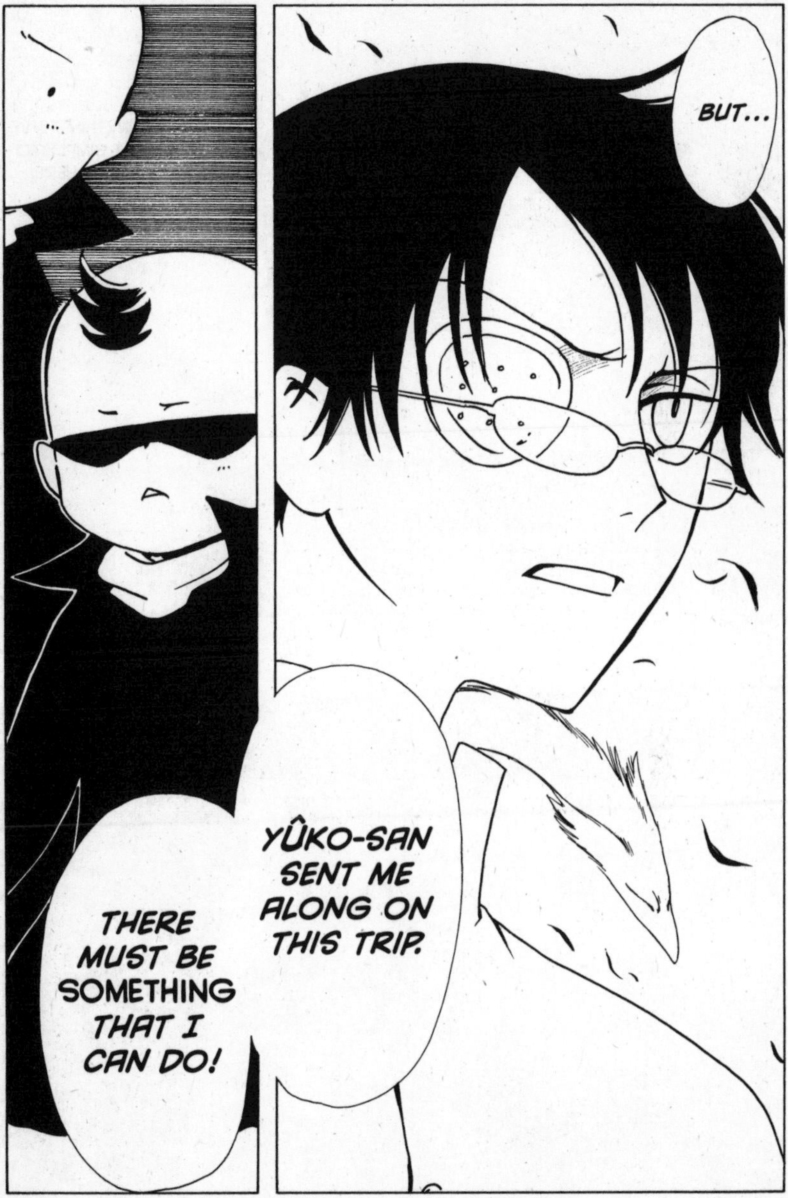
BUT...
YÛKO-SAN SENT ME ALONG ON THIS TRIP.
THERE MUST BE SOMETHING THAT I CAN DO!
...

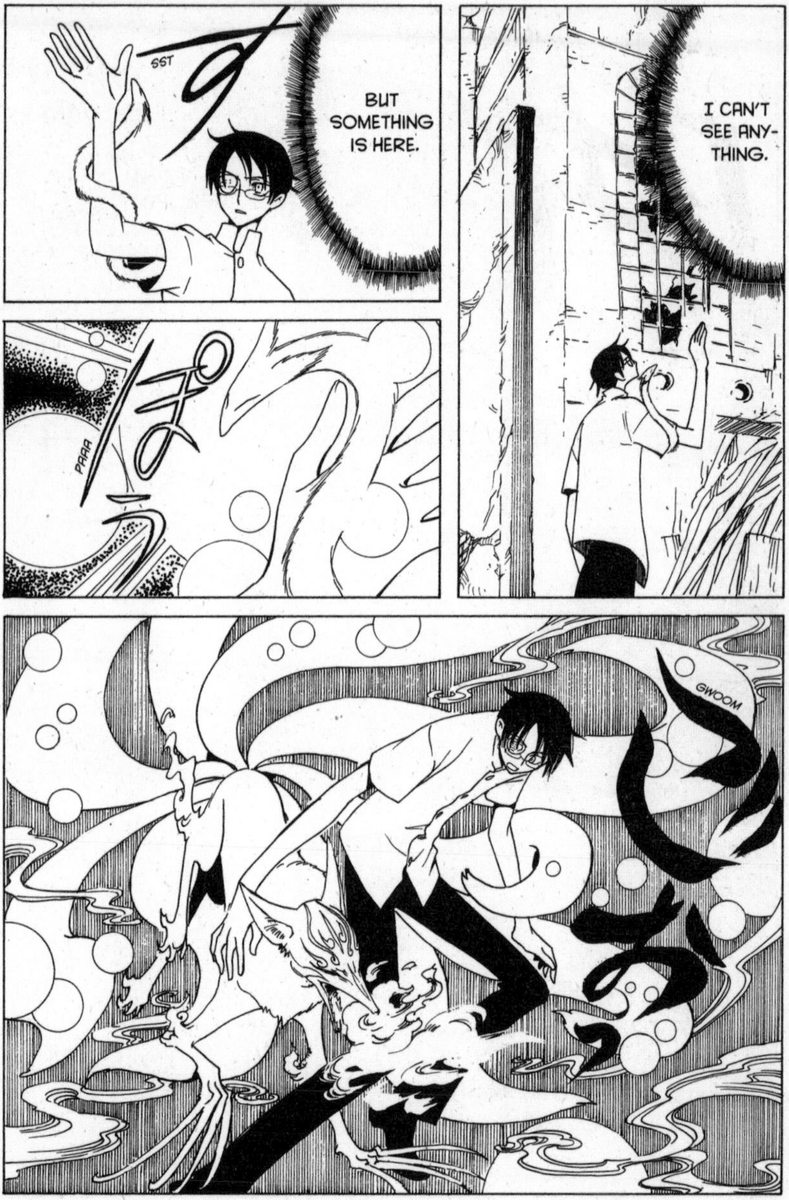
I CAN'T SEE ANY-THING.
SST
BUT SOMETHING IS HERE.
PAAA
GWOOM

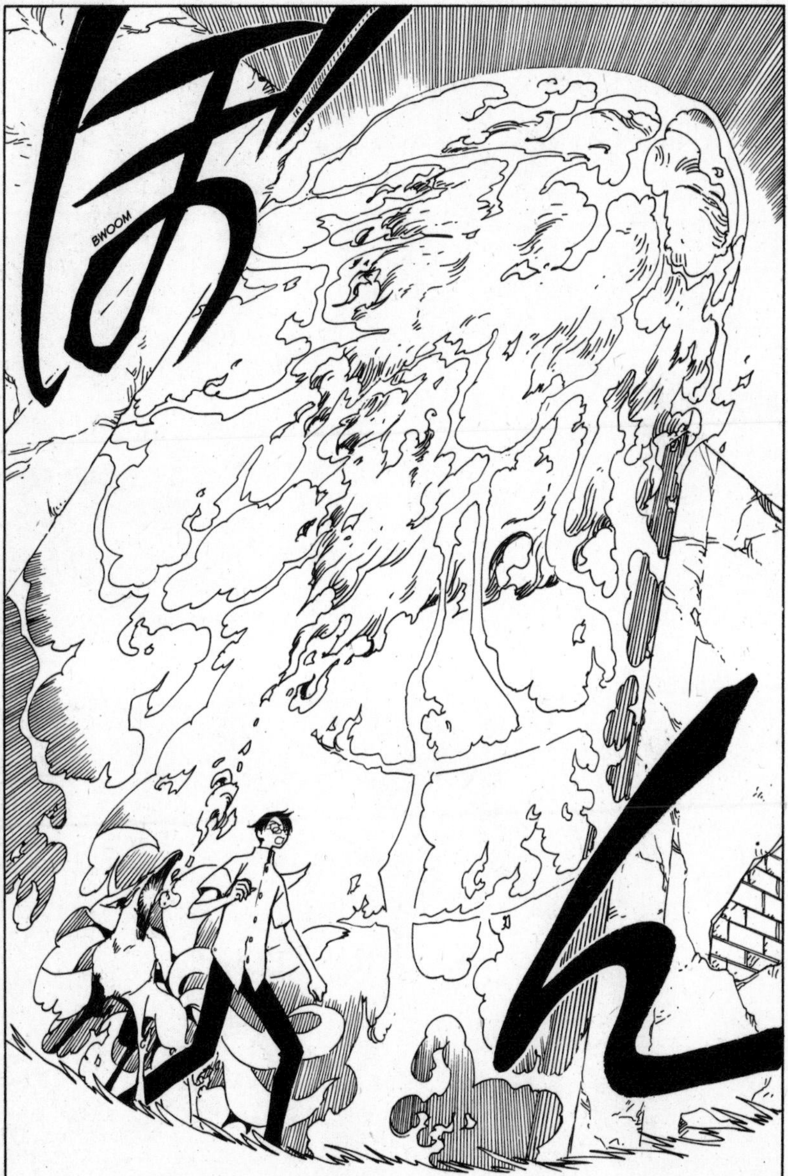
BWOOM

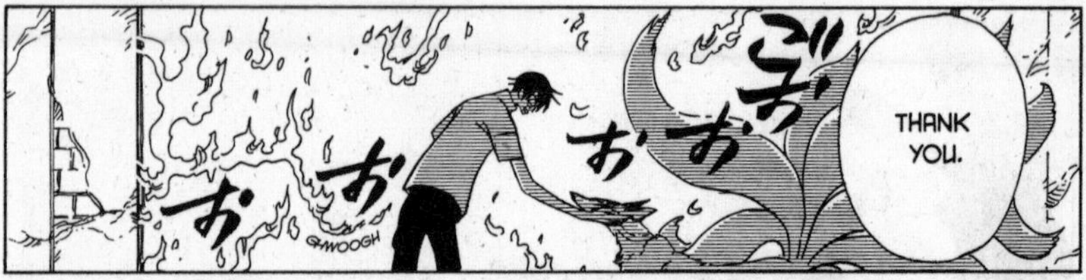
THANK YOU.
GWOOGH

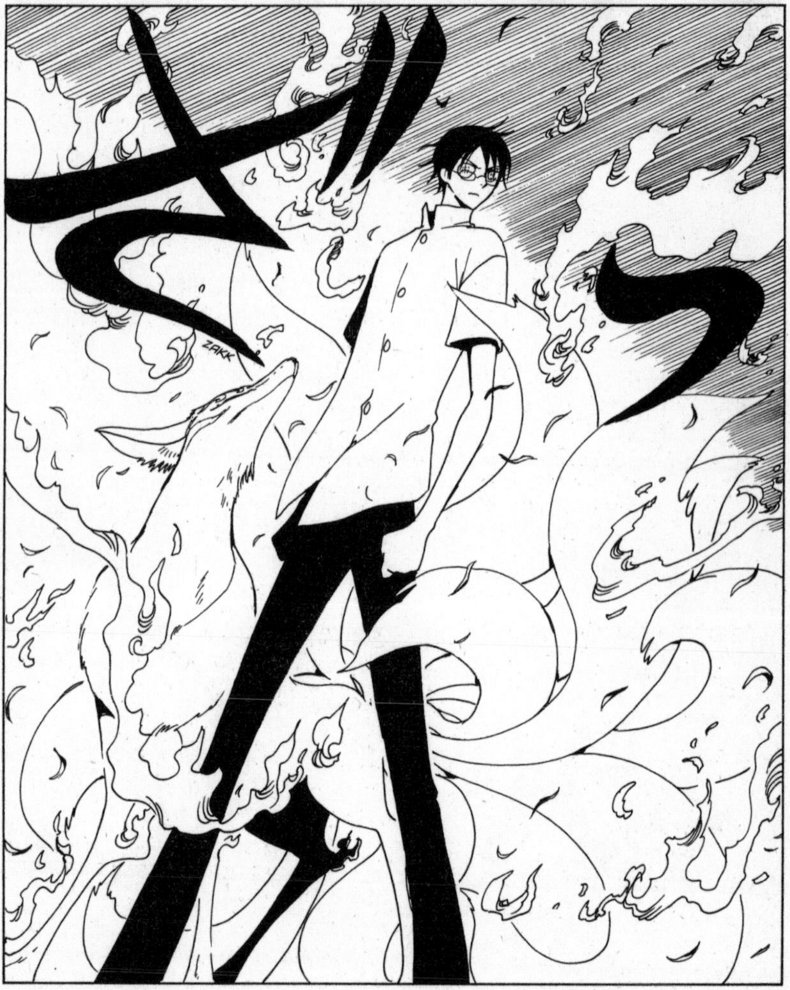
ZAKK

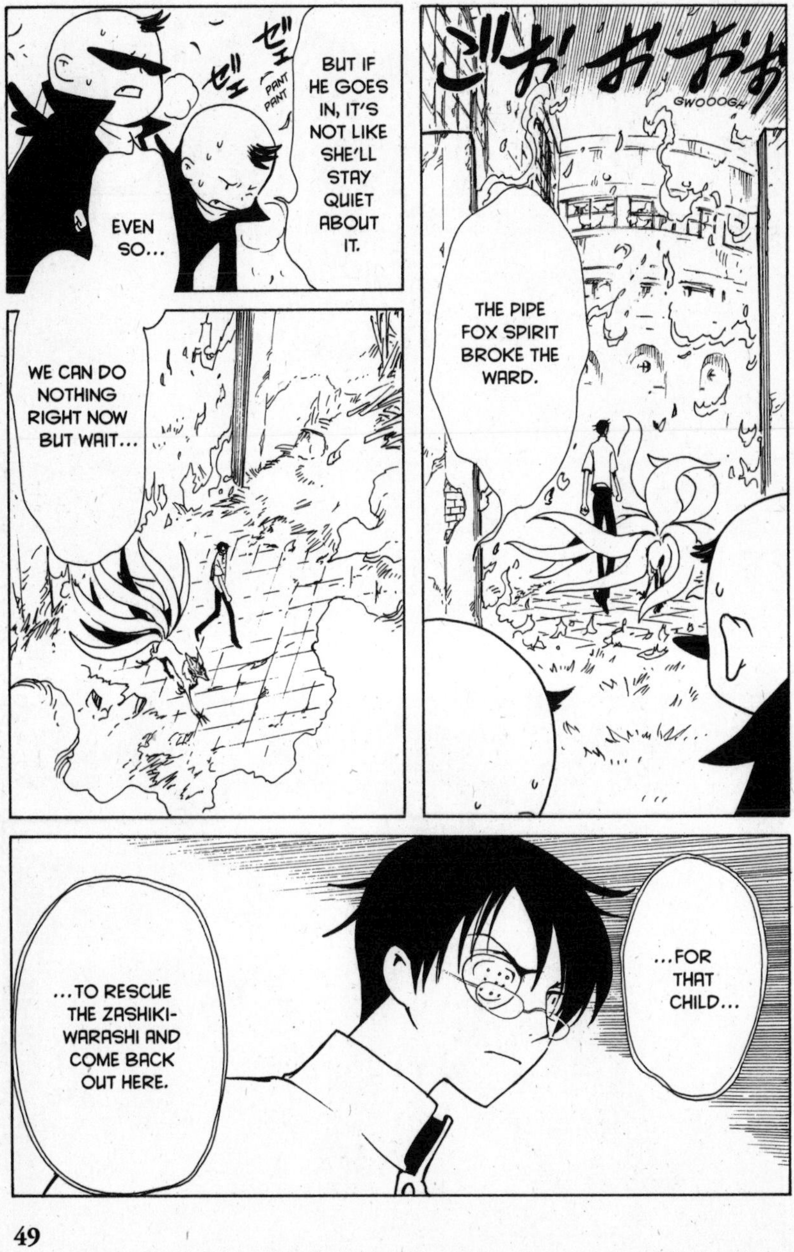
ごおおお
GWOOOGH
THE PIPE FOX SPIRIT BROKE THE WARD.
BUT IF HE GOES IN, IT'S NOT LIKE SHE'LL STAY QUIET ABOUT IT.
ゼェゼェ
PANT PANT
EVEN SO...
WE CAN DO NOTHING RIGHT NOW BUT WAIT...
...FOR THAT CHILD...
...TO RESCUE THE ZASHIKI-WARASHI AND COME BACK OUT HERE.

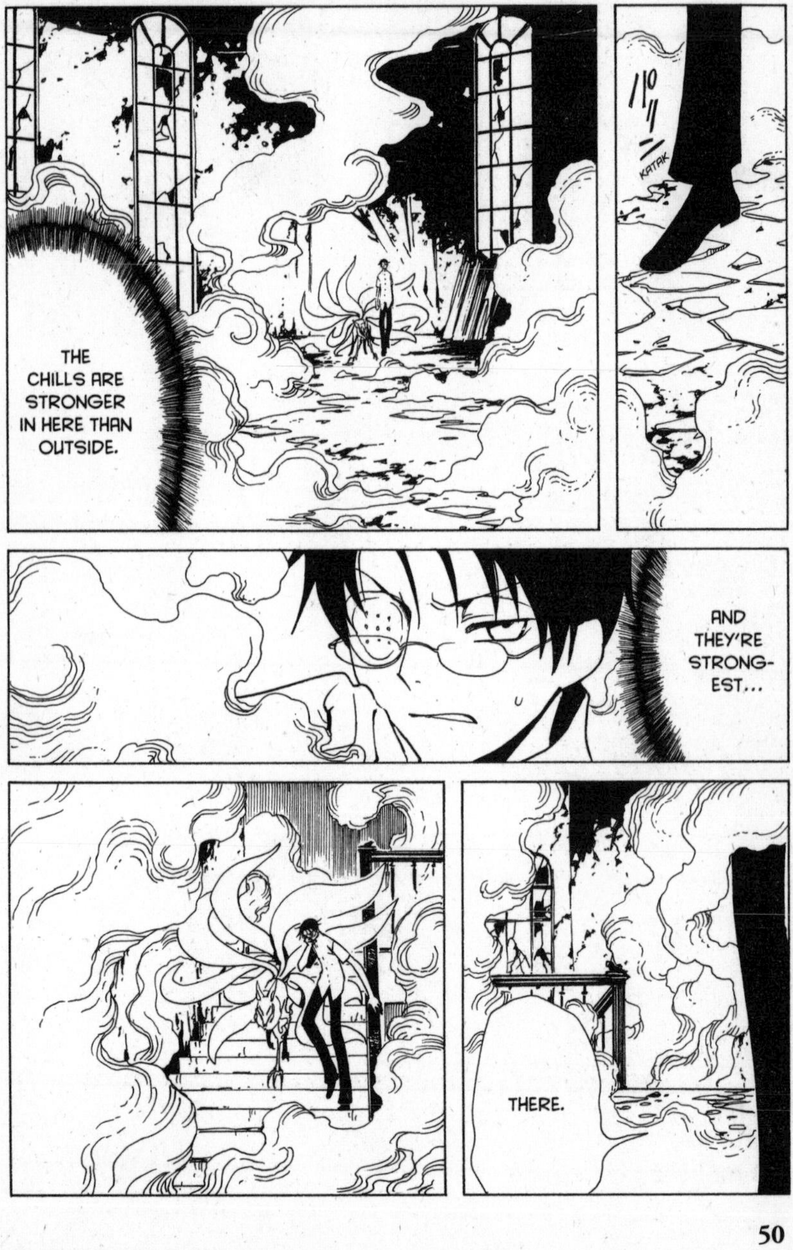
KATAK
THE CHILLS ARE STRONGER IN HERE THAN OUTSIDE.
AND THEY'RE STRONG-EST...
THERE.

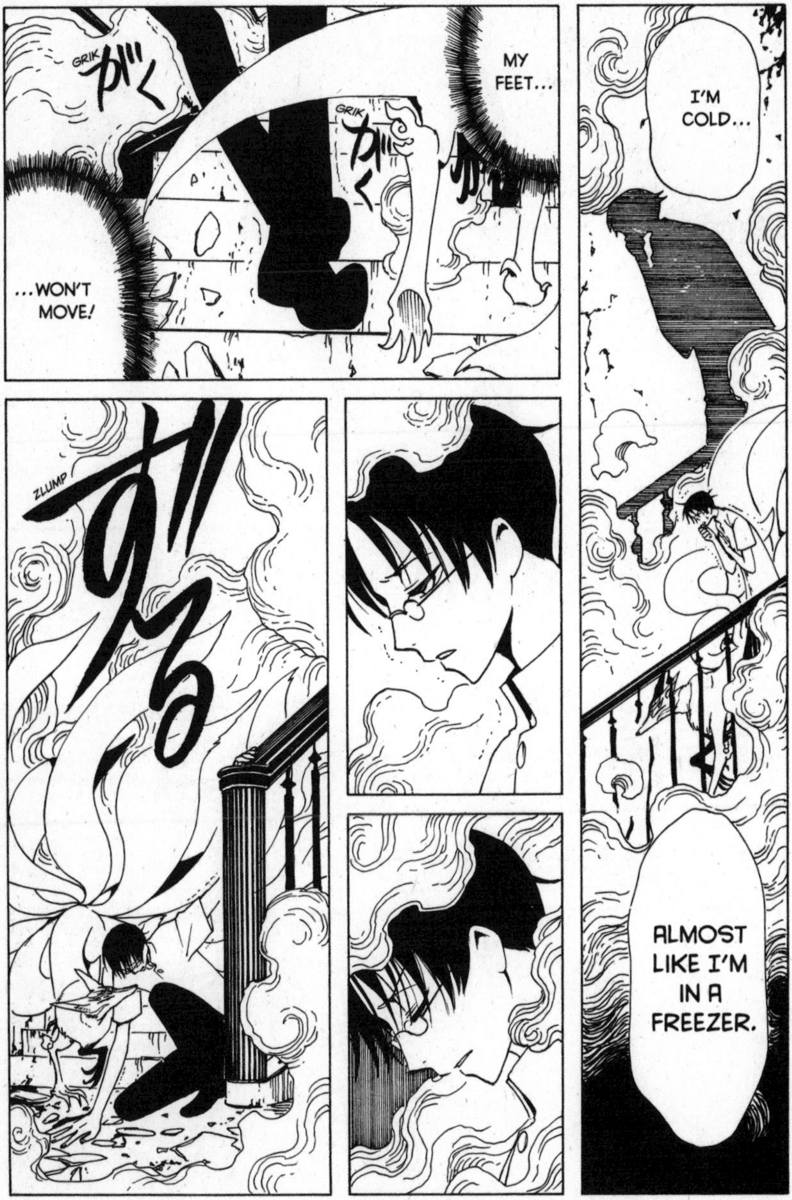
I'M COLD...
ALMOST LIKE I'M IN A FREEZER.
MY FEET...
GRIK
がく
GRIK
がく
...WON'T MOVE!
ZLUMP
ずる

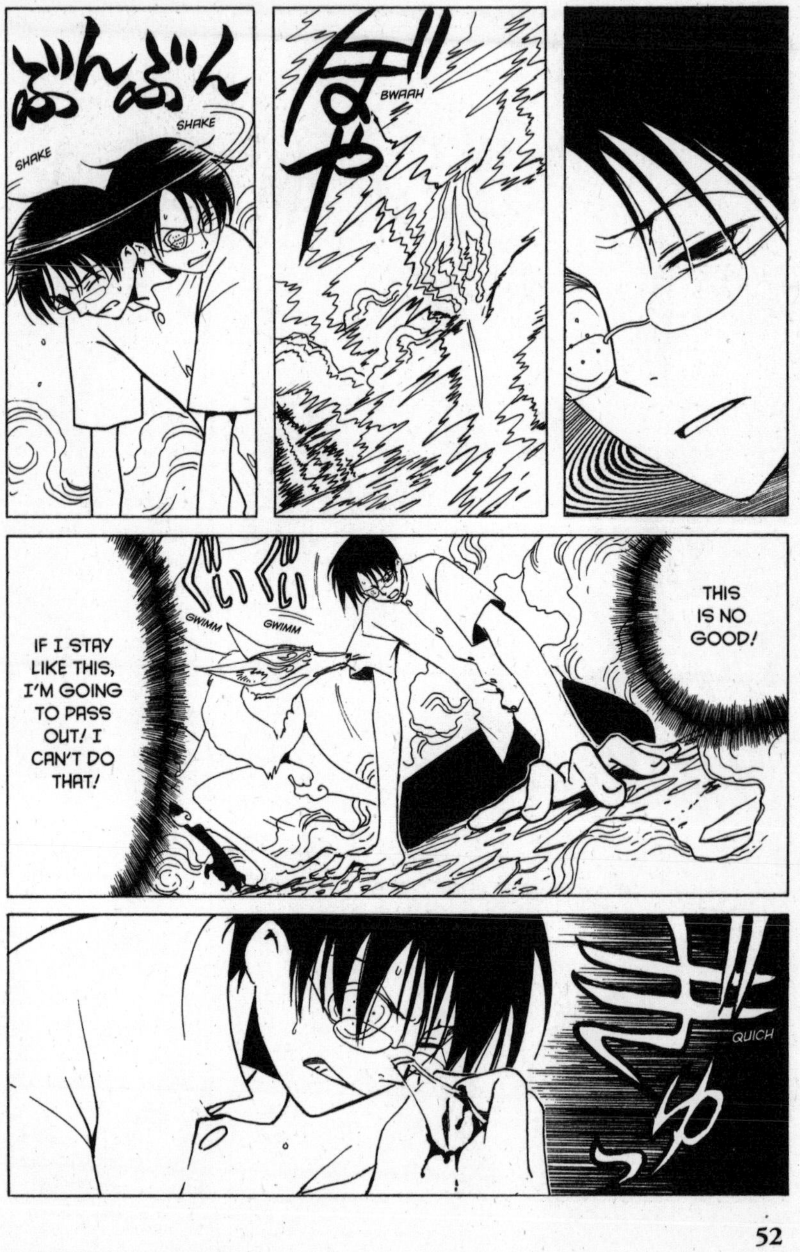
BWAAH
ぶんぶん
SHAKE
SHAKE
THIS IS NO GOOD!
GWIMM
GWIMM
IF I STAY LIKE THIS, I'M GOING TO PASS OUT! I CAN'T DO THAT!
QUICH

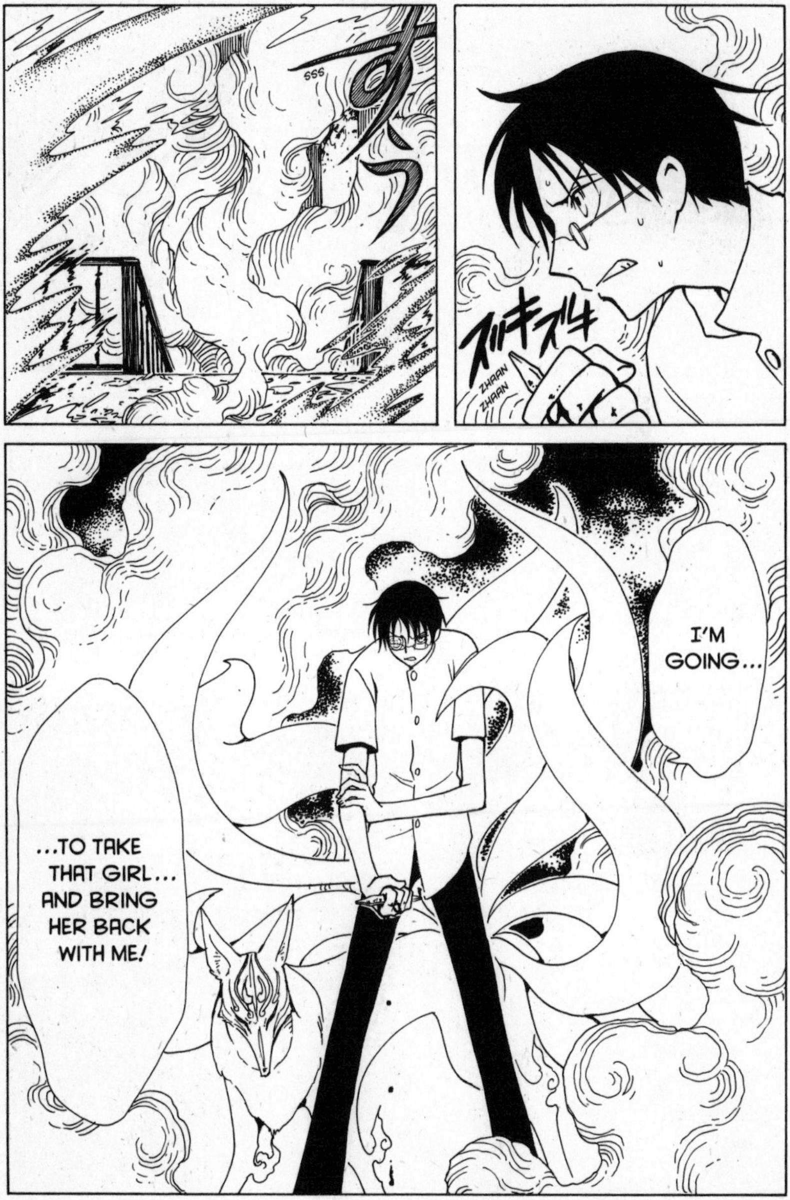
ズキズキ
ZHAAN
ZHAAN
SSS
I'M GOING...
...TO TAKE THAT GIRL... AND BRING HER BACK WITH ME!

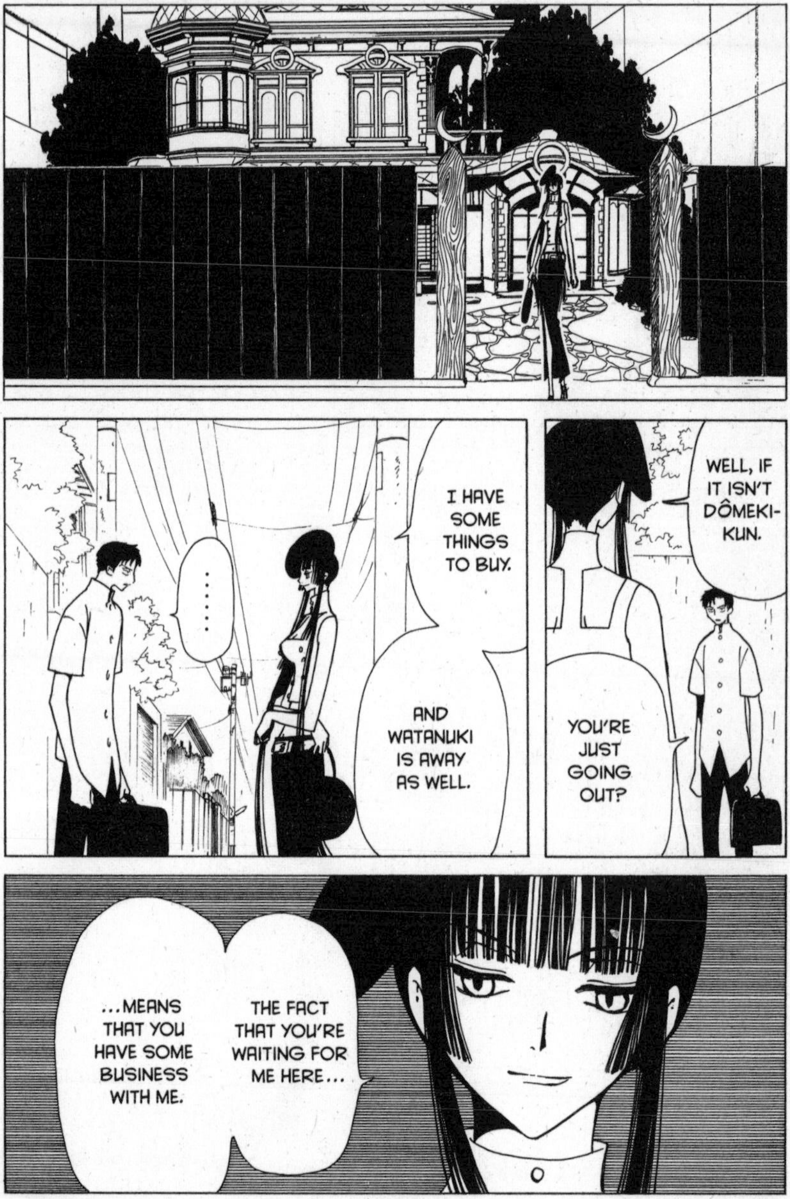
WELL, IF IT ISN'T DÔMEKI-KUN.
YOU'RE JUST GOING OUT?
I HAVE SOME THINGS TO BUY.
AND WATANUKI IS AWAY AS WELL.
......
THE FACT THAT YOU'RE WAITING FOR ME HERE...
...MEANS THAT YOU HAVE SOME BUSINESS WITH ME.

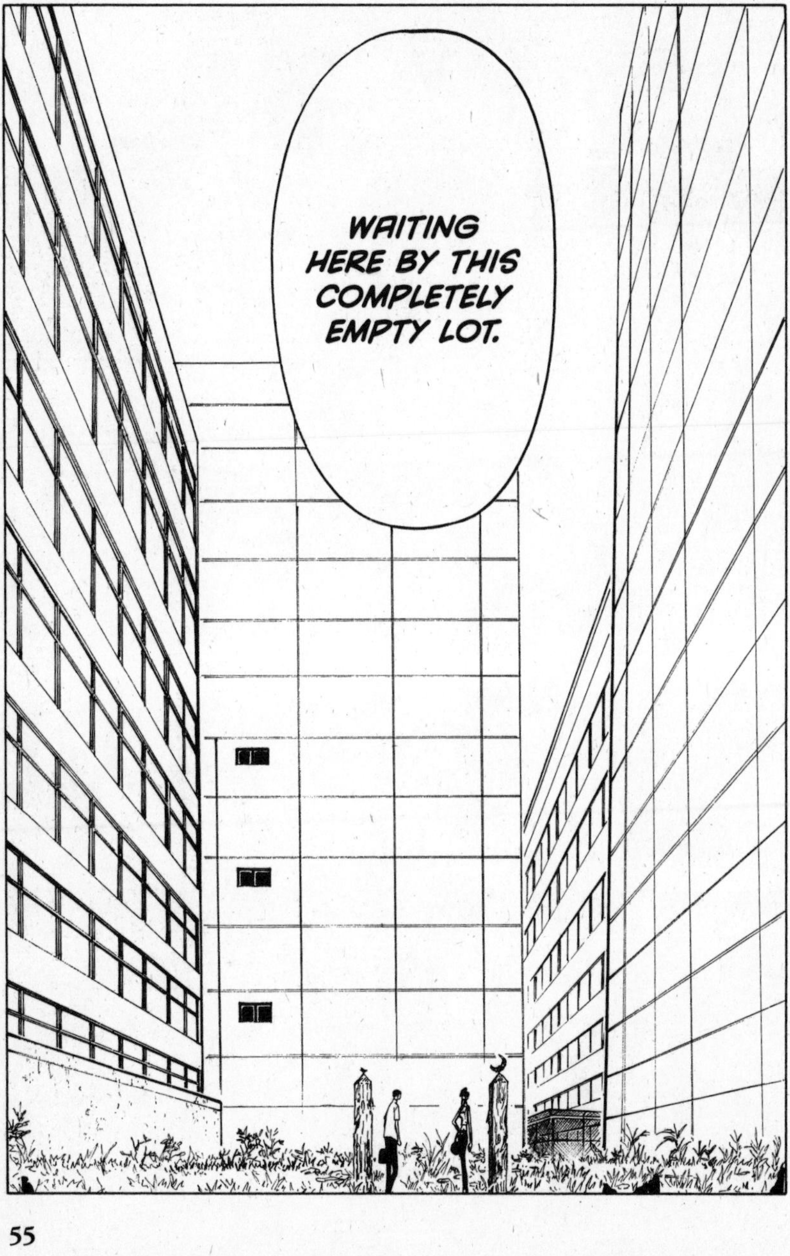
WAITING HERE BY THIS COMPLETELY EMPTY LOT.

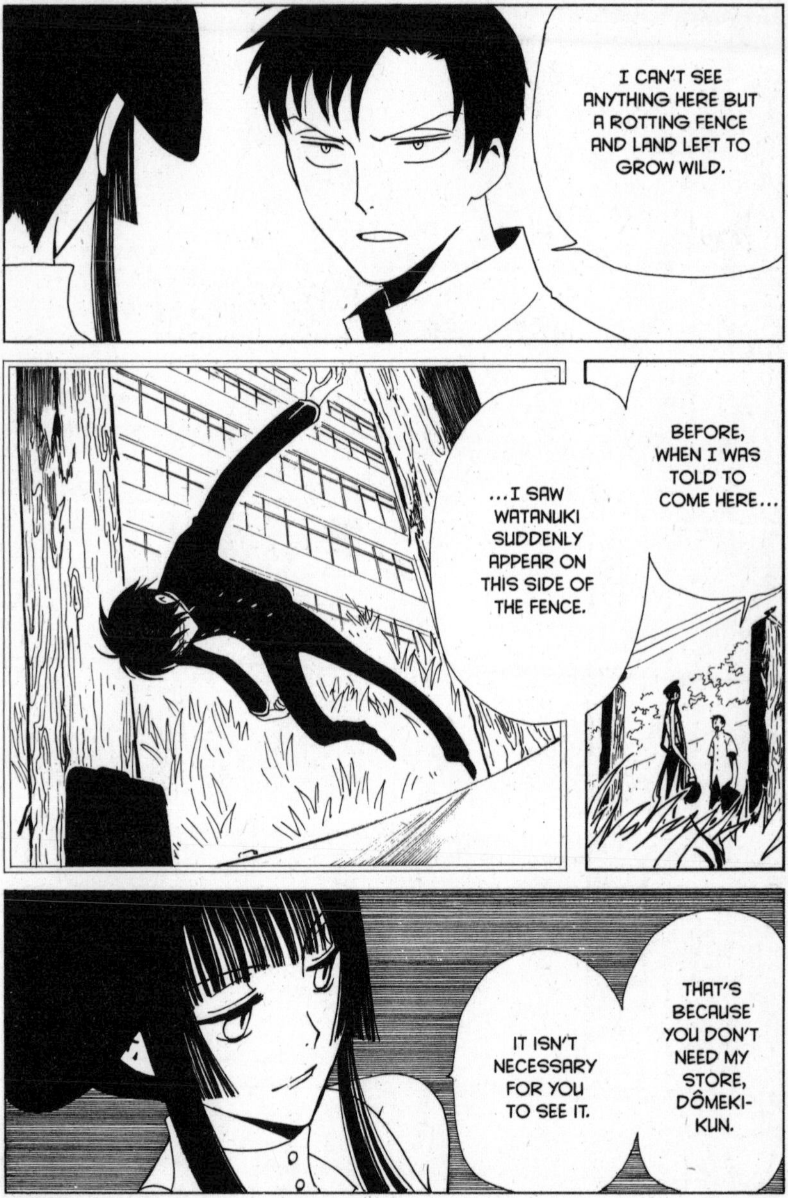
I CAN'T SEE ANYTHING HERE BUT A ROTTING FENCE AND LAND LEFT TO GROW WILD.
BEFORE, WHEN I WAS TOLD TO COME HERE...
...I SAW WATANUKI SUDDENLY APPEAR ON THIS SIDE OF THE FENCE.
THAT'S BECAUSE YOU DON'T NEED MY STORE, DÔMEKI-KUN.
IT ISN'T NECESSARY FOR YOU TO SEE IT.

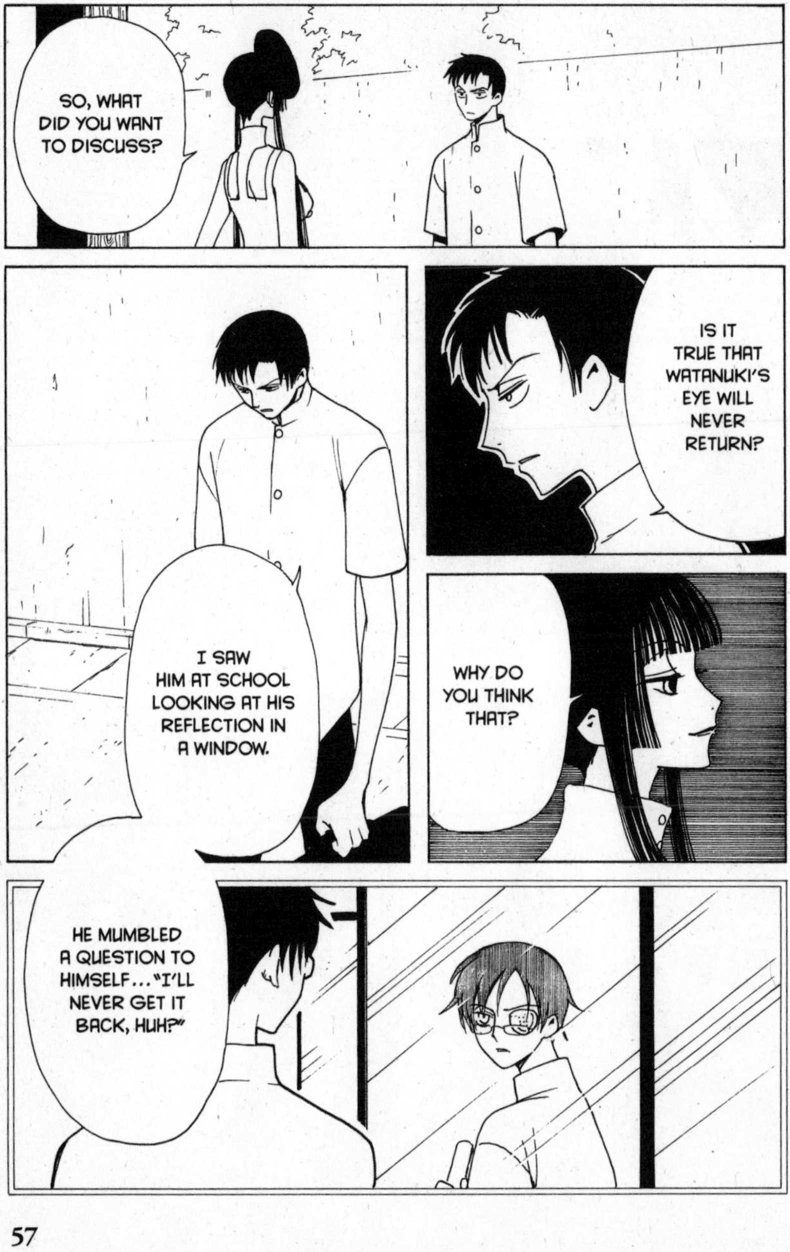
SO, WHAT DID YOU WANT TO DISCUSS?
IS IT TRUE THAT WATANUKI'S EYE WILL NEVER RETURN?
WHY DO YOU THINK THAT?
I SAW HIM AT SCHOOL LOOKING AT HIS REFLECTION IN A WINDOW.
HE MUMBLED A QUESTION TO HIMSELF... "I'LL NEVER GET IT BACK, HUH?"

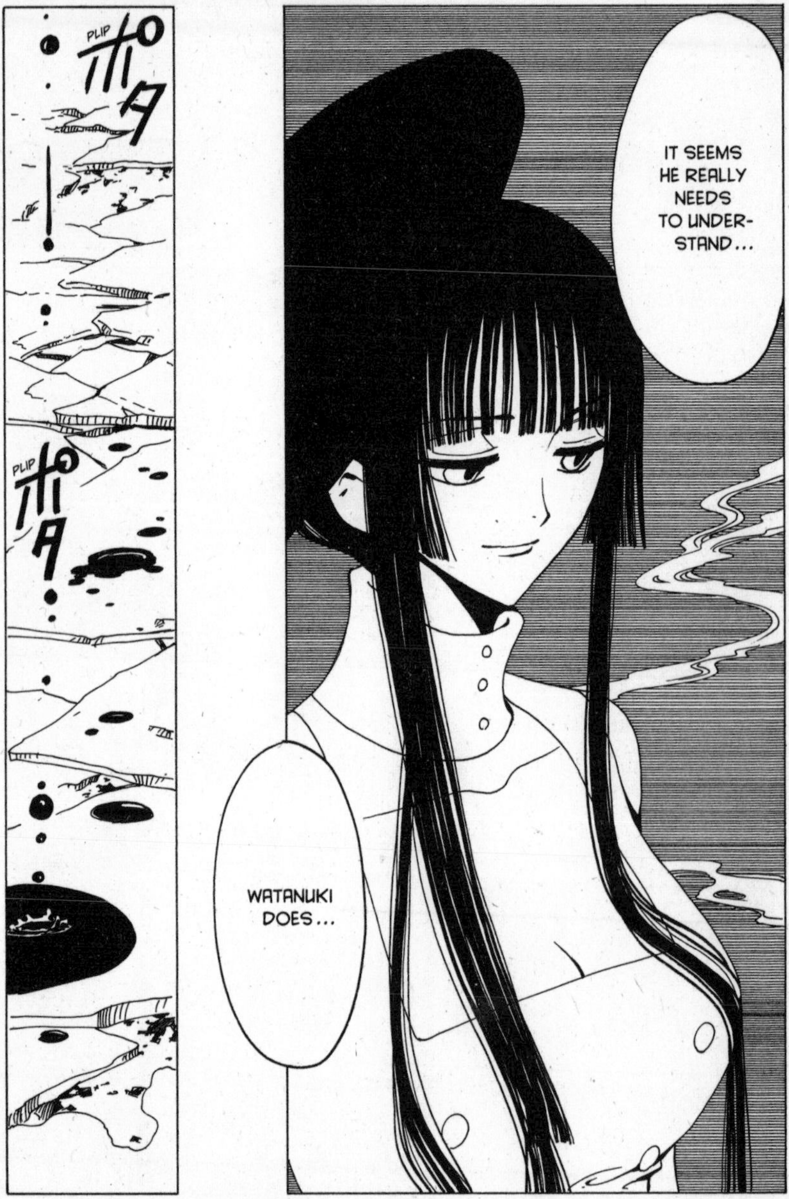
IT SEEMS HE REALLY NEEDS TO UNDER-STAND...
WATANUKI DOES...
PLIP
ポタ
PLIP
ポタ

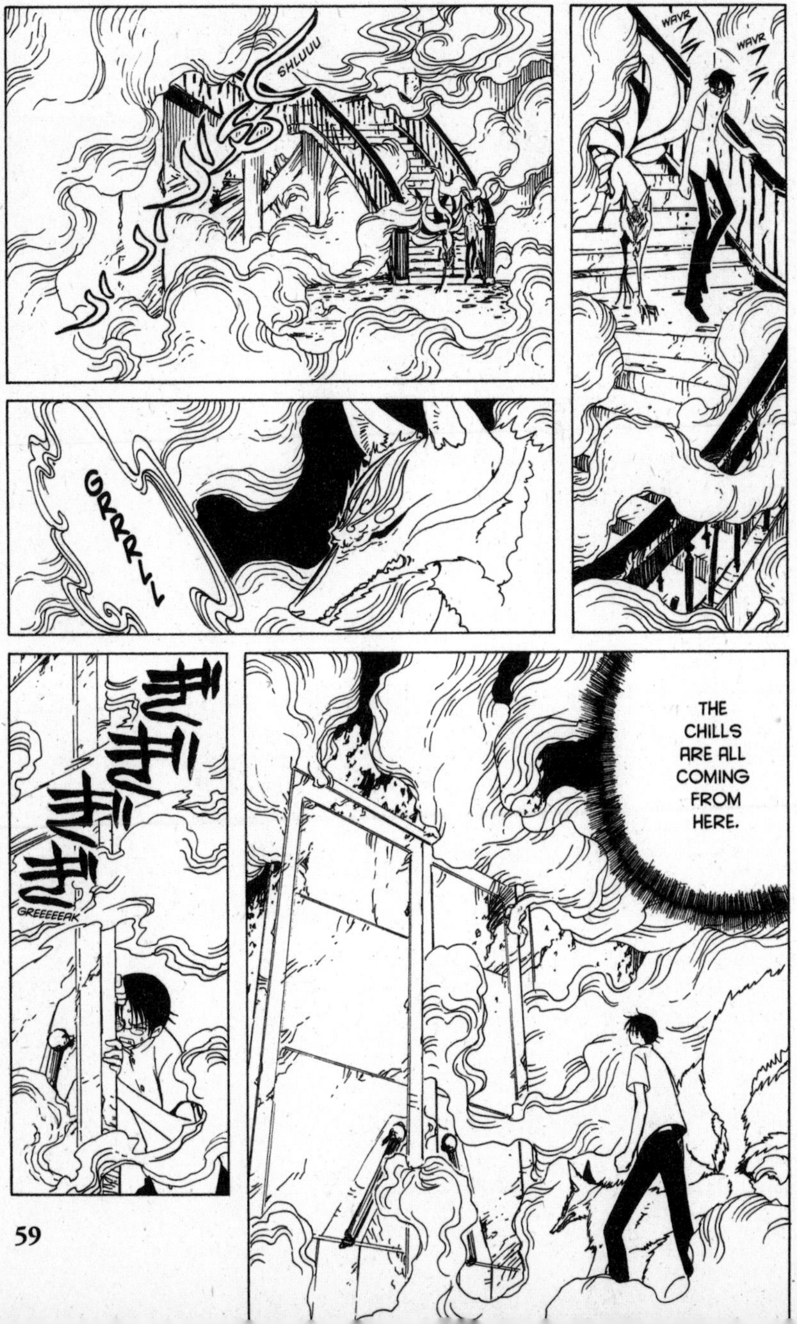
WAVR
WAVR
SHLUUU
GRRRLLL
THE CHILLS ARE ALL COMING FROM HERE.
GREEEEEAK

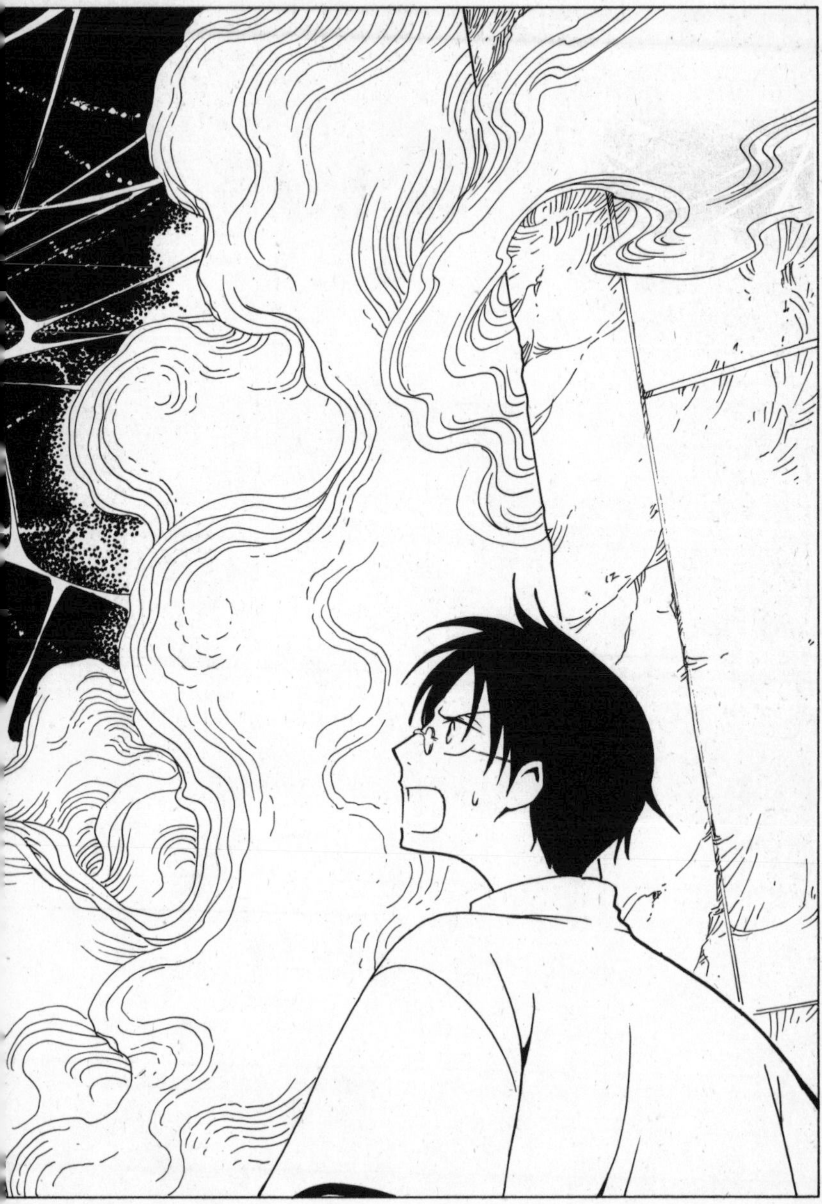

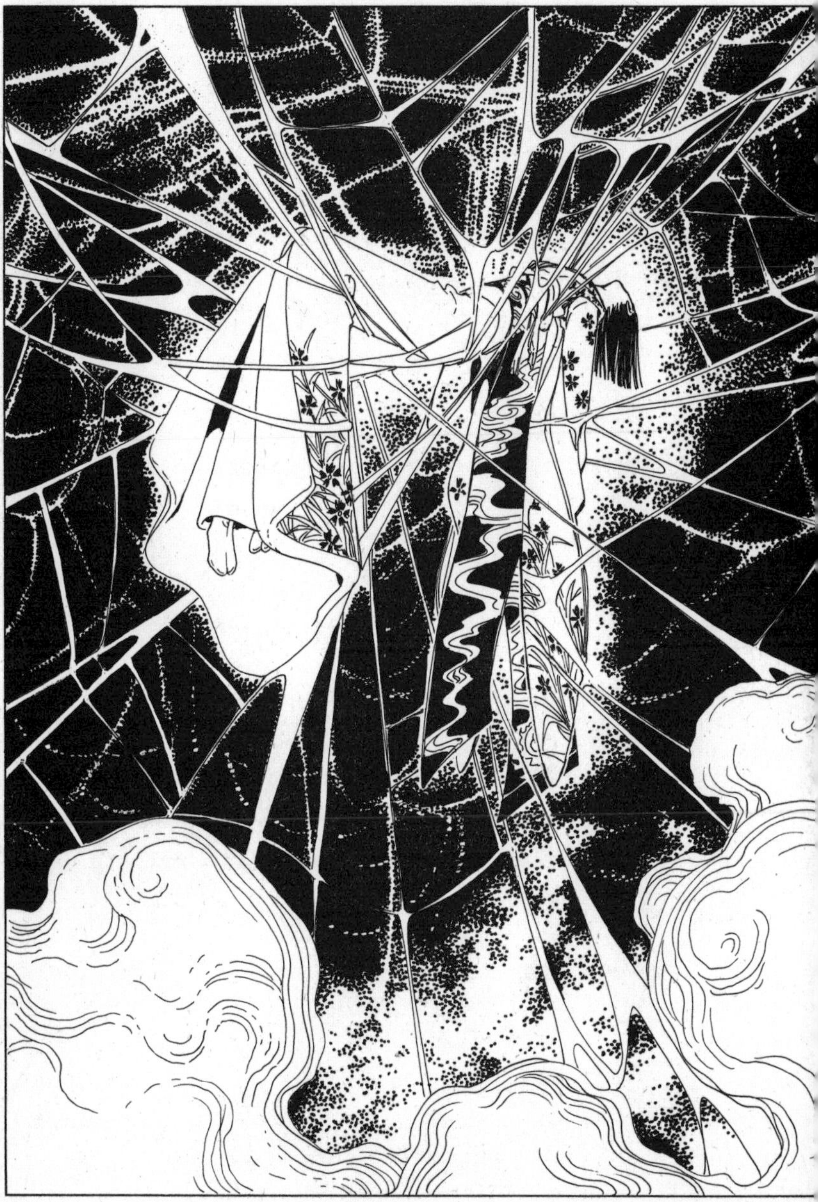

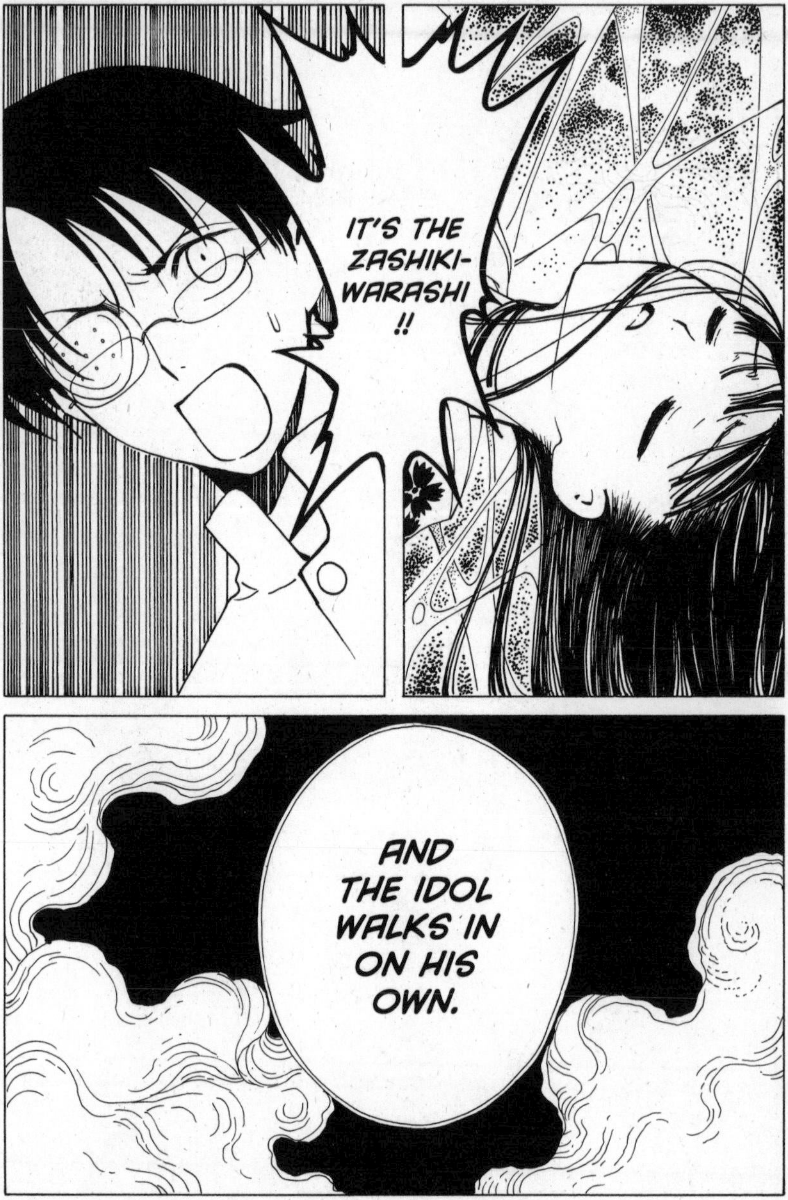
IT'S THE ZASHIKI-WARASHI !!
AND THE IDOL WALKS IN ON HIS OWN.

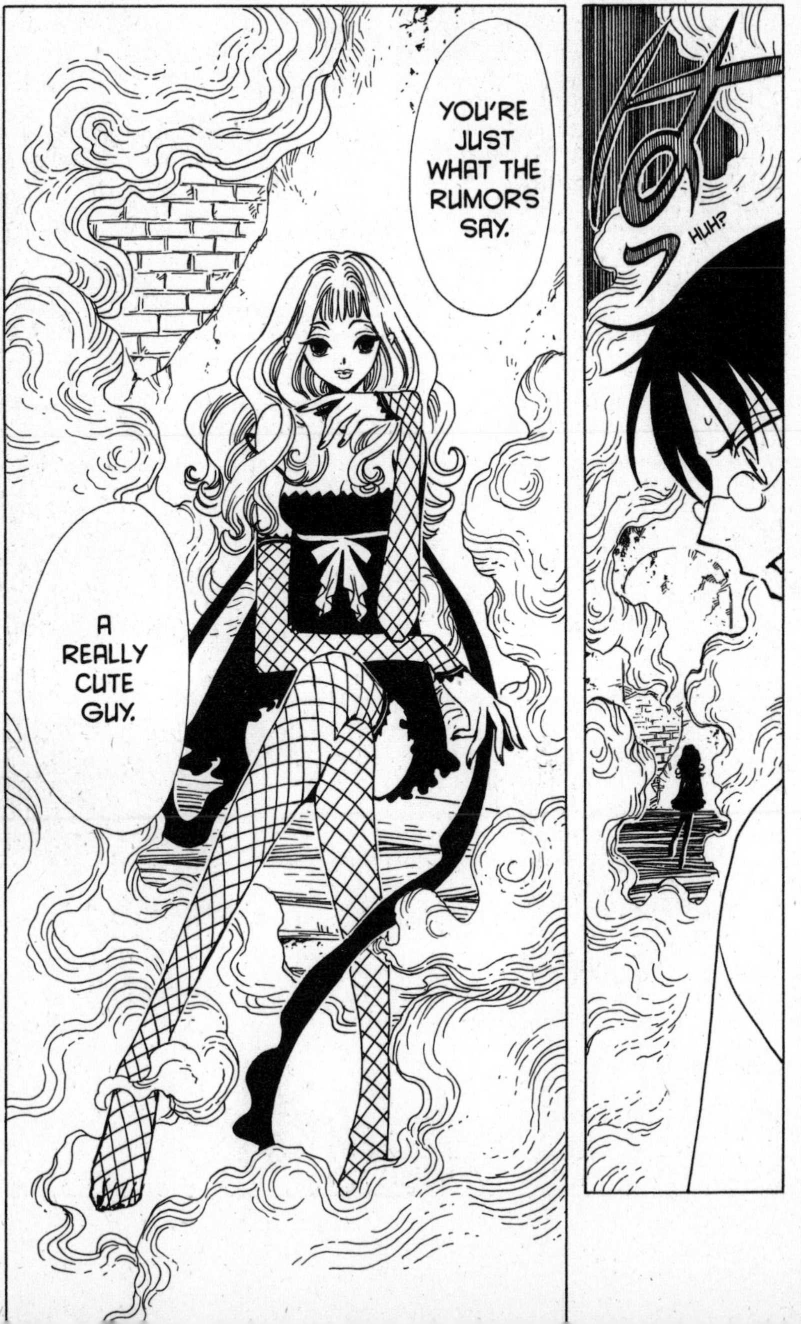
HUH?
YOU'RE JUST WHAT THE RUMORS SAY.
A REALLY CUTE GUY.

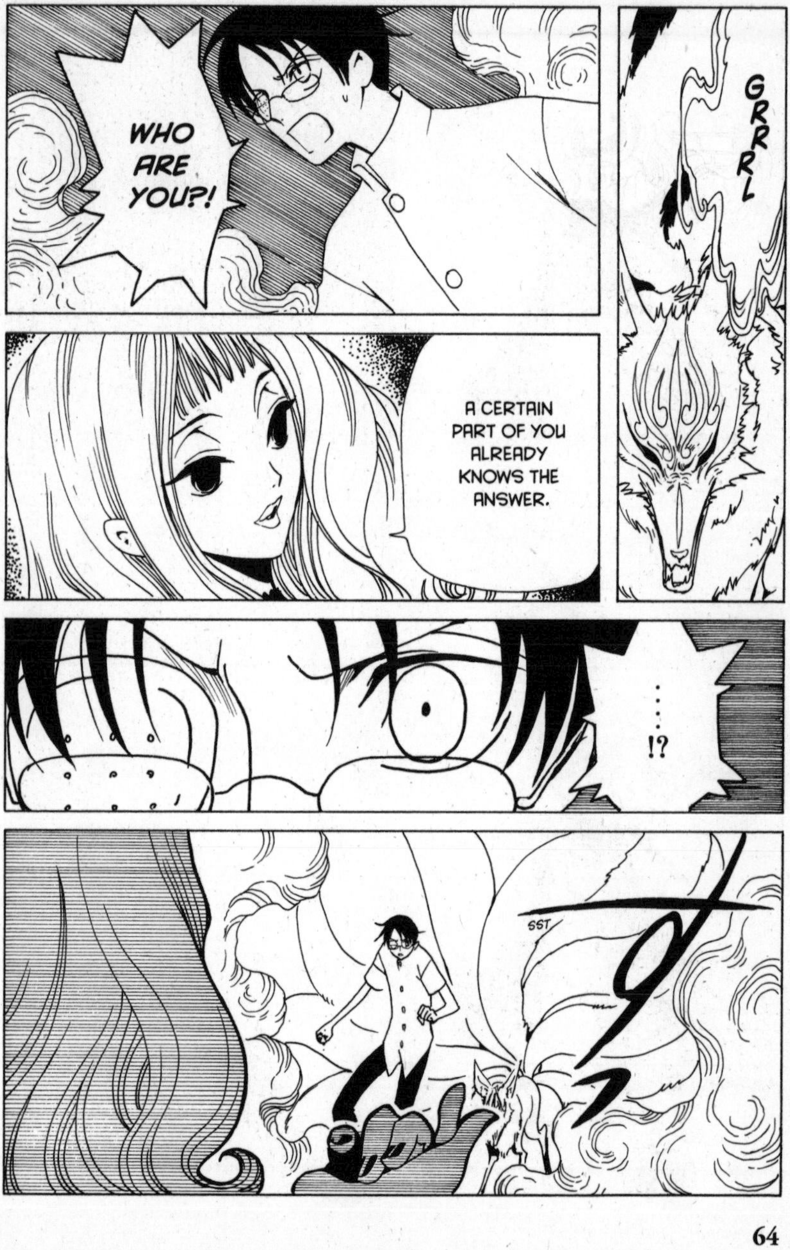
GRRRL
WHO ARE YOU?!
A CERTAIN PART OF YOU ALREADY KNOWS THE ANSWER.
......!?
SST

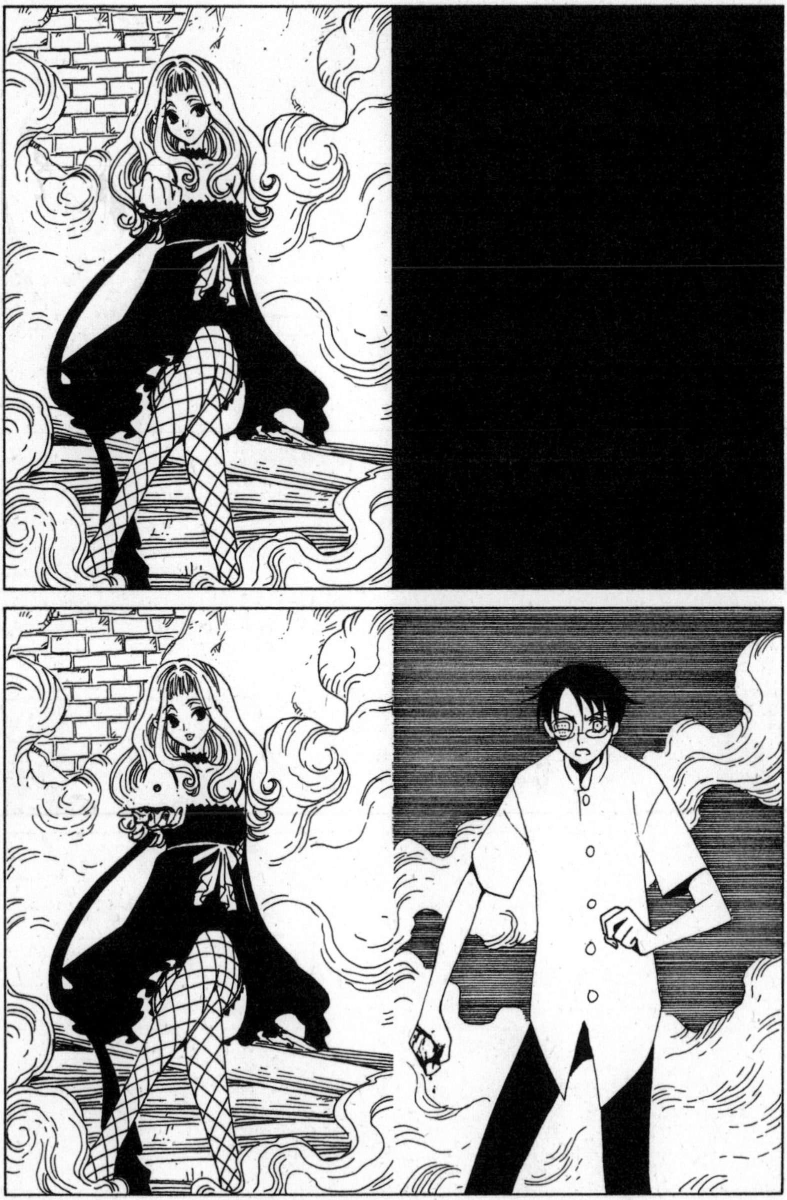

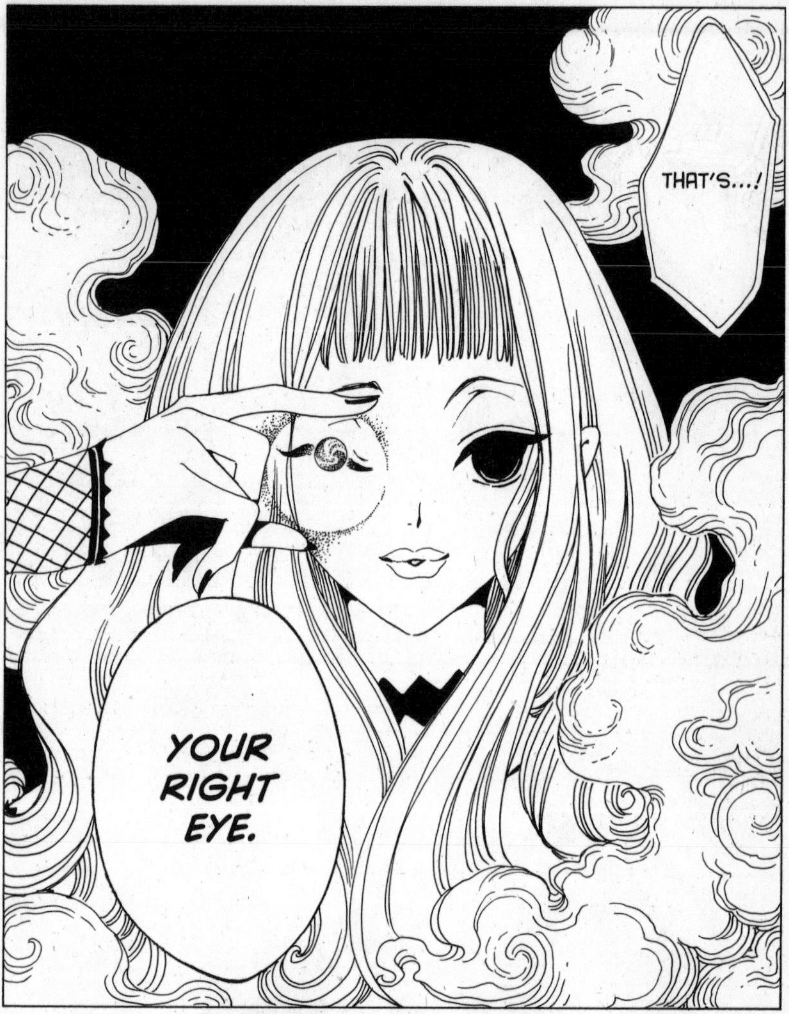
THAT'S...!
YOUR RIGHT EYE.
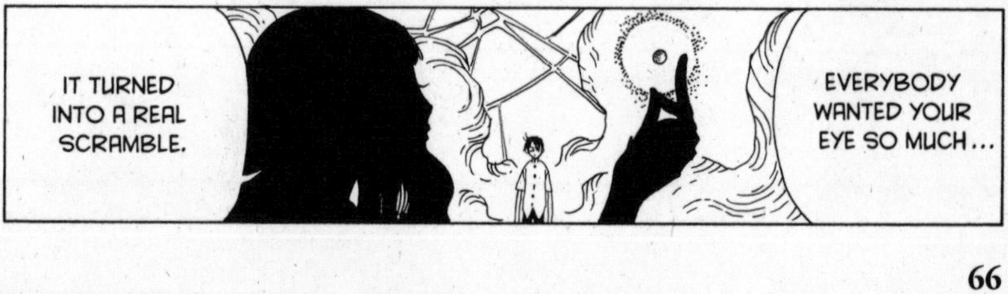
EVERYBODY WANTED YOUR EYE SO MUCH...
IT TURNED INTO A REAL SCRAMBLE.

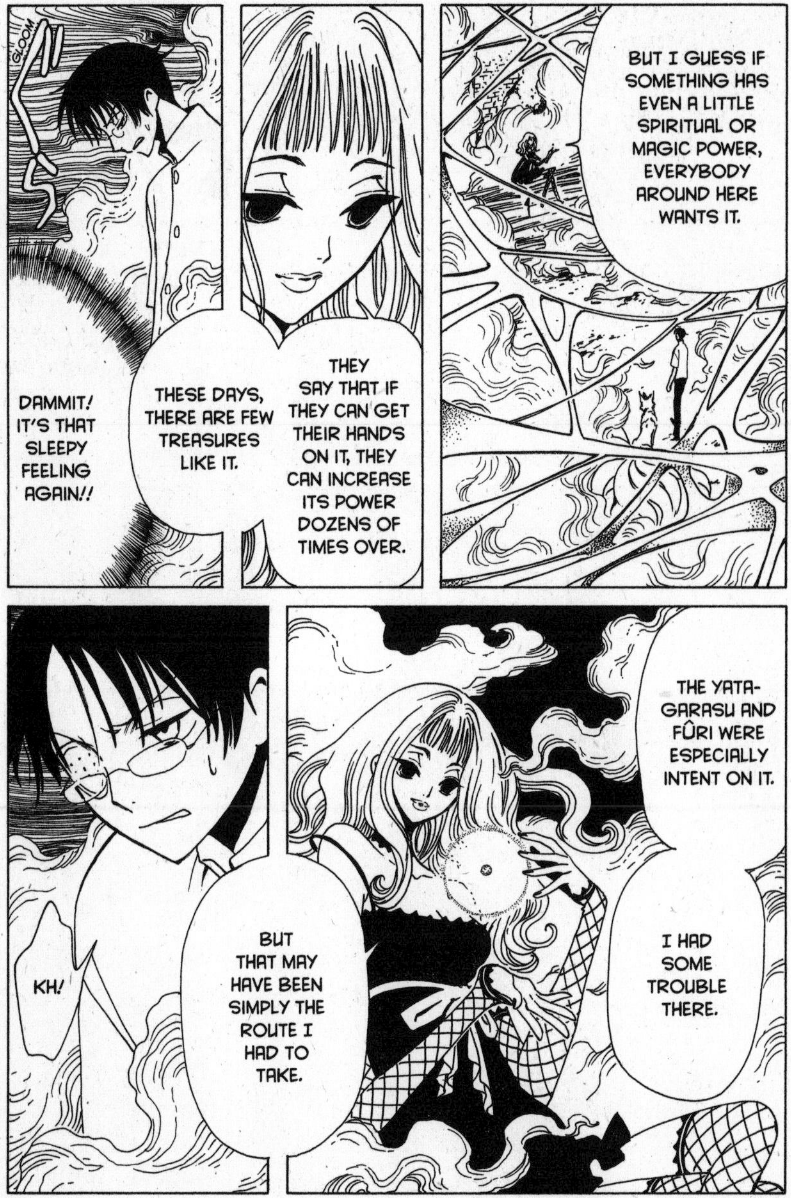
BUT I GUESS IF SOMETHING HAS EVEN A LITTLE SPIRITUAL OR MAGIC POWER, EVERYBODY AROUND HERE WANTS IT.
THEY SAY THAT IF THEY CAN GET THEIR HANDS ON IT, THEY CAN INCREASE ITS POWER DOZENS OF TIMES OVER.
THESE DAYS, THERE ARE FEW TREASURES LIKE IT.
GLOOM
DAMMIT! IT'S THAT SLEEPY FEELING AGAIN!!
THE YATA-GARASU AND FÛRI WERE ESPECIALLY INTENT ON IT.
I HAD SOME TROUBLE THERE.
BUT THAT MAY HAVE BEEN SIMPLY THE ROUTE I HAD TO TAKE.
KH!

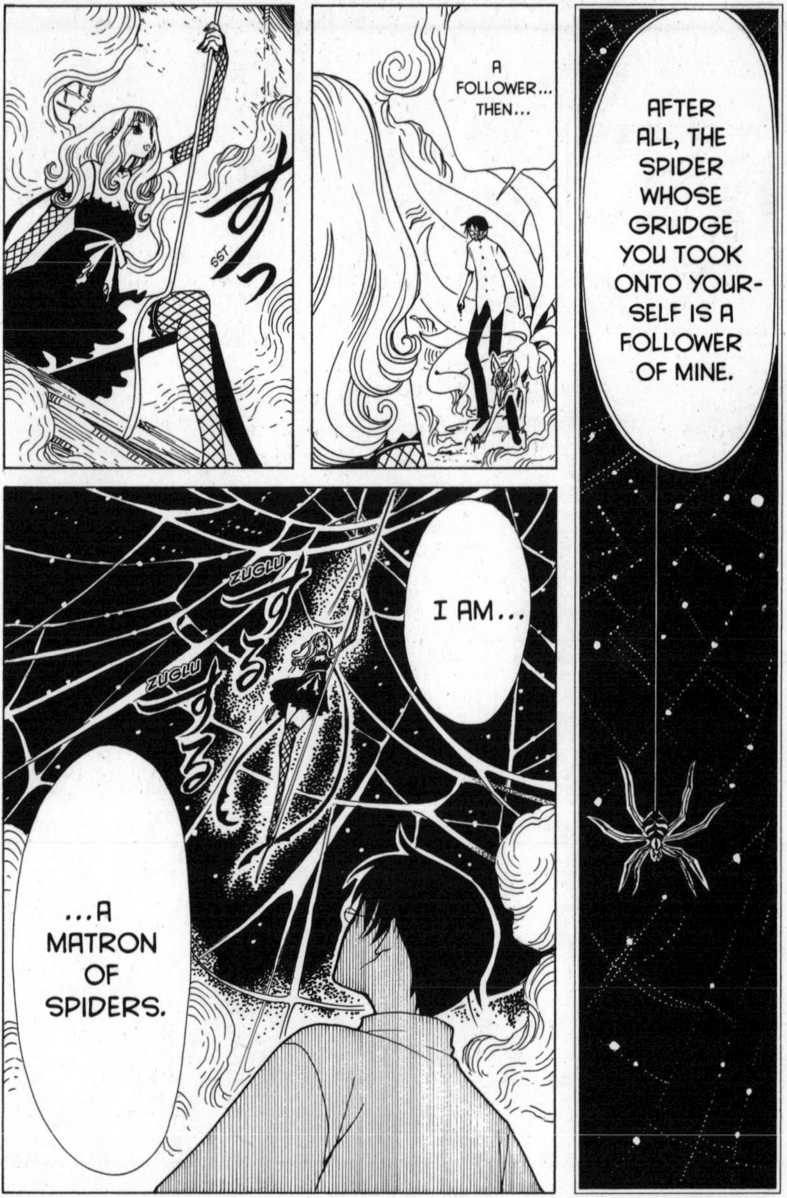
AFTER ALL, THE SPIDER WHOSE GRUDGE YOU TOOK ONTO YOUR-SELF IS A FOLLOWER OF MINE.
A FOLLOWER... THEN...
すっ
SST
I AM...
するする
ZUGLU
ZUGLU
...A MATRON OF SPIDERS.

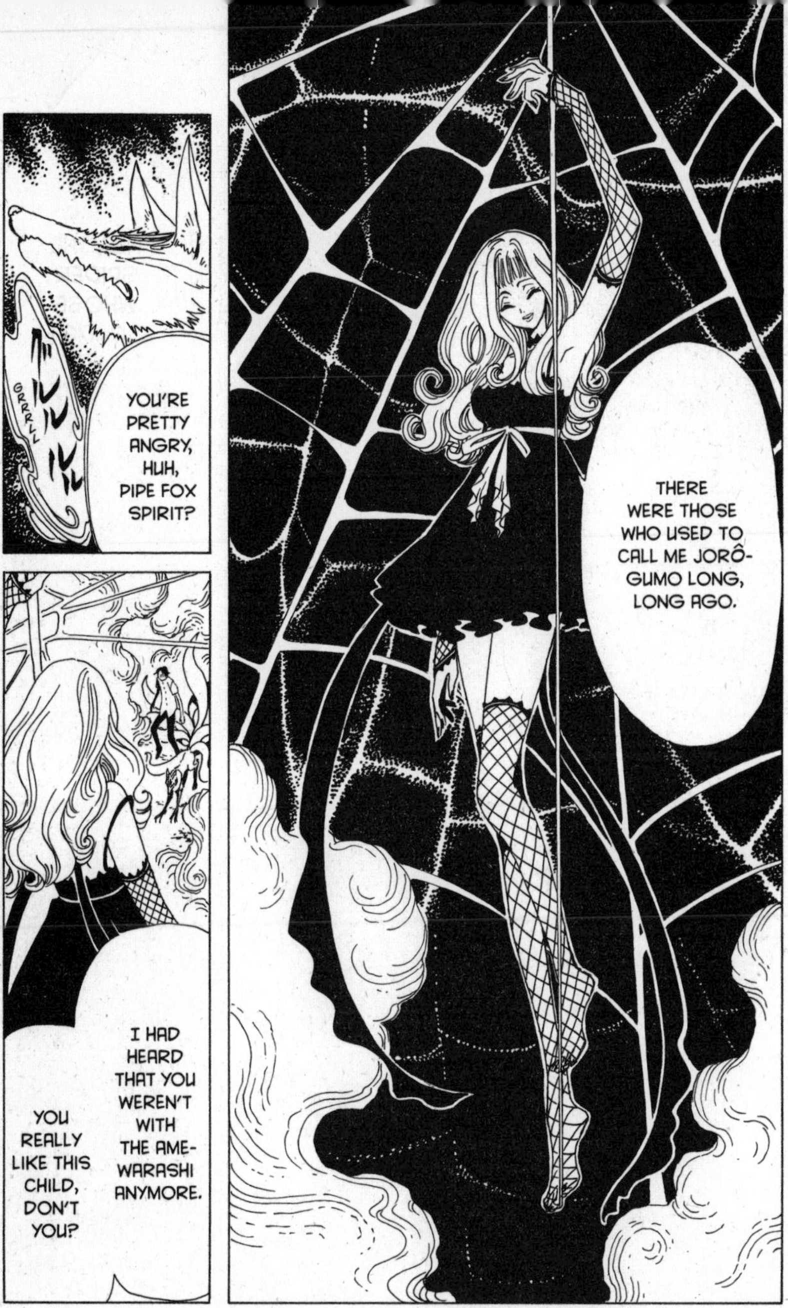
THERE WERE THOSE WHO USED TO CALL ME JORÔ-GUMO LONG, LONG AGO.
グルルルル
GRRRLL
YOU'RE PRETTY ANGRY, HUH, PIPE FOX SPIRIT?
I HAD HEARD THAT YOU WEREN'T WITH THE AME-WARASHI ANYMORE.
YOU REALLY LIKE THIS CHILD, DON'T YOU?

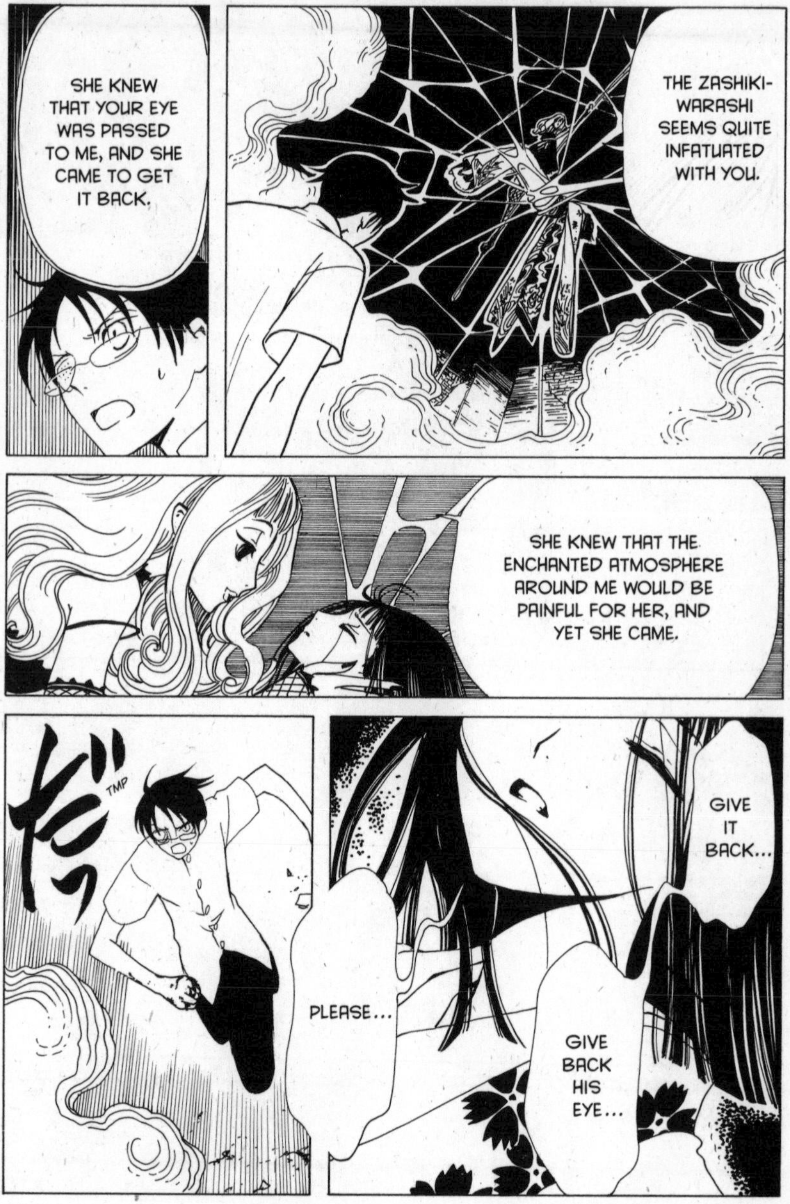
THE ZASHIKI-WARASHI SEEMS QUITE INFATUATED WITH YOU.
SHE KNEW THAT YOUR EYE WAS PASSED TO ME, AND SHE CAME TO GET IT BACK.
SHE KNEW THAT THE ENCHANTED ATMOSPHERE AROUND ME WOULD BE PAINFUL FOR HER, AND YET SHE CAME.
GIVE IT BACK...
GIVE BACK HIS EYE...
PLEASE...
TMP

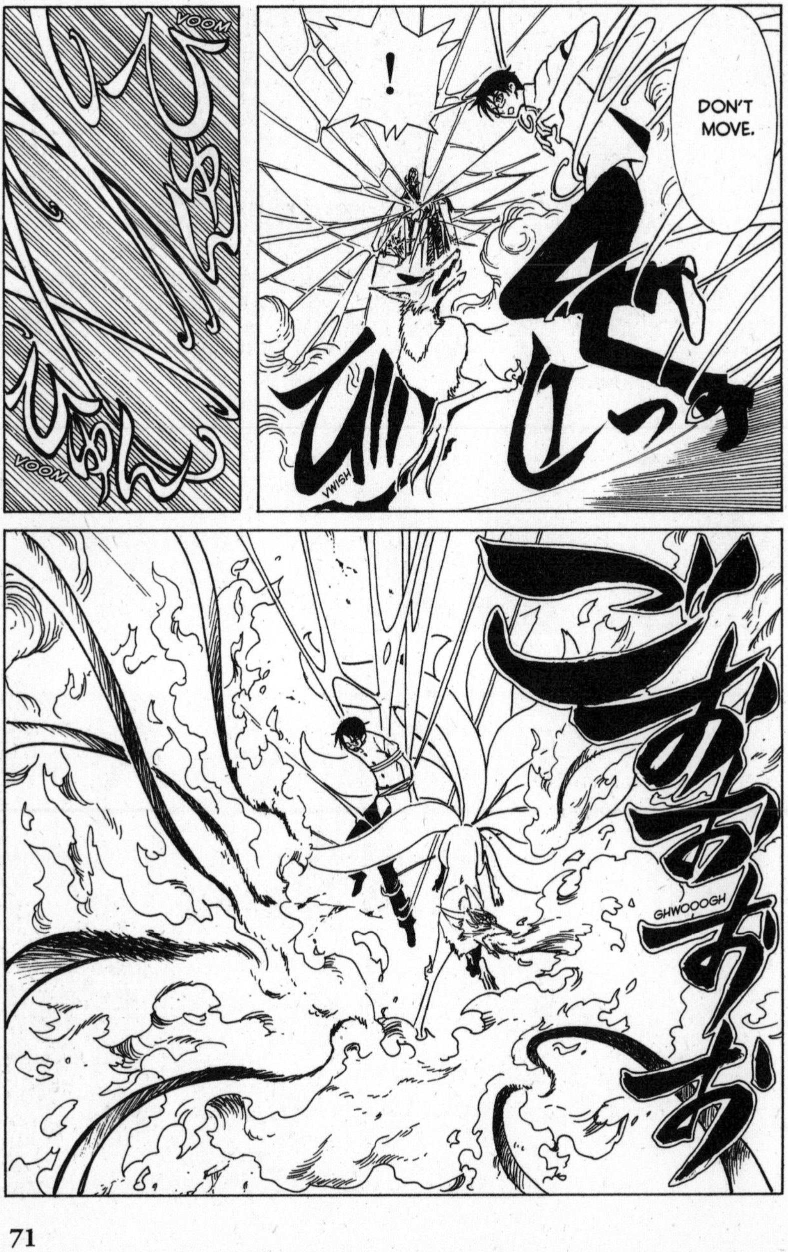
!
DON'T MOVE.
VWISH
VOOM
VOOM
GHWOOOGH

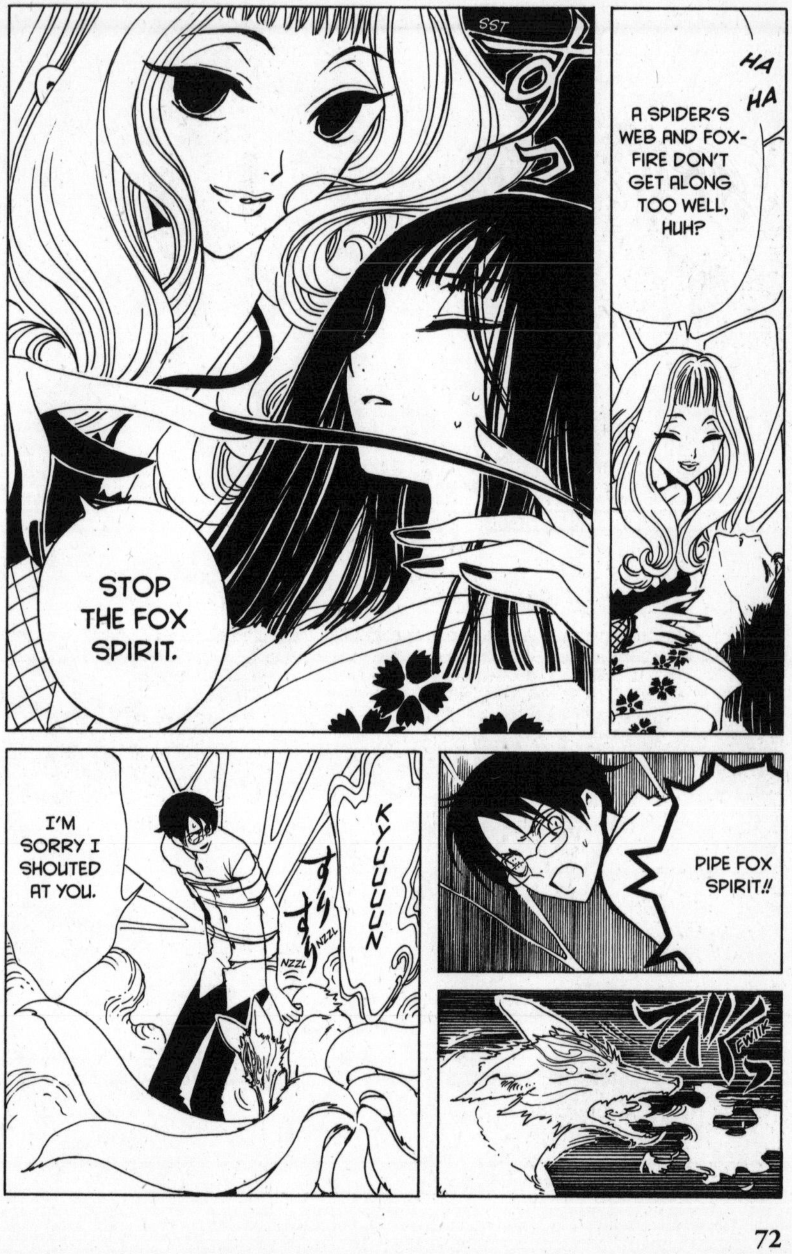
HA HA
A SPIDER'S WEB AND FOX-FIRE DON'T GET ALONG TOO WELL, HUH?
SST
STOP THE FOX SPIRIT.
PIPE FOX SPIRIT!!
FWIIK
KYUUUUUN
NZZL
NZZL
I'M SORRY I SHOUTED AT YOU.

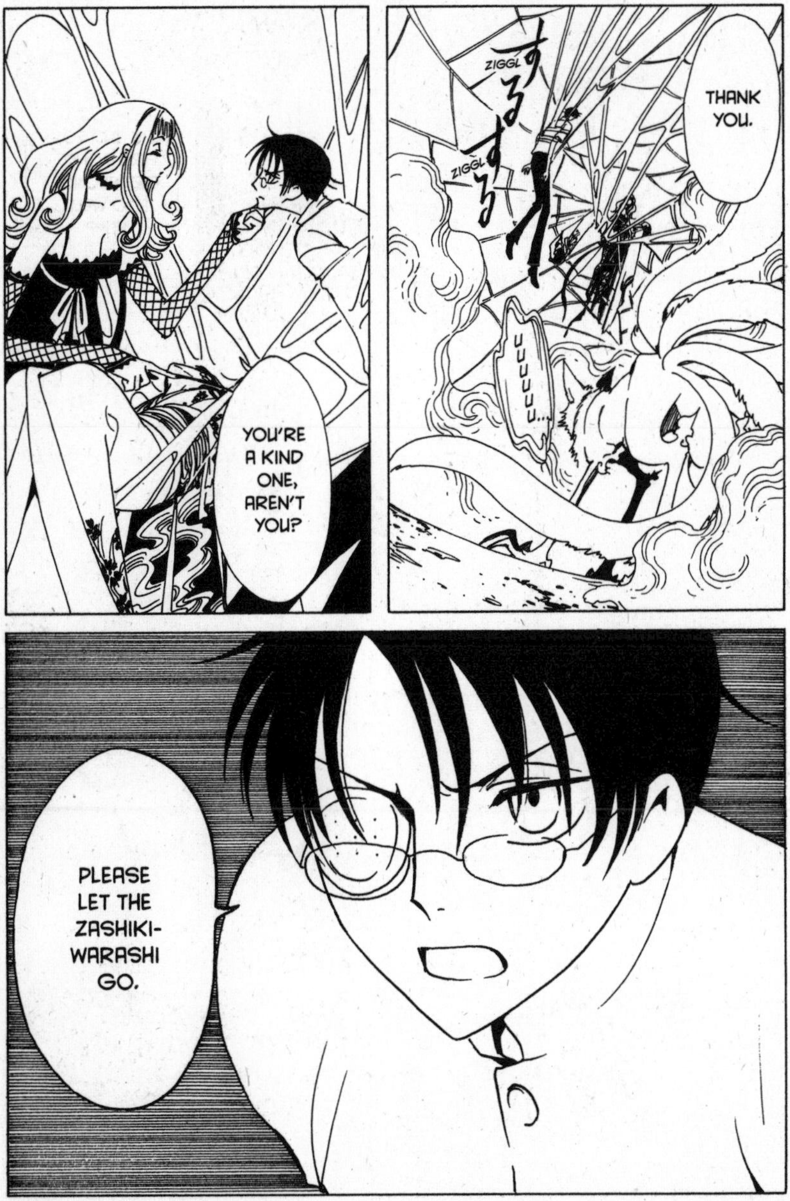
THANK YOU.
するするするする
ZIGGL ZIGGL
UUUUUU...
YOU'RE A KIND ONE, AREN'T YOU?
PLEASE LET THE ZASHIKI-WARASHI GO.

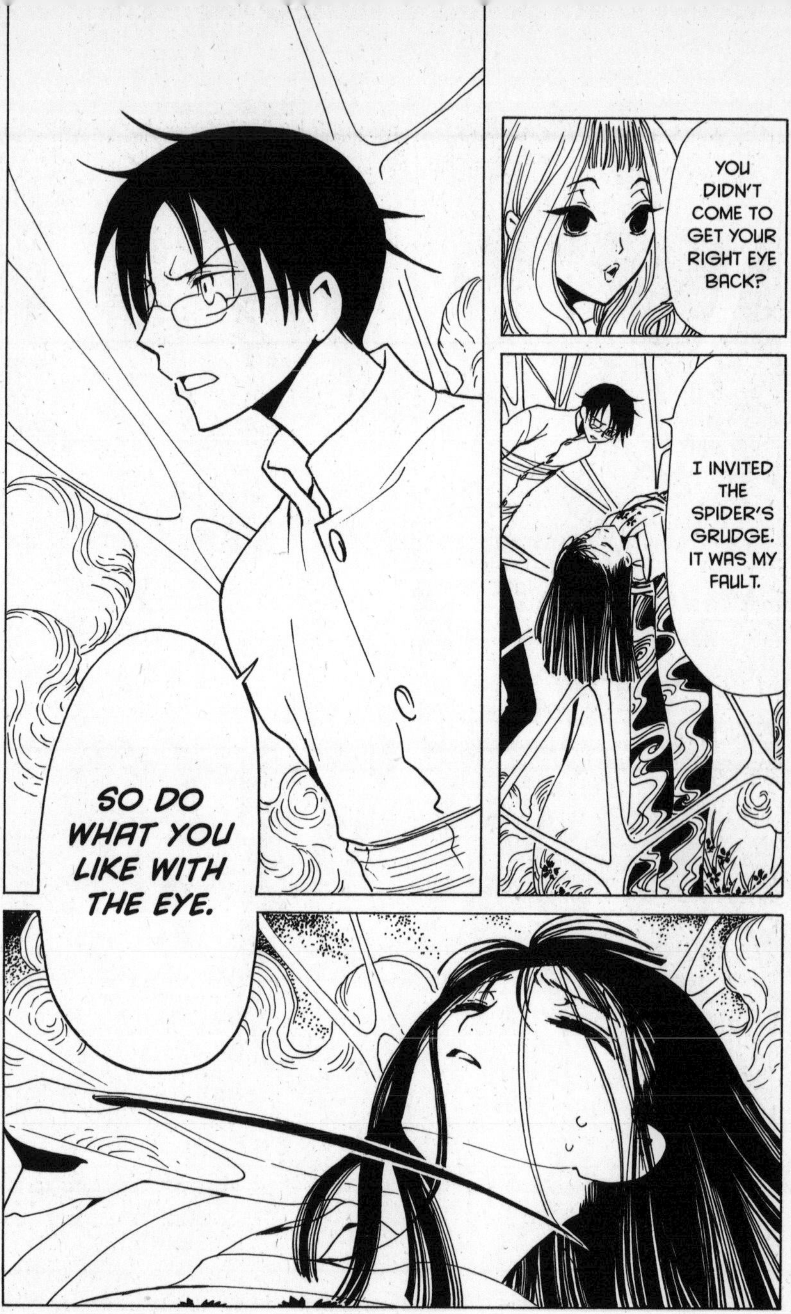
YOU DIDN'T COME TO GET YOUR RIGHT EYE BACK?
I INVITED THE SPIDER'S GRUDGE. IT WAS MY FAULT.
SO DO WHAT YOU LIKE WITH THE EYE.

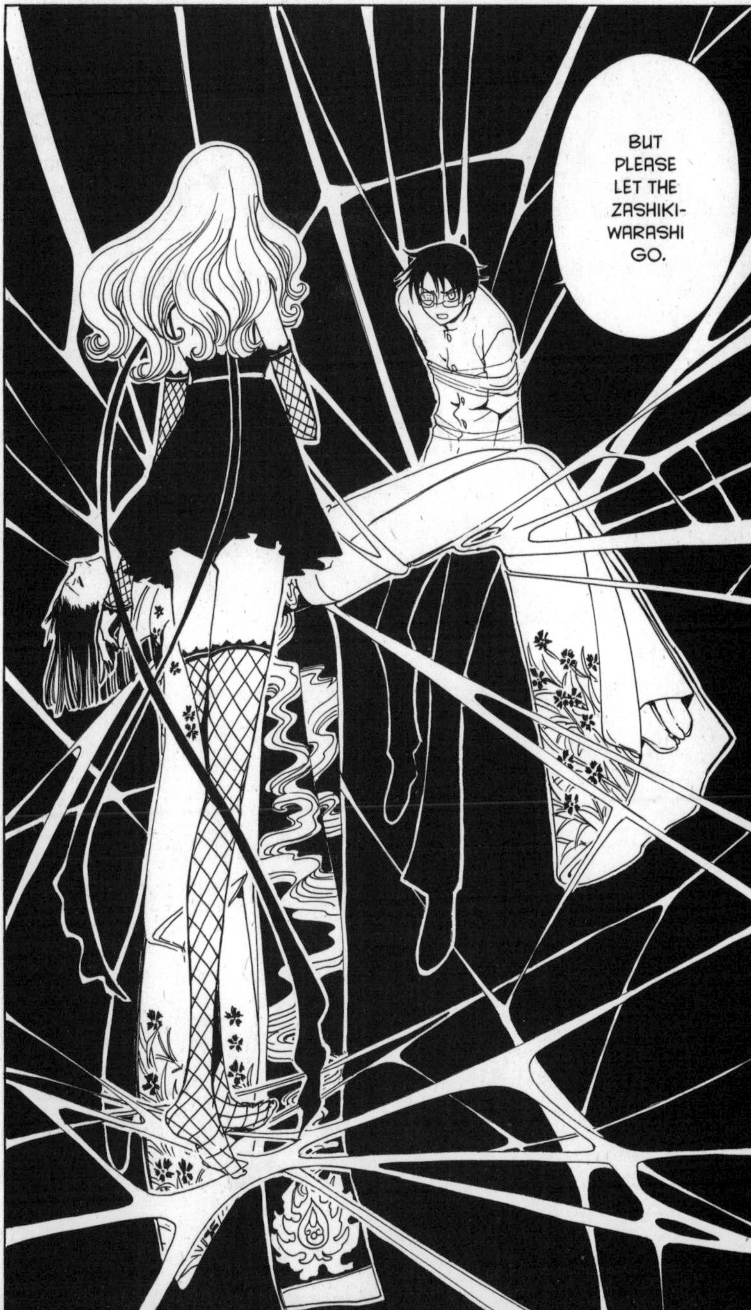
BUT PLEASE LET THE ZASHIKI-WARASHI GO.

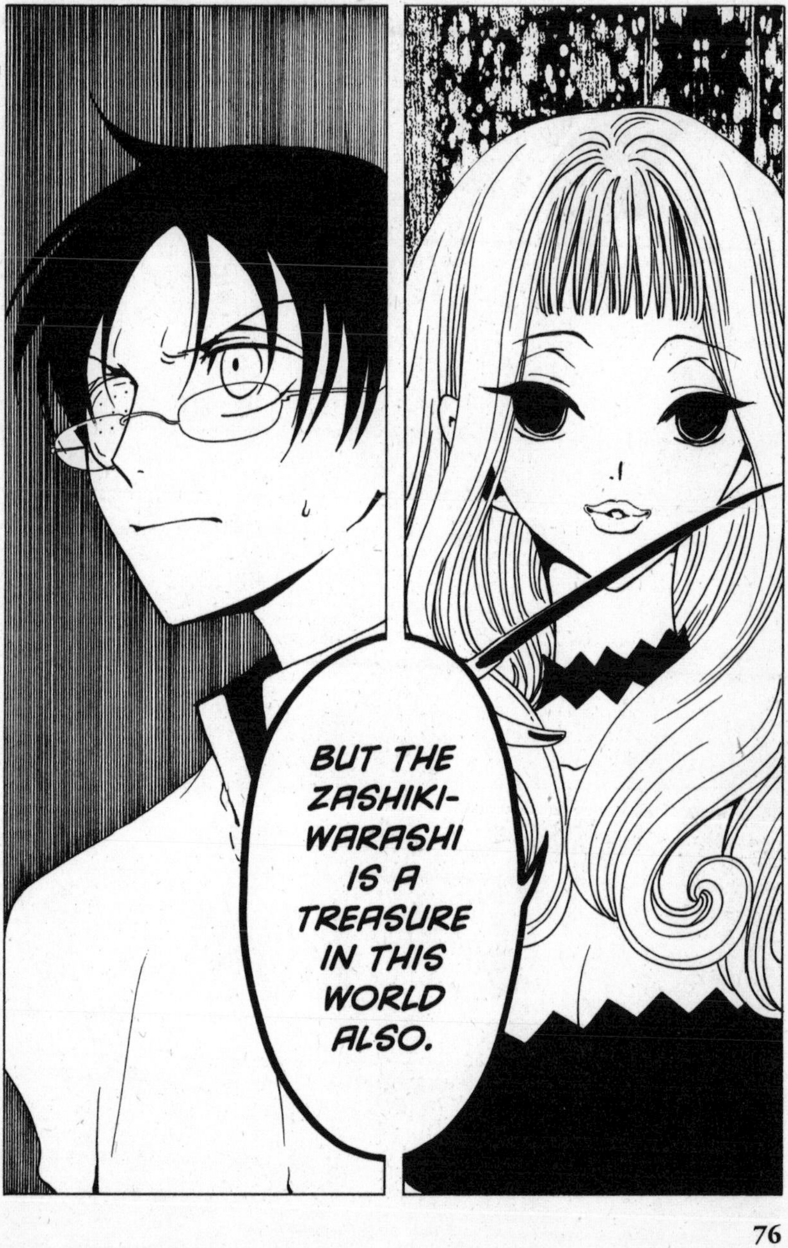
BUT THE ZASHIKI-WARASHI IS A TREASURE IN THIS WORLD ALSO.

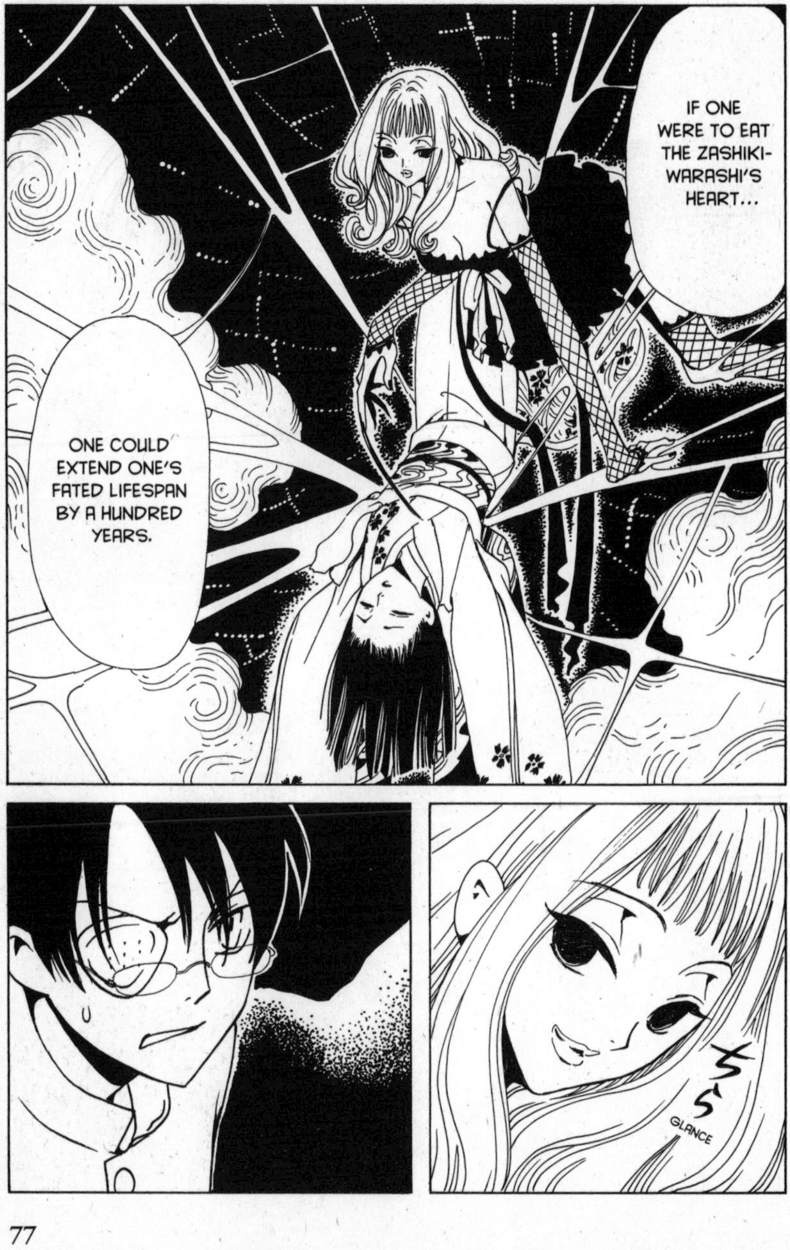
IF ONE WERE TO EAT THE ZASHIKI-WARASHI'S HEART...
ONE COULD EXTEND ONE'S FATED LIFESPAN BY A HUNDRED YEARS.
ちら
GLANCE

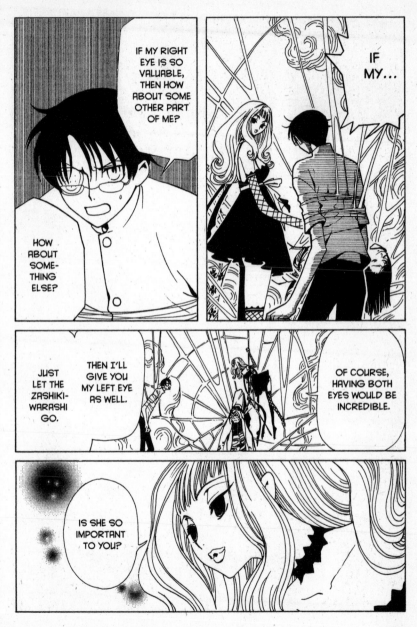

IF MY...
IF MY RIGHT EYE IS SO VALUABLE, THEN HOW ABOUT SOME OTHER PART OF ME?
HOW ABOUT SOME-THING ELSE?
OF COURSE, HAVING BOTH EYES WOULD BE INCREDIBLE.
THEN I'LL GIVE YOU MY LEFT EYE AS WELL.
JUST LET THE ZASHIKI-WARASHI GO.
IS SHE SO IMPORTANT TO YOU?

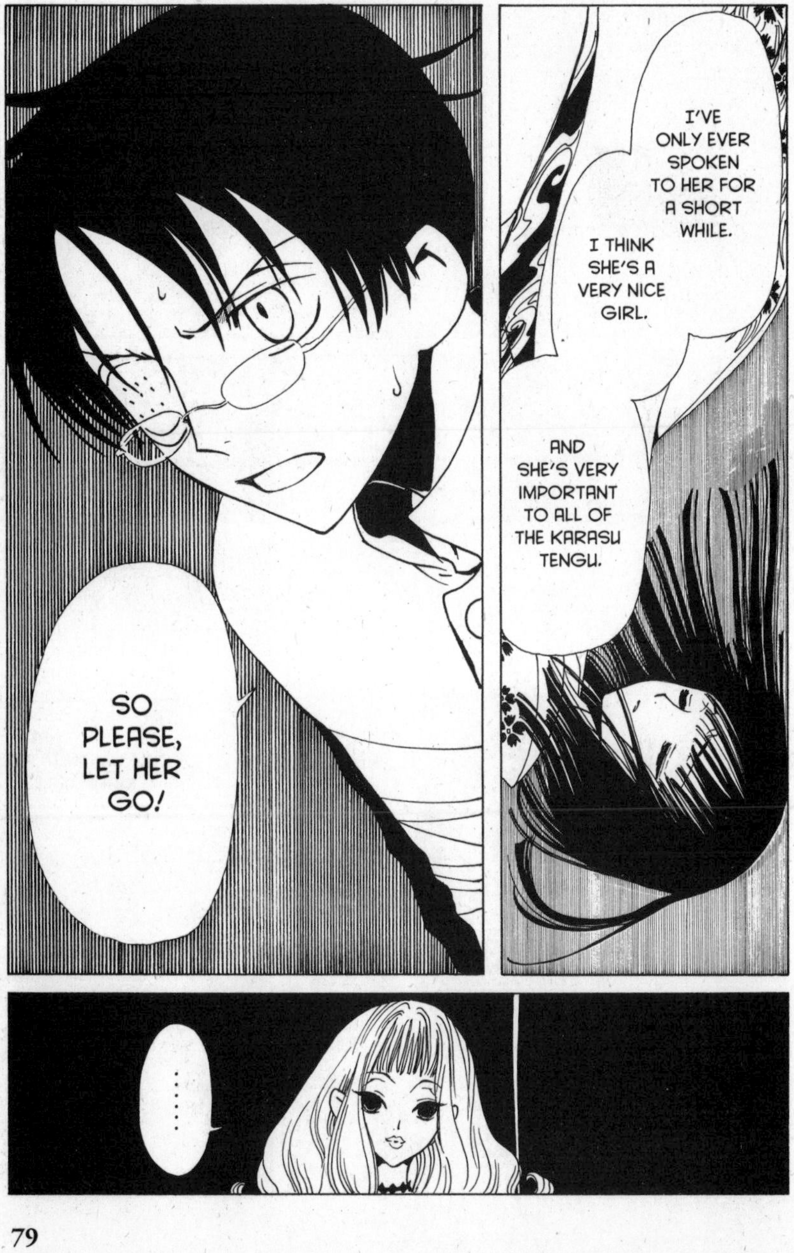
I'VE ONLY EVER SPOKEN TO HER FOR A SHORT WHILE.
I THINK SHE'S A VERY NICE GIRL.
AND SHE'S VERY IMPORTANT TO ALL OF THE KARASU TENGU.
SO PLEASE, LET HER GO!
......

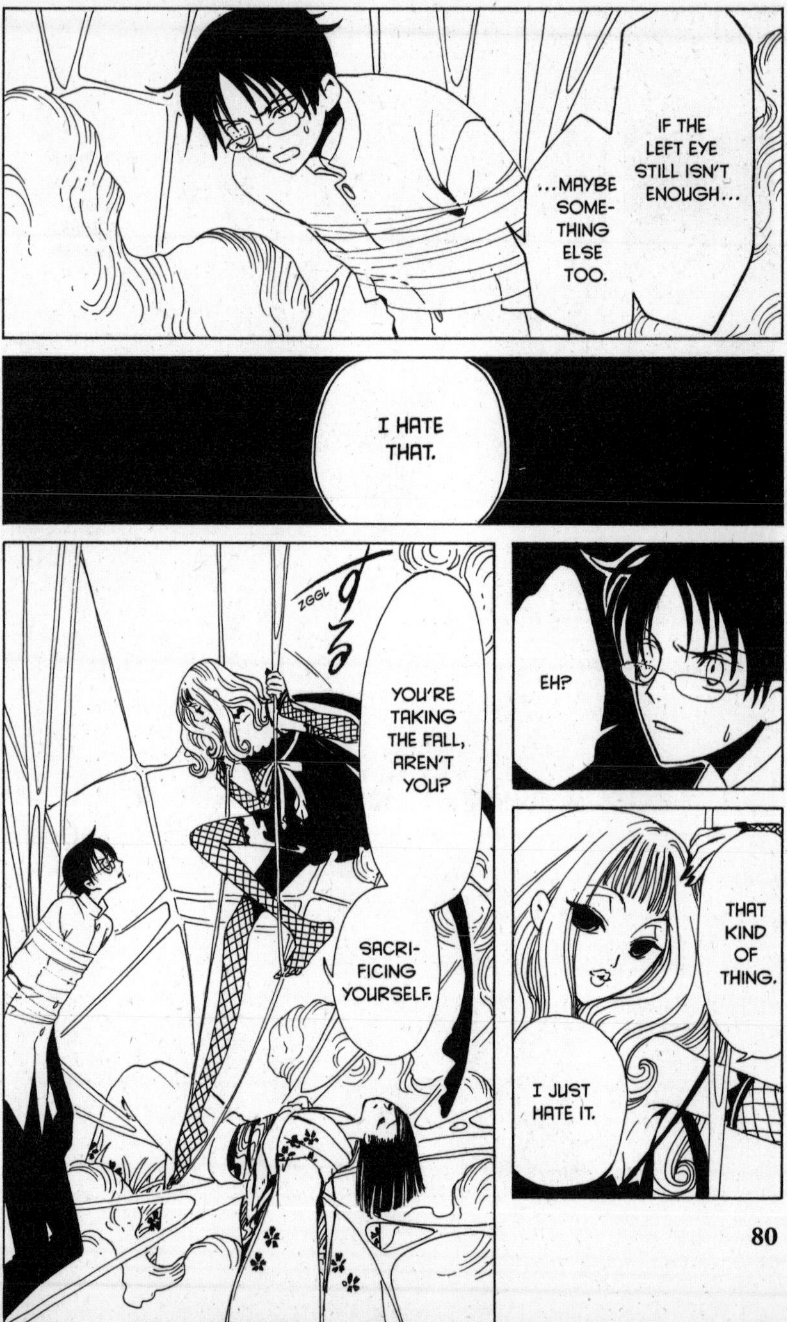
IF THE LEFT EYE STILL ISN'T ENOUGH...
...MAYBE SOME-THING ELSE TOO.
I HATE THAT.
EH?
ZGGL
YOU'RE TAKING THE FALL, AREN'T YOU?
SACRI-FICING YOURSELF.
THAT KIND OF THING.
I JUST HATE IT.

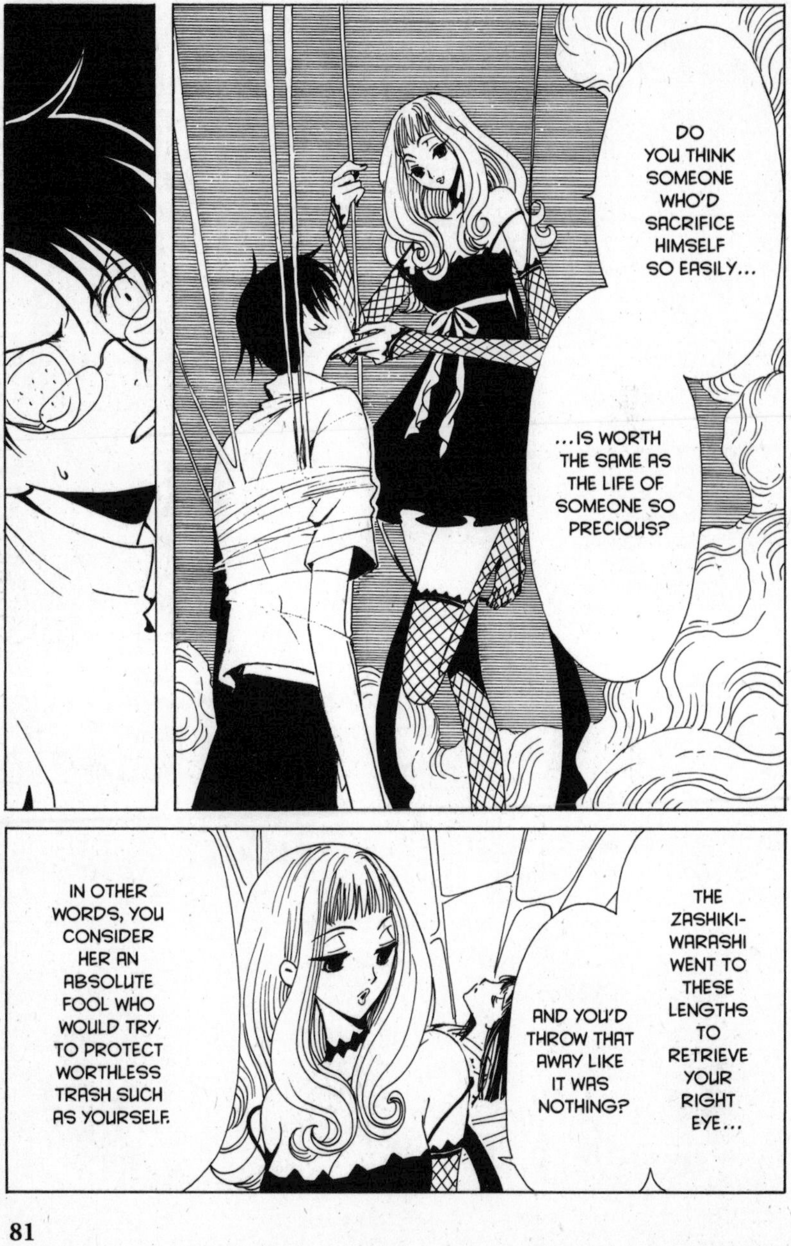
DO YOU THINK SOMEONE WHO'D SACRIFICE HIMSELF SO EASILY...
...IS WORTH THE SAME AS THE LIFE OF SOMEONE SO PRECIOUS?
THE ZASHIKI-WARASHI WENT TO THESE LENGTHS TO RETRIEVE YOUR RIGHT EYE...
AND YOU'D THROW THAT AWAY LIKE IT WAS NOTHING?
IN OTHER WORDS, YOU CONSIDER HER AN ABSOLUTE FOOL WHO WOULD TRY TO PROTECT WORTHLESS TRASH SUCH AS YOURSELF.

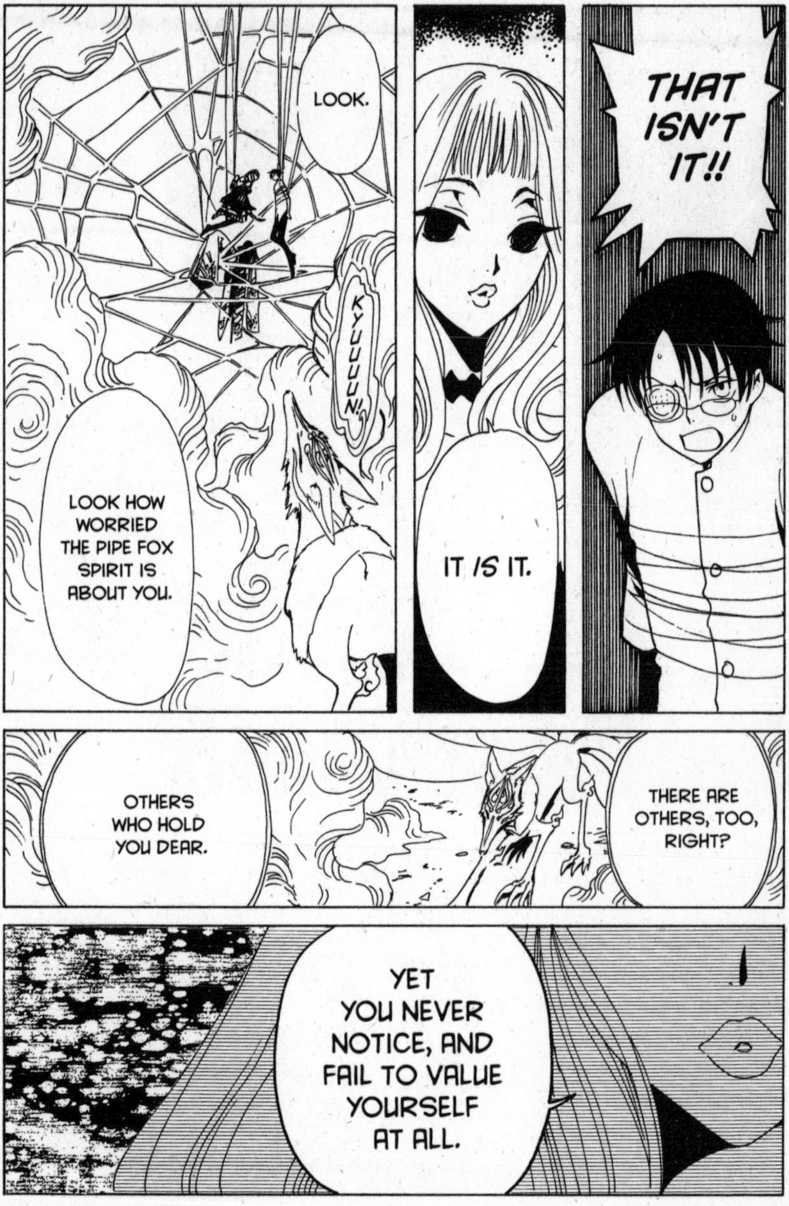
THAT ISN'T IT!!
IT IS IT.
LOOK.
KYUUUUN!!
LOOK HOW WORRIED THE PIPE FOX SPIRIT IS ABOUT YOU.
THERE ARE OTHERS, TOO, RIGHT?
OTHERS WHO HOLD YOU DEAR.
YET YOU NEVER NOTICE, AND FAIL TO VALUE YOURSELF AT ALL.

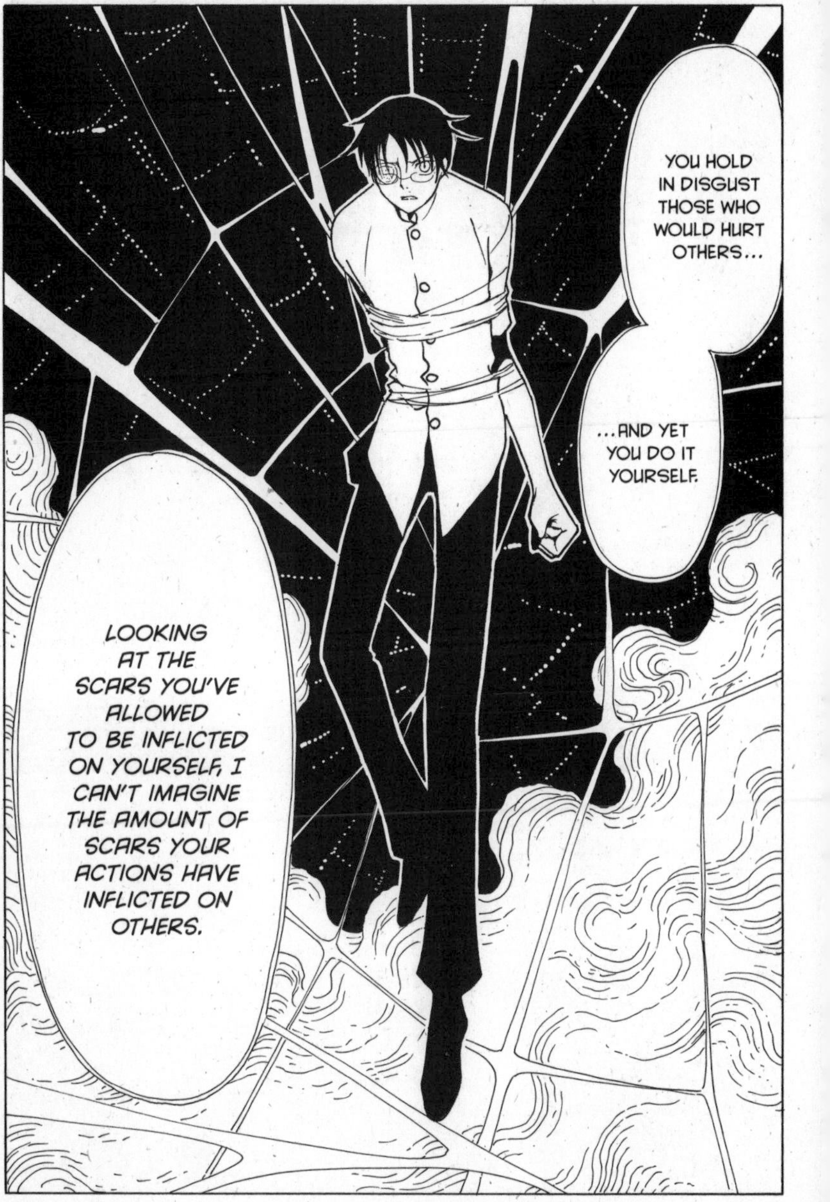
YOU HOLD IN DISGUST THOSE WHO WOULD HURT OTHERS...
...AND YET YOU DO IT YOURSELF.
LOOKING AT THE SCARS YOU'VE ALLOWED TO BE INFLICTED ON YOURSELF, I CAN'T IMAGINE THE AMOUNT OF SCARS YOUR ACTIONS HAVE INFLICTED ON OTHERS.

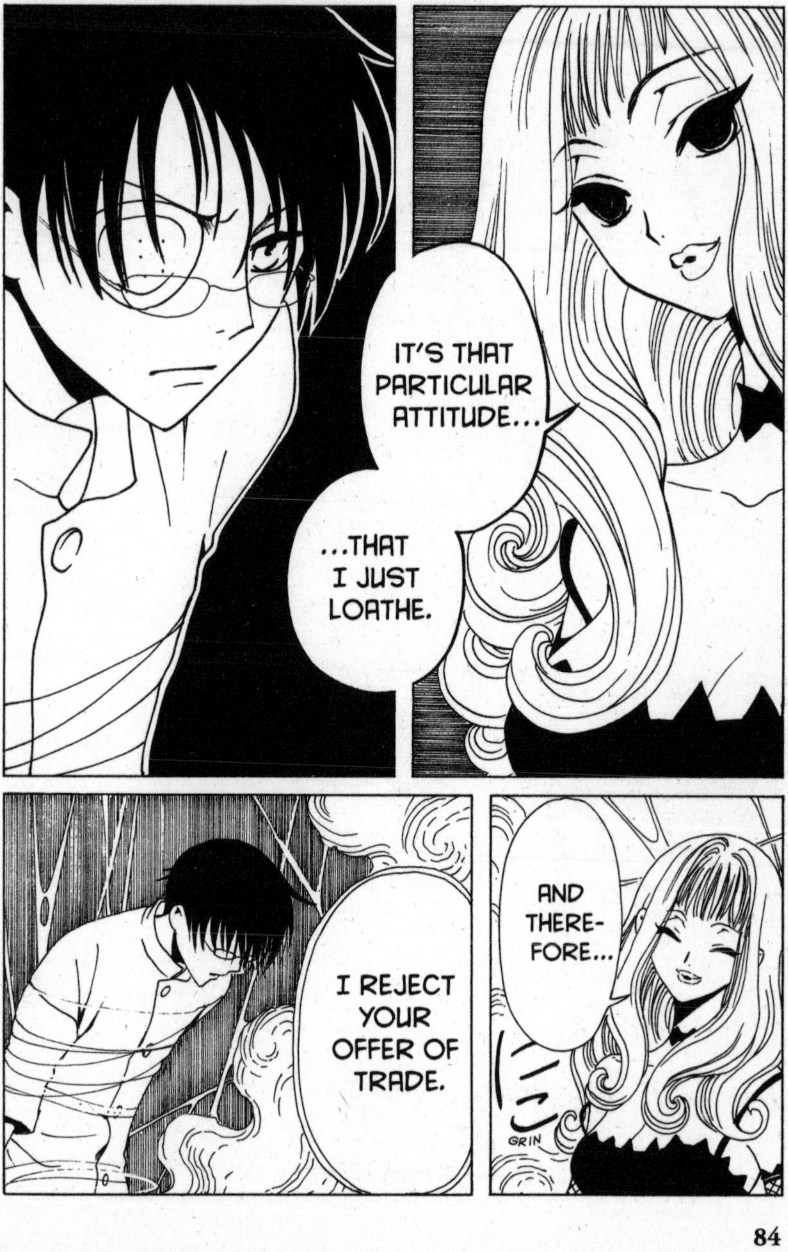
IT'S THAT PARTICULAR ATTITUDE...
...THAT I JUST LOATHE.
AND THERE-FORE...
GRIN
I REJECT YOUR OFFER OF TRADE.

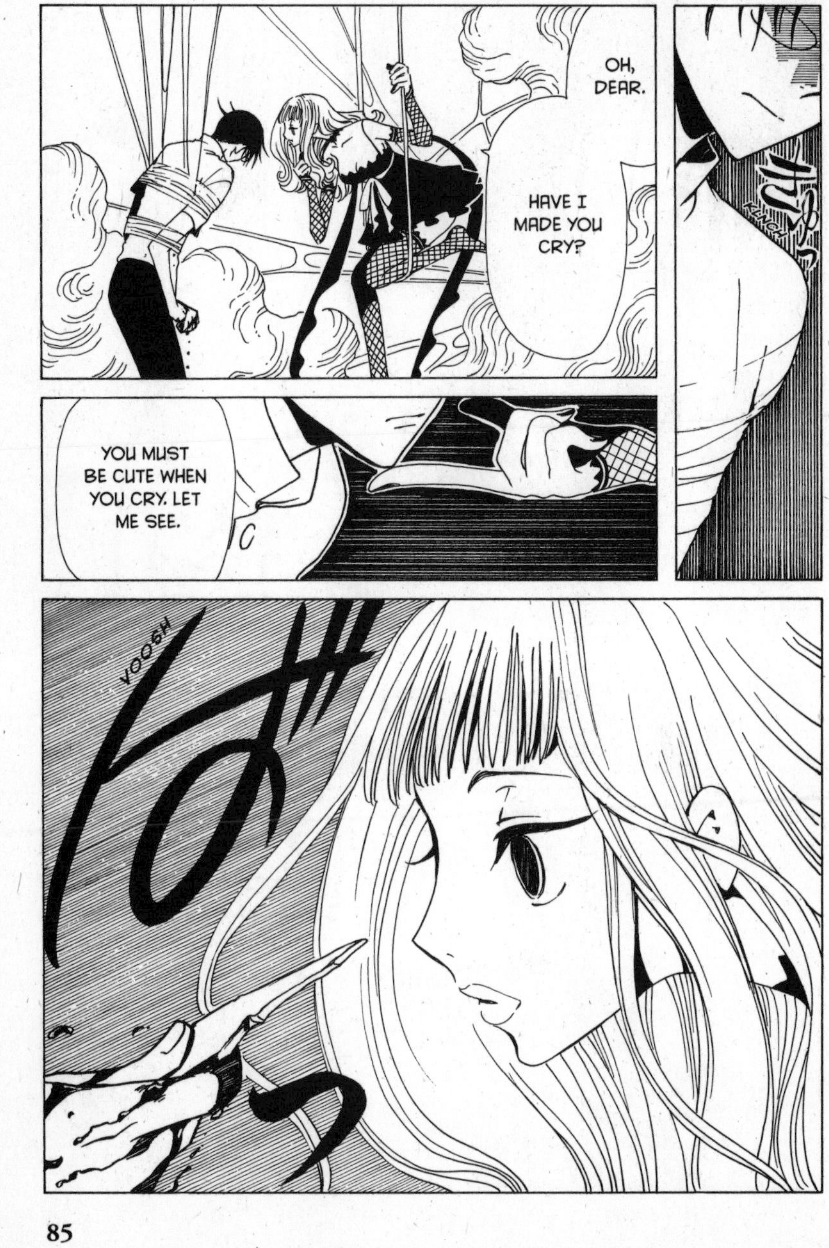
KLINCH
OH, DEAR.
HAVE I MADE YOU CRY?
YOU MUST BE CUTE WHEN YOU CRY. LET ME SEE.
VOOSH

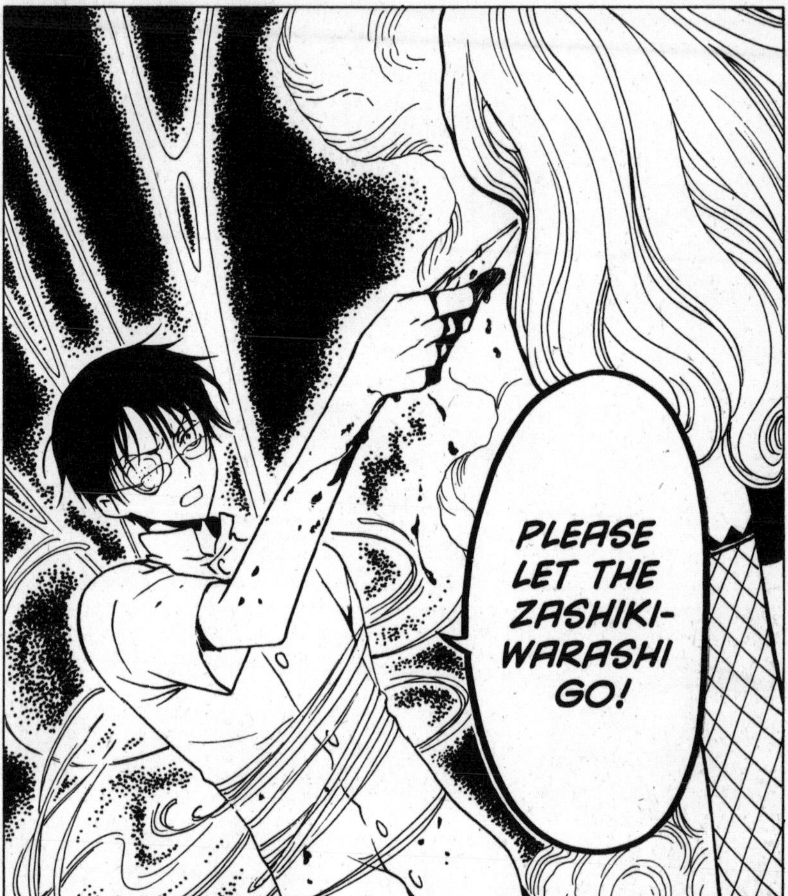
PLEASE LET THE ZASHIKI-WARASHI GO!

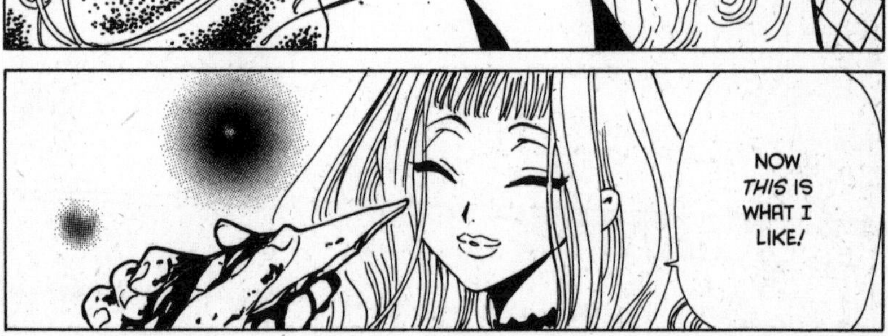
NOW *THIS* IS WHAT I LIKE!

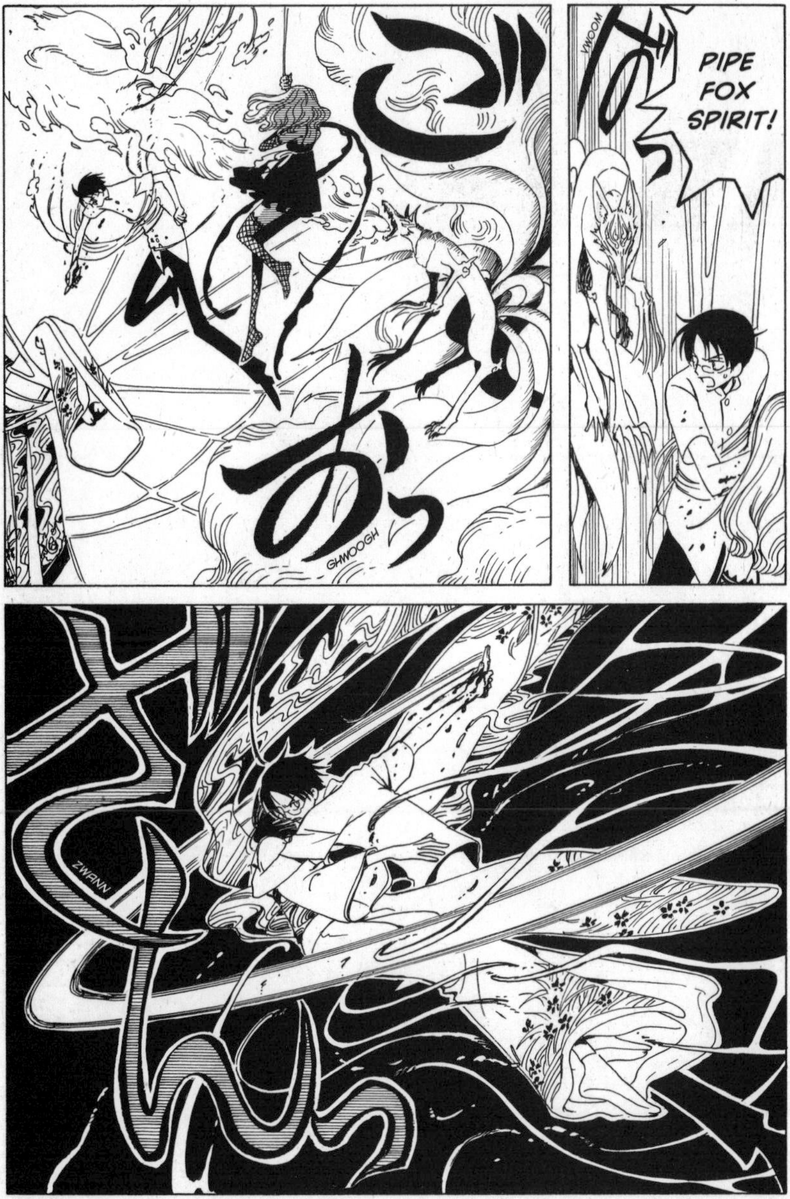
VWOOM
PIPE FOX SPIRIT!
GHWOOGH
ZWANN

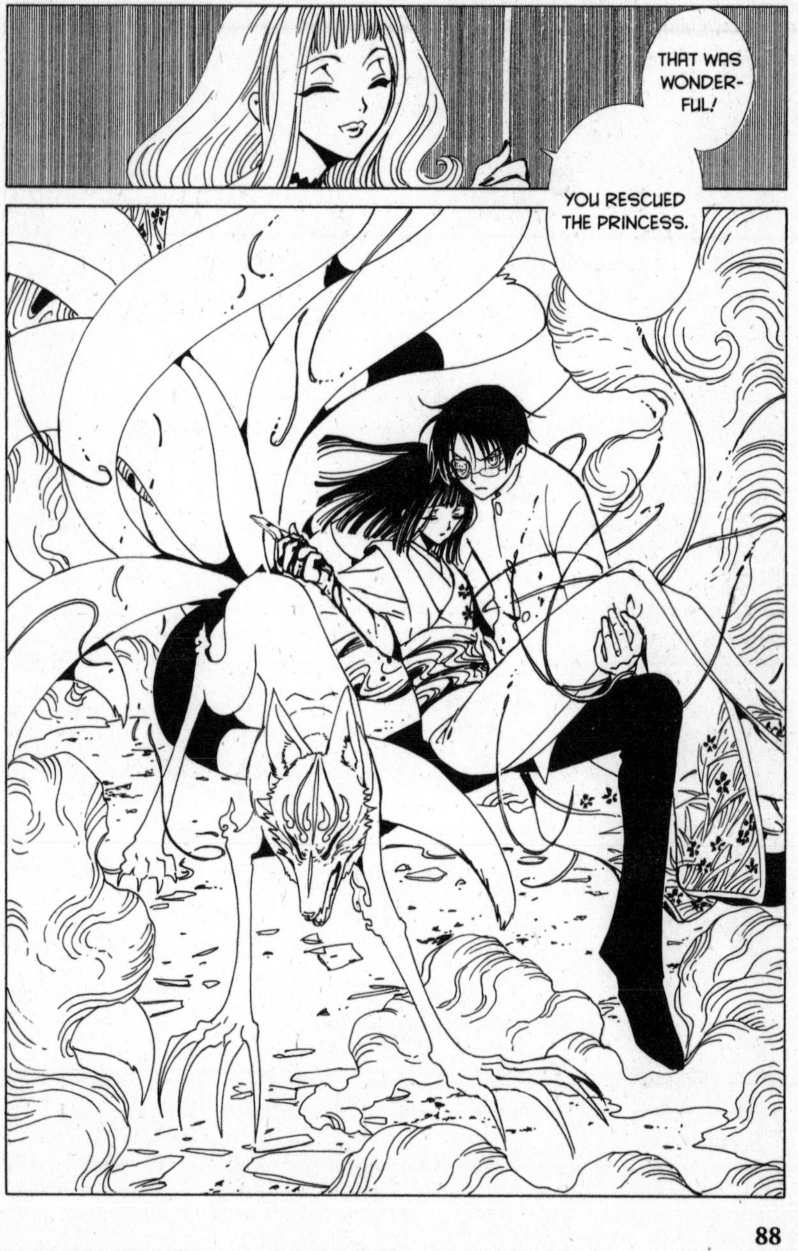
THAT WAS WONDER-FUL!
YOU RESCUED THE PRINCESS.

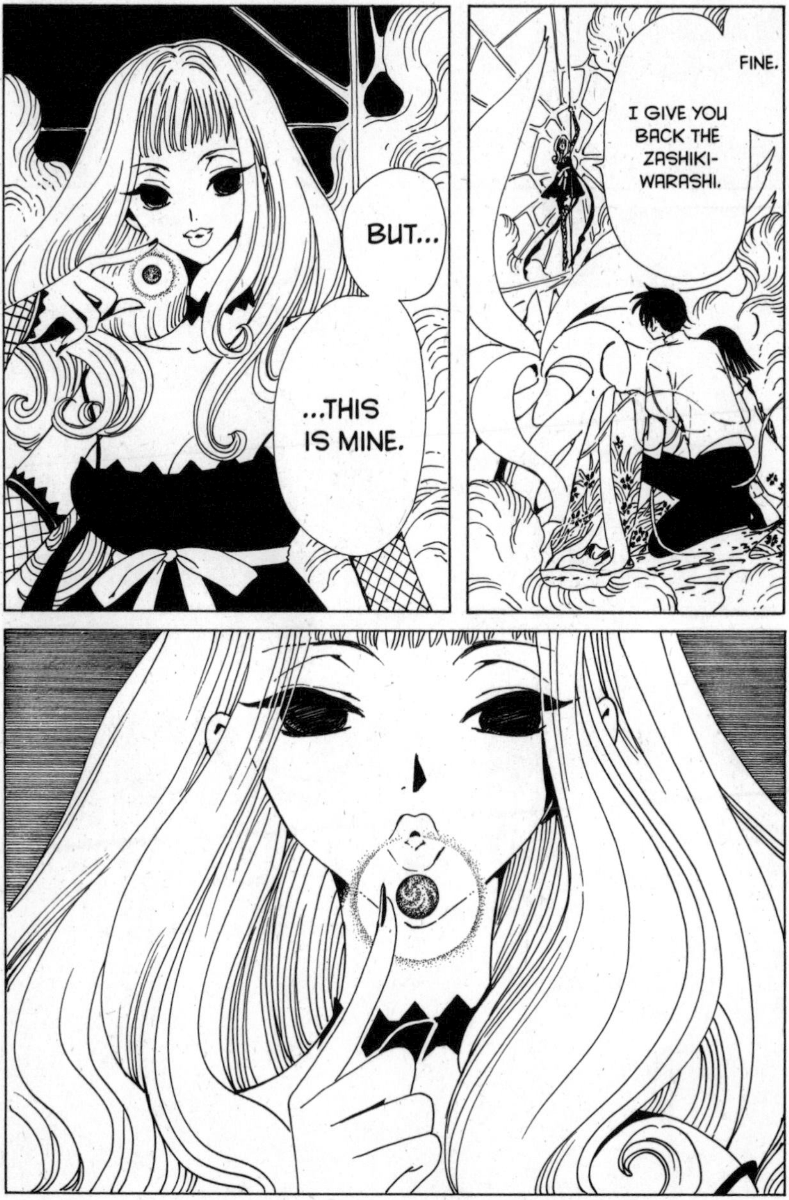
FINE.
I GIVE YOU BACK THE ZASHIKI-WARASHI.
BUT...
...THIS IS MINE.

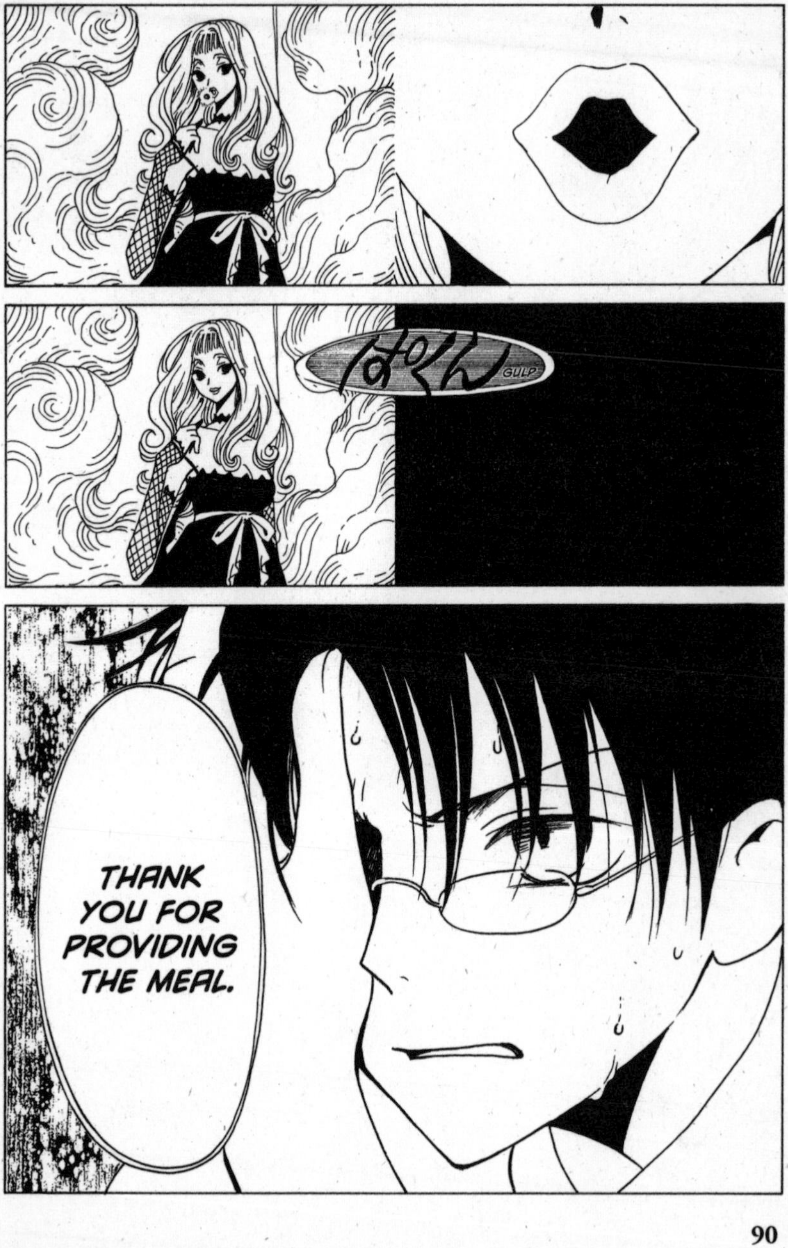
はぐん
GULP
THANK YOU FOR PROVIDING THE MEAL.

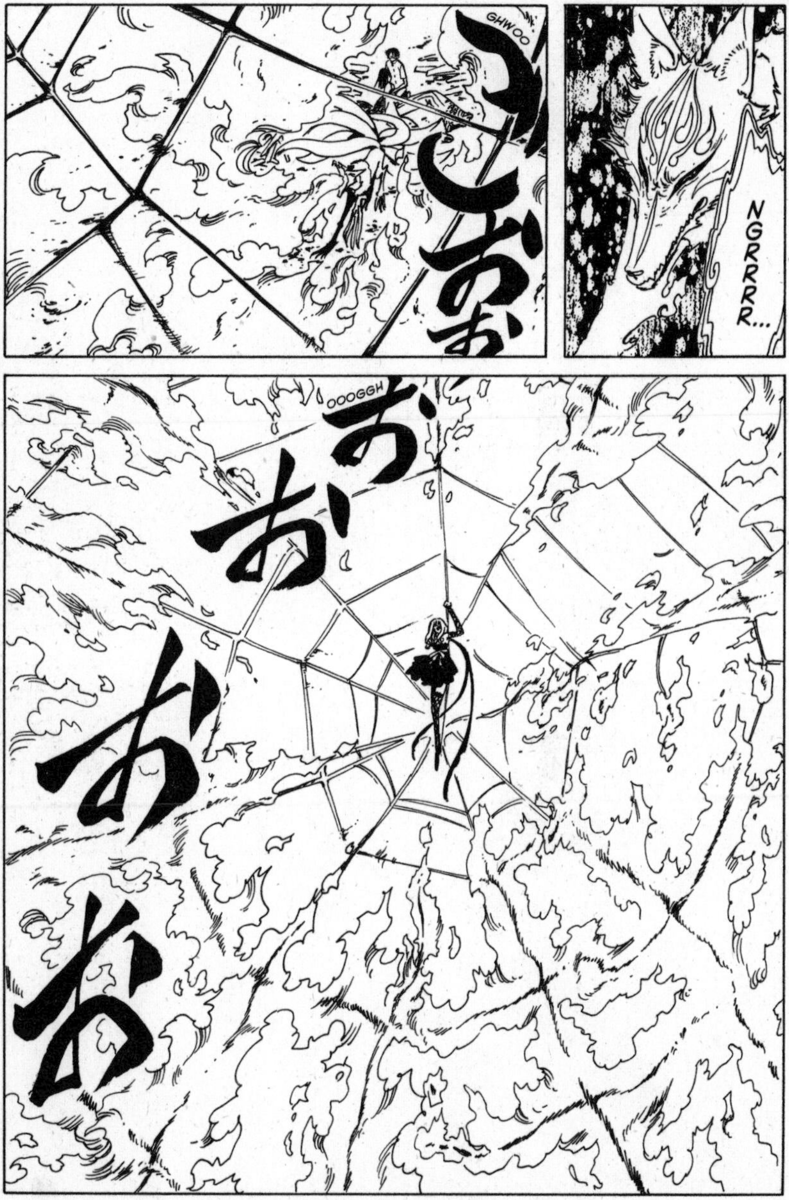
NGRRRR...
GHWOO
OOOGGH

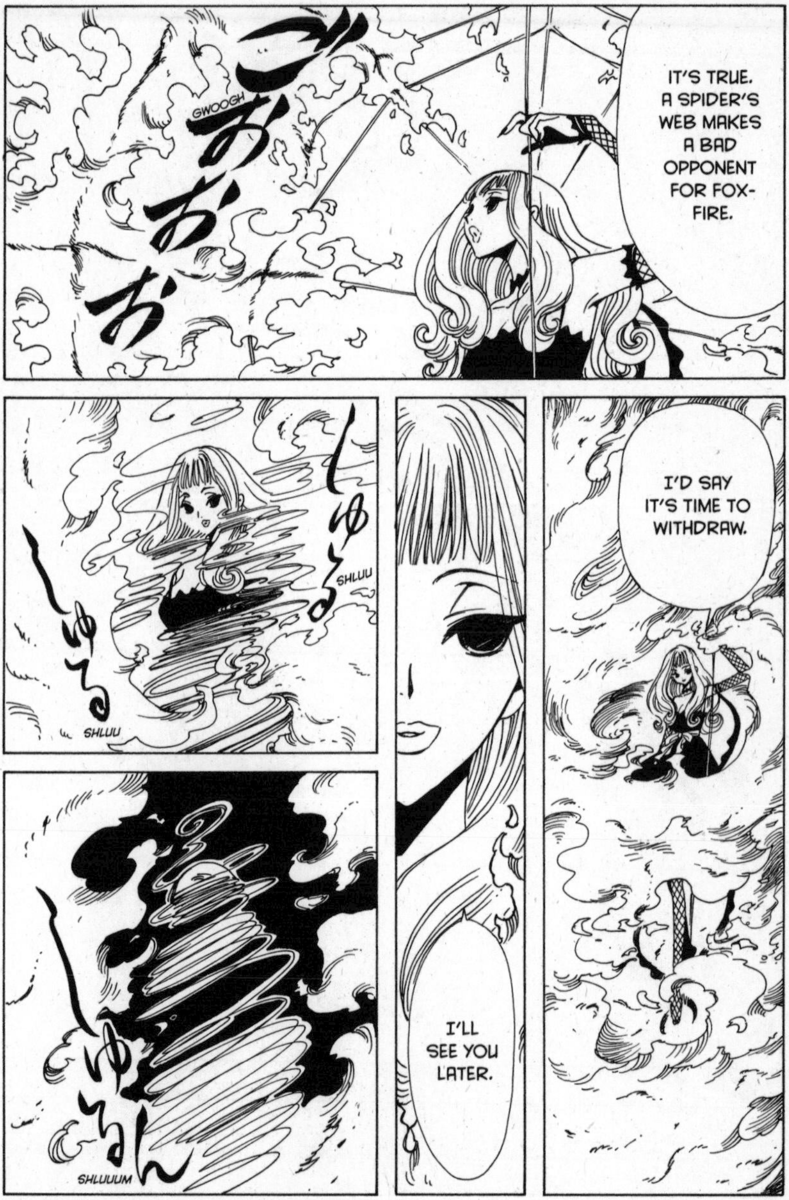
IT'S TRUE. A SPIDER'S WEB MAKES A BAD OPPONENT FOR FOX-FIRE.
GWOOGH
I'D SAY IT'S TIME TO WITHDRAW.
I'LL SEE YOU LATER.
SHLUU
SHLUU
SHLUUUM

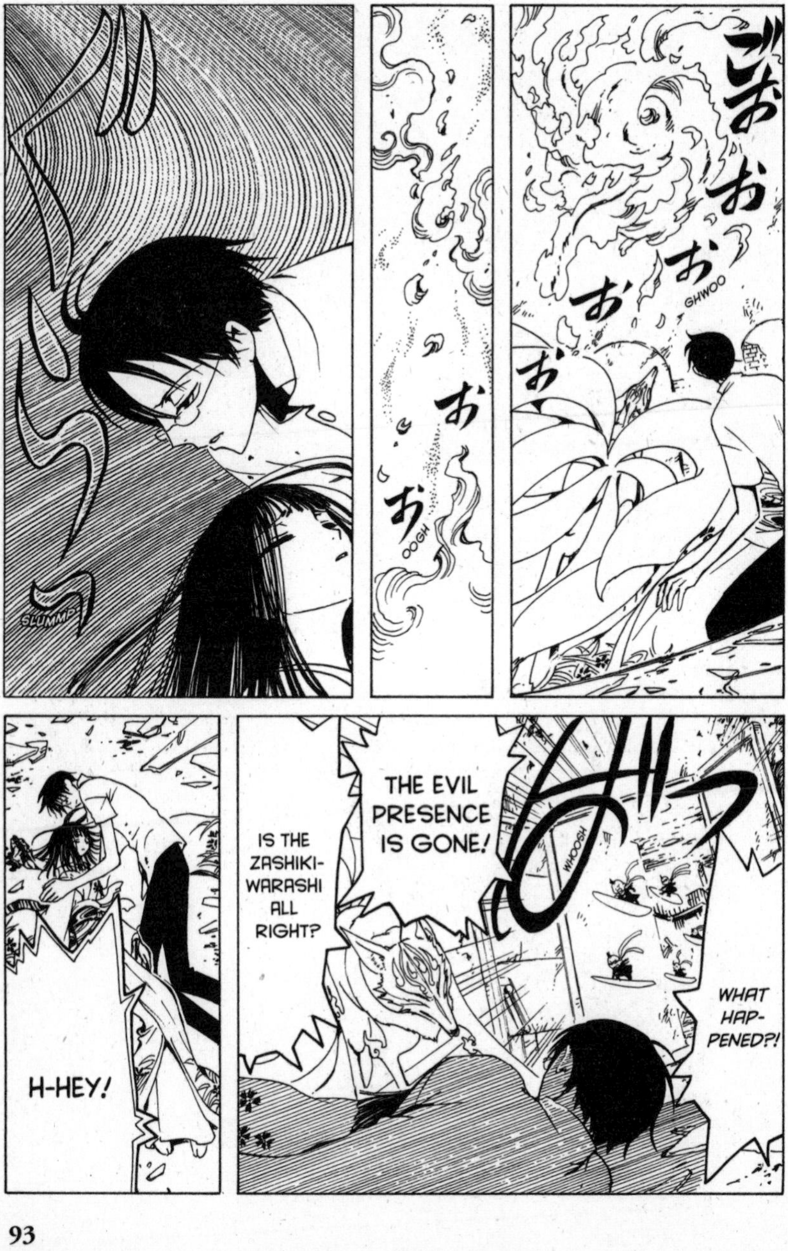
GHWOO
OOGH
SLUMMP
WHOOSH
WHAT HAP-PENED?!
THE EVIL PRESENCE IS GONE!
IS THE ZASHIKI-WARASHI ALL RIGHT?
H-HEY!

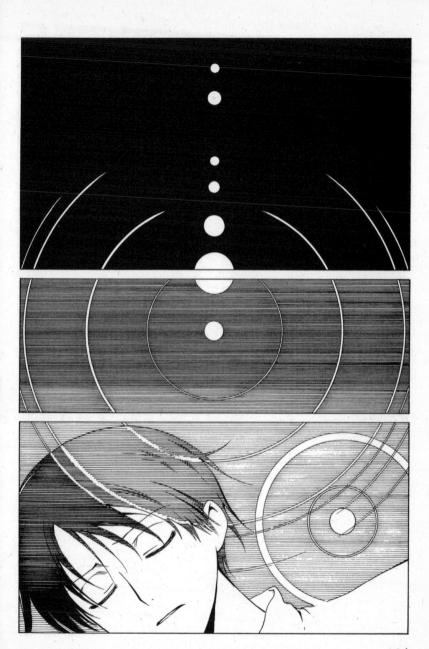

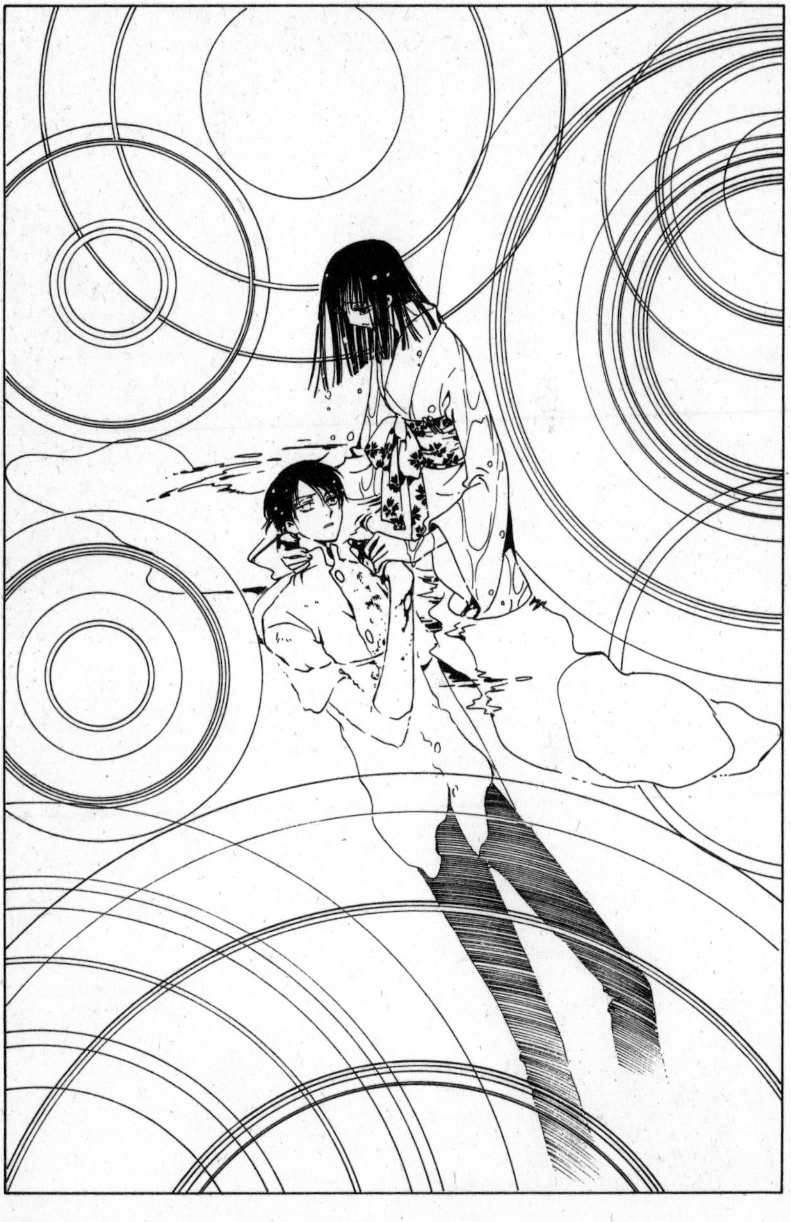

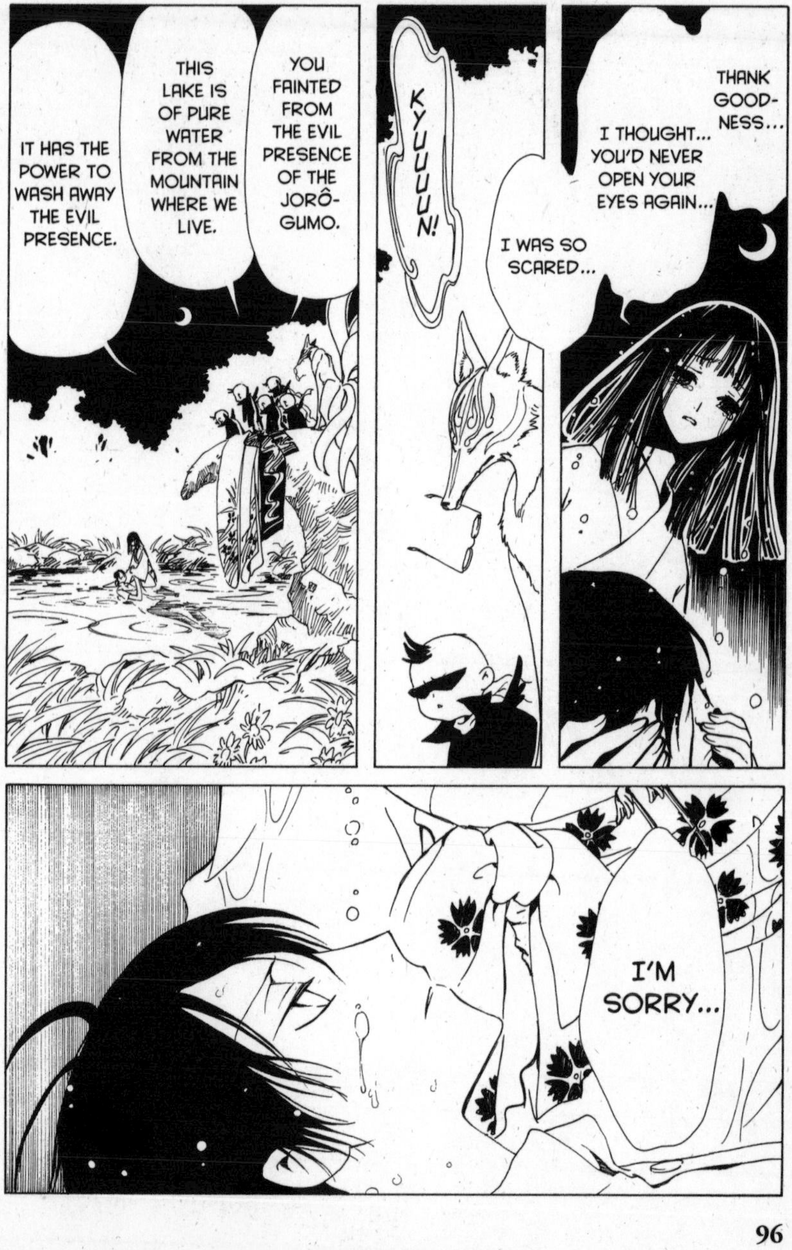
THANK GOODNESS...
I THOUGHT... YOU'D NEVER OPEN YOUR EYES AGAIN...
I WAS SO SCARED...
KYUUUUN!
YOU FAINTED FROM THE EVIL PRESENCE OF THE JORÔ-GUMO.
THIS LAKE IS OF PURE WATER FROM THE MOUNTAIN WHERE WE LIVE.
IT HAS THE POWER TO WASH AWAY THE EVIL PRESENCE.
I'M SORRY...

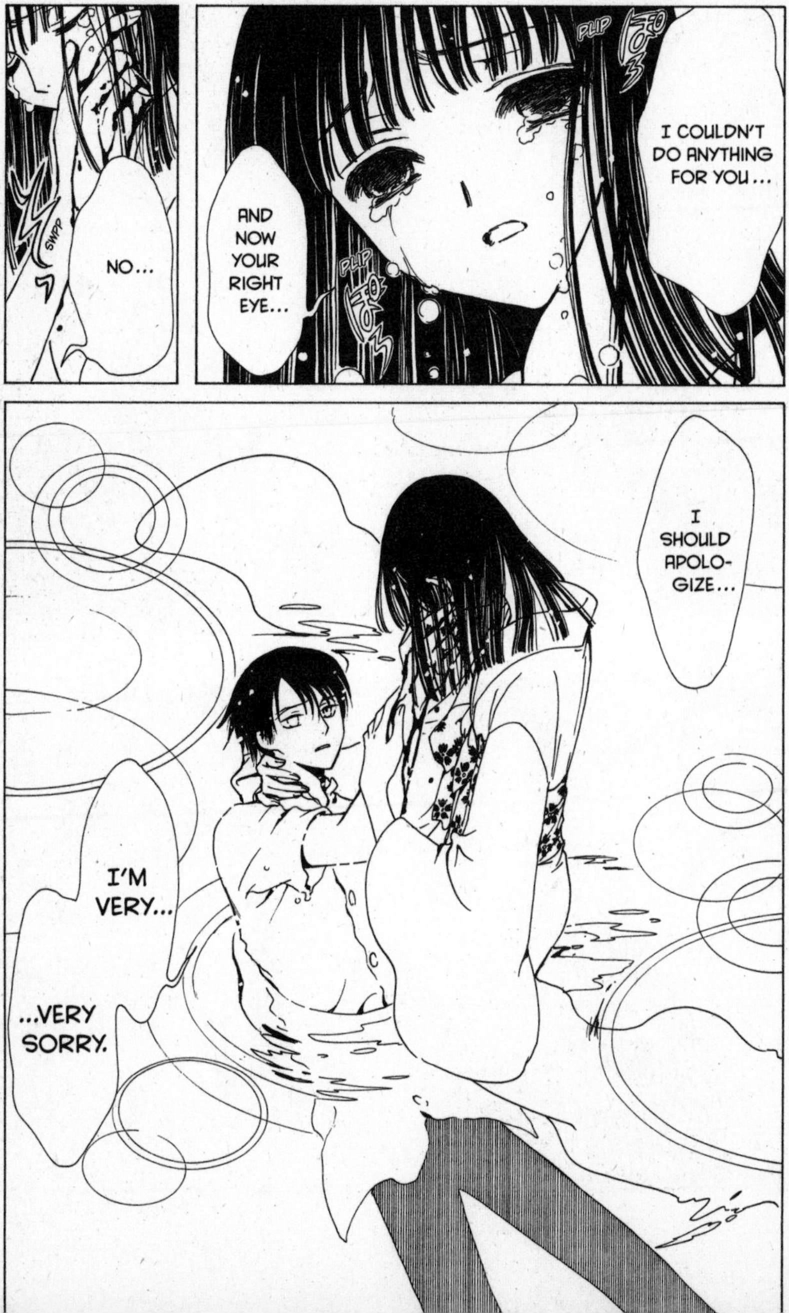
PLIP
I COULDN'T DO ANYTHING FOR YOU...
AND NOW YOUR RIGHT EYE...
PLIP
SWPP
NO...
I SHOULD APOLO-GIZE...
I'M VERY...
...VERY SORRY.

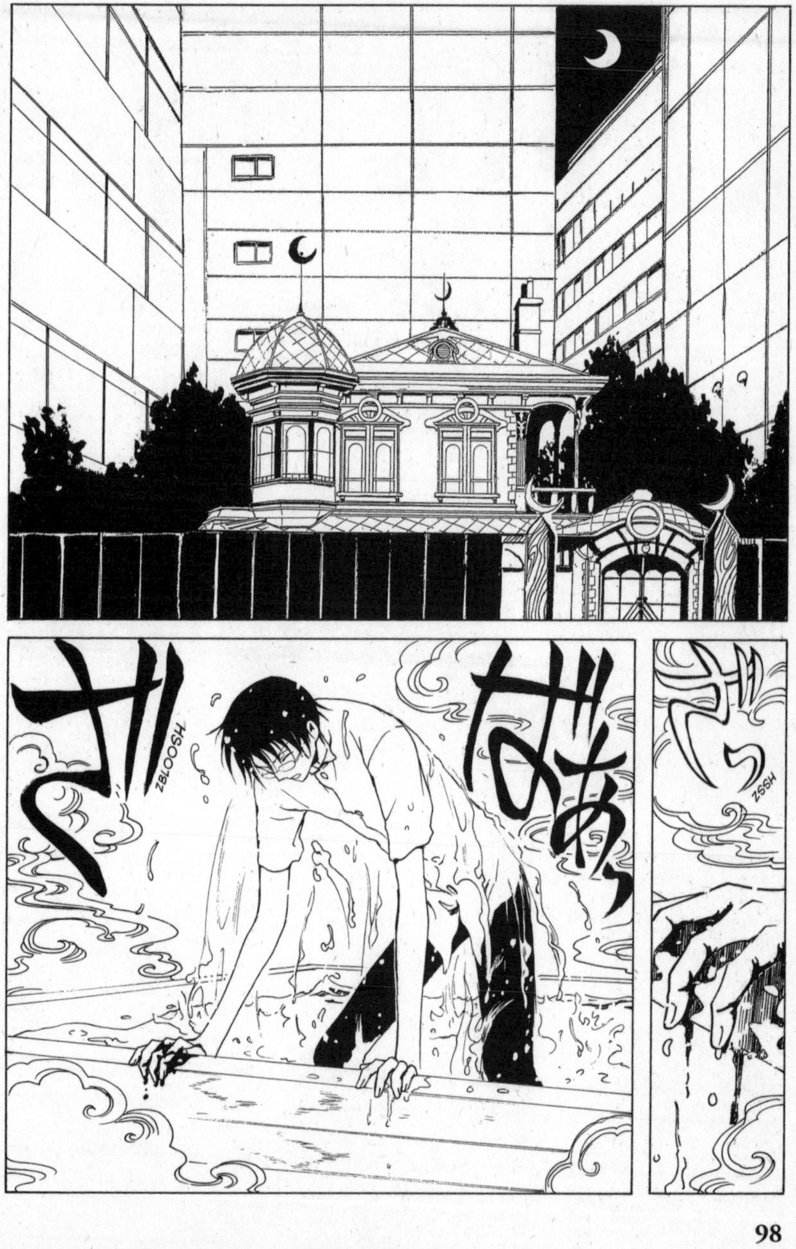
ZSSH
ZBLOOSH

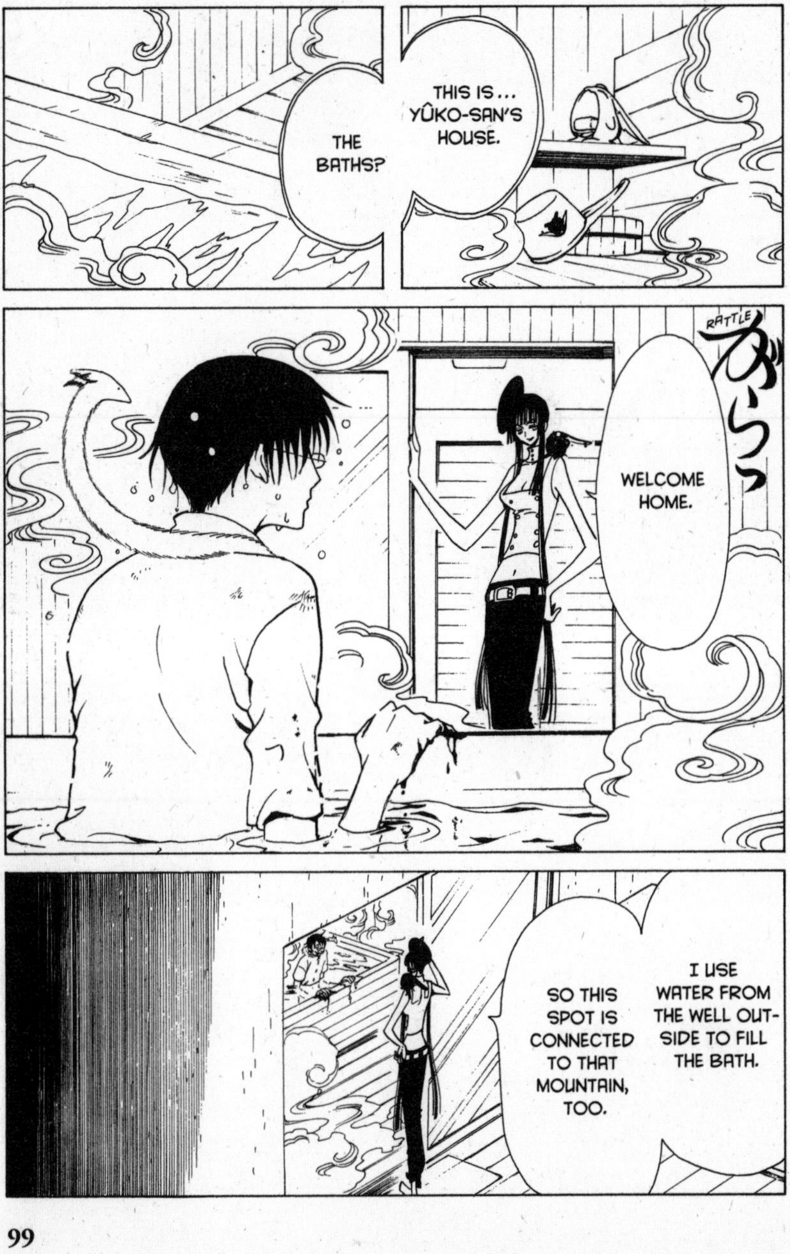

THIS IS... YÛKO-SAN'S HOUSE.
THE BATHS?
RATTLE
がらっ
WELCOME HOME.
I USE WATER FROM THE WELL OUT-SIDE TO FILL THE BATH.
SO THIS SPOT IS CONNECTED TO THAT MOUNTAIN, TOO.

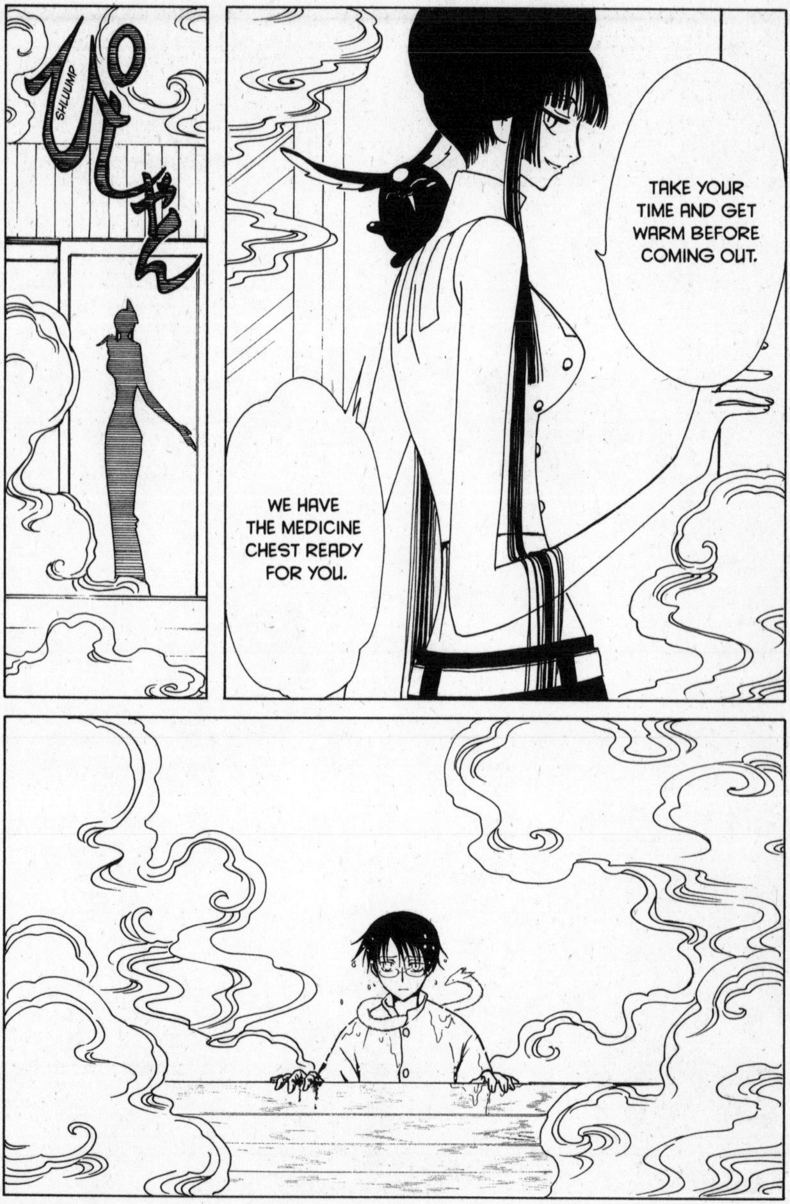
TAKE YOUR TIME AND GET WARM BEFORE COMING OUT.
WE HAVE THE MEDICINE CHEST READY FOR YOU.
ぴしゃん
SHLUUMP

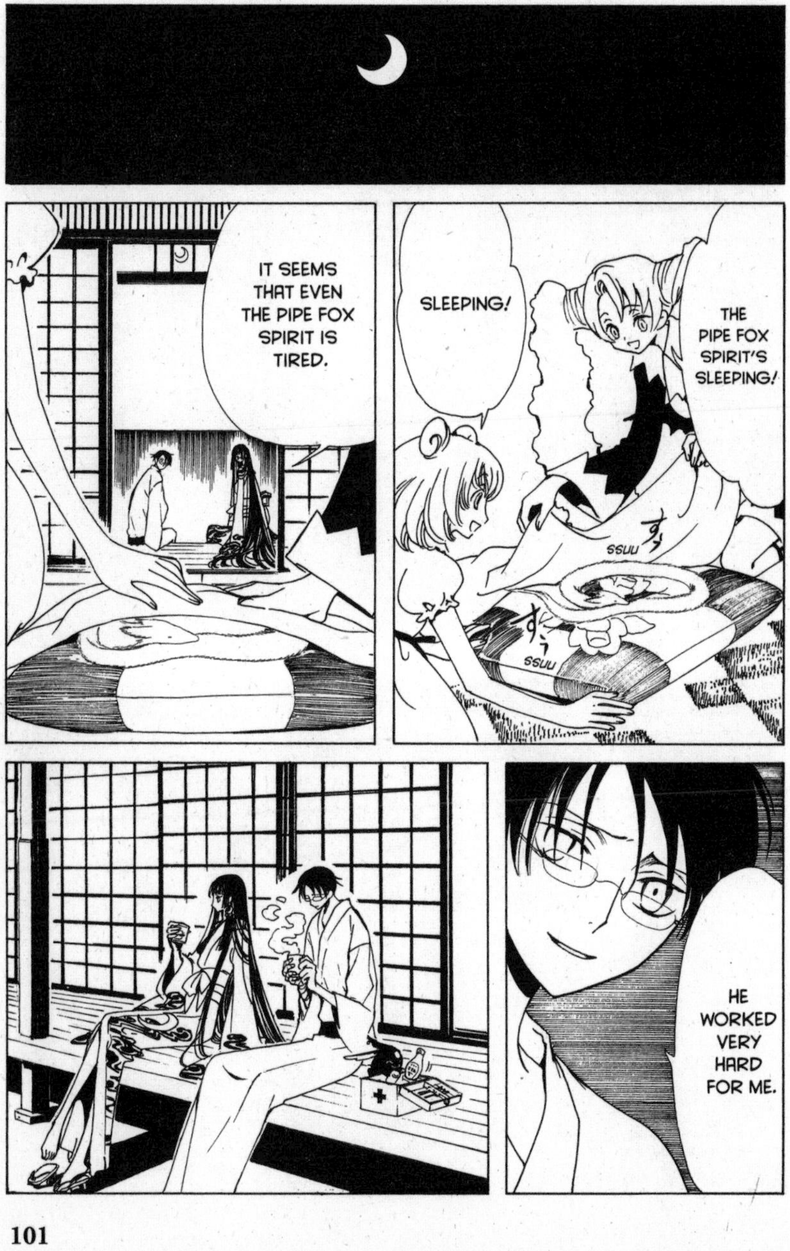
THE PIPE FOX SPIRIT'S SLEEPING!
SLEEPING!
SSUU
SSUU
IT SEEMS THAT EVEN THE PIPE FOX SPIRIT IS TIRED.
HE WORKED VERY HARD FOR ME.

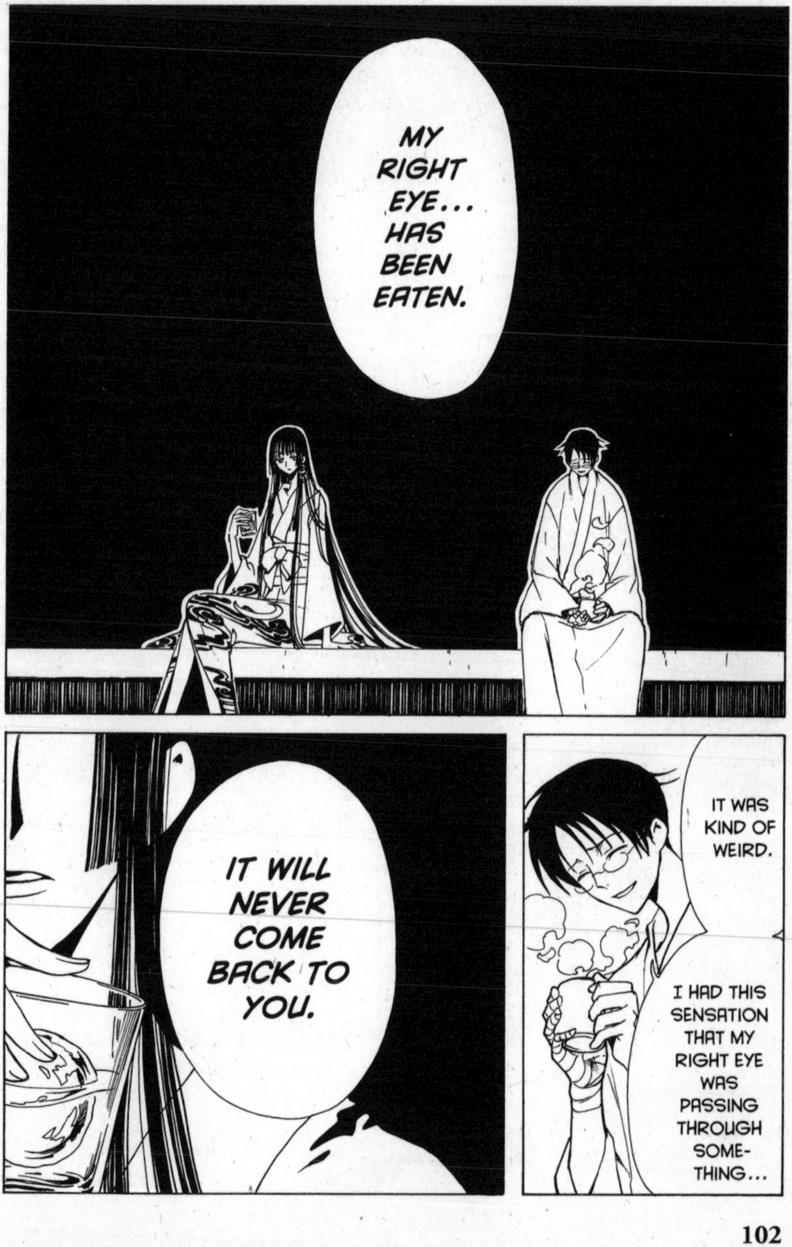
MY RIGHT EYE... HAS BEEN EATEN.
IT WAS KIND OF WEIRD.
I HAD THIS SENSATION THAT MY RIGHT EYE WAS PASSING THROUGH SOME-THING...
IT WILL NEVER COME BACK TO YOU.

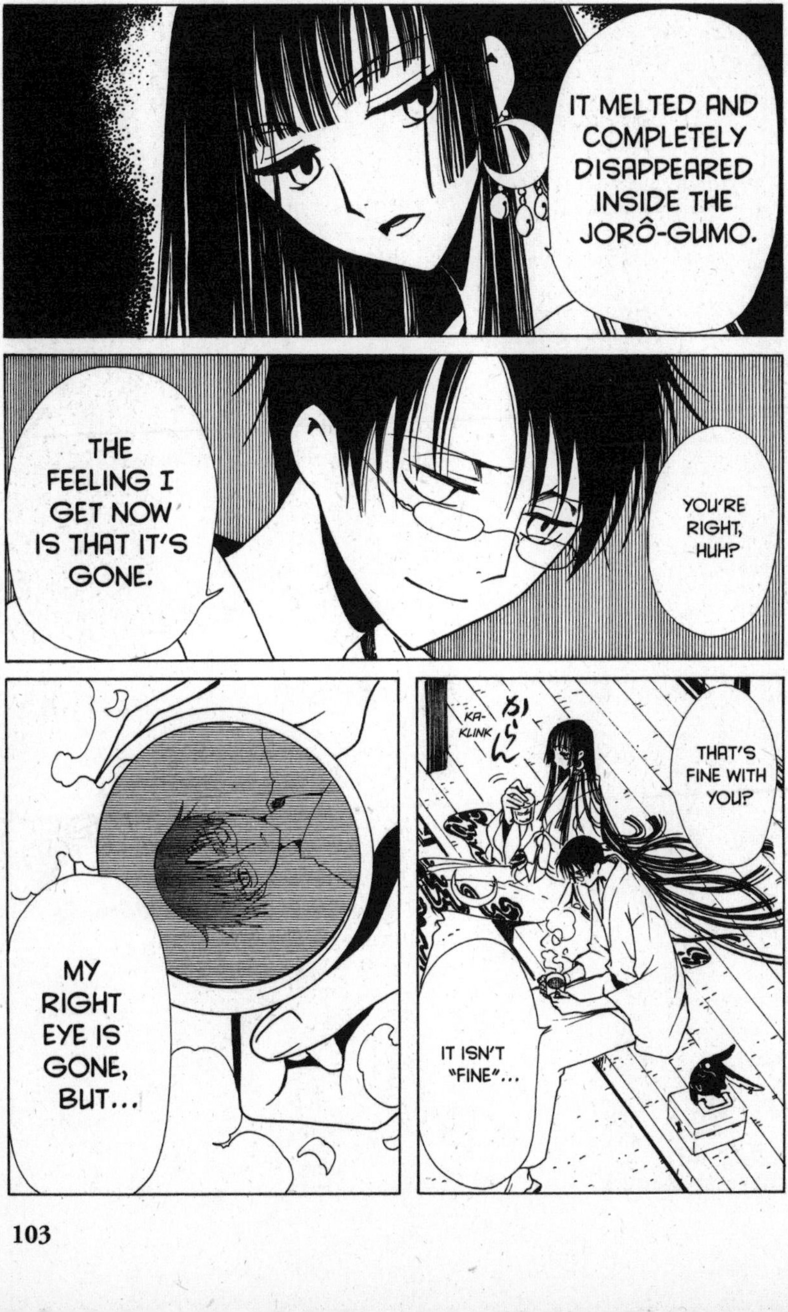
IT MELTED AND COMPLETELY DISAPPEARED INSIDE THE JORÔ-GUMO.
YOU'RE RIGHT, HUH?
THE FEELING I GET NOW IS THAT IT'S GONE.
からん
KA-KLINK
THAT'S FINE WITH YOU?
IT ISN'T "FINE"...
MY RIGHT EYE IS GONE, BUT...

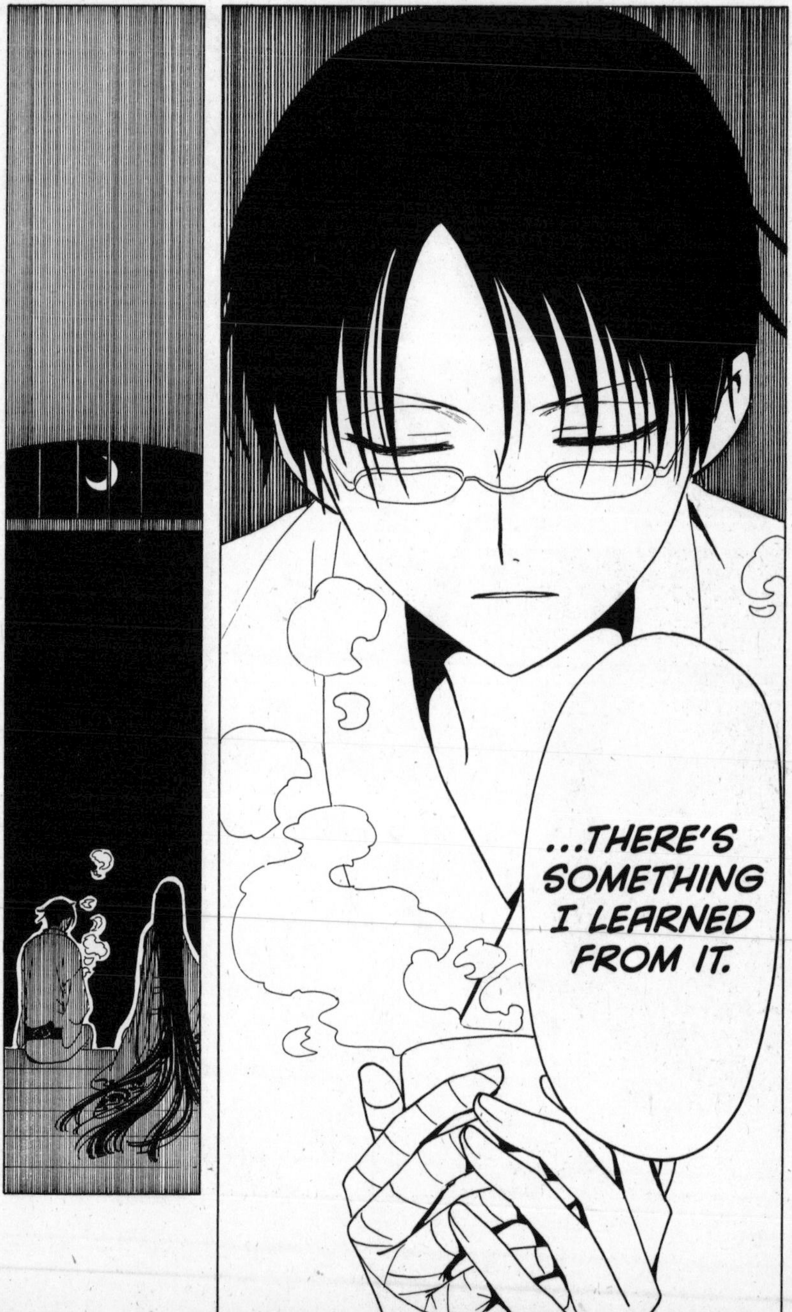
...THERE'S SOMETHING I LEARNED FROM IT.

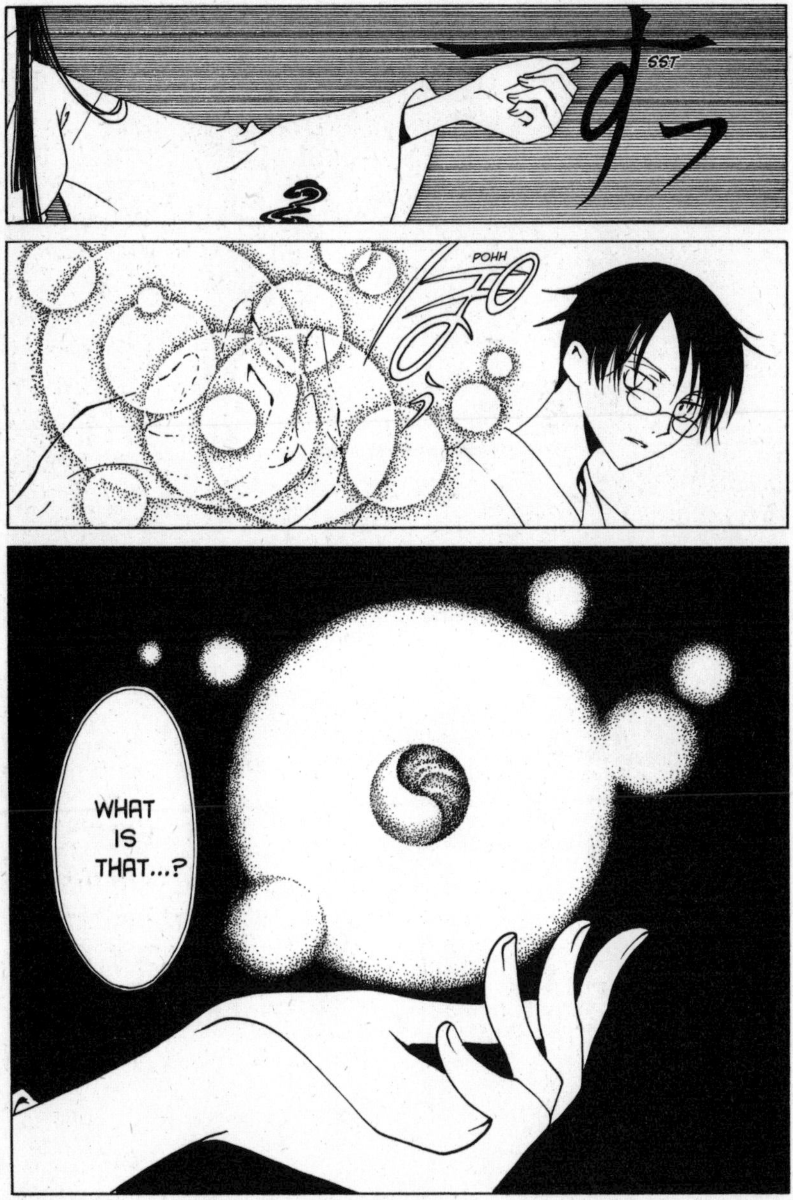
すっ
SST
ぽぉ
POHH
WHAT IS THAT...?

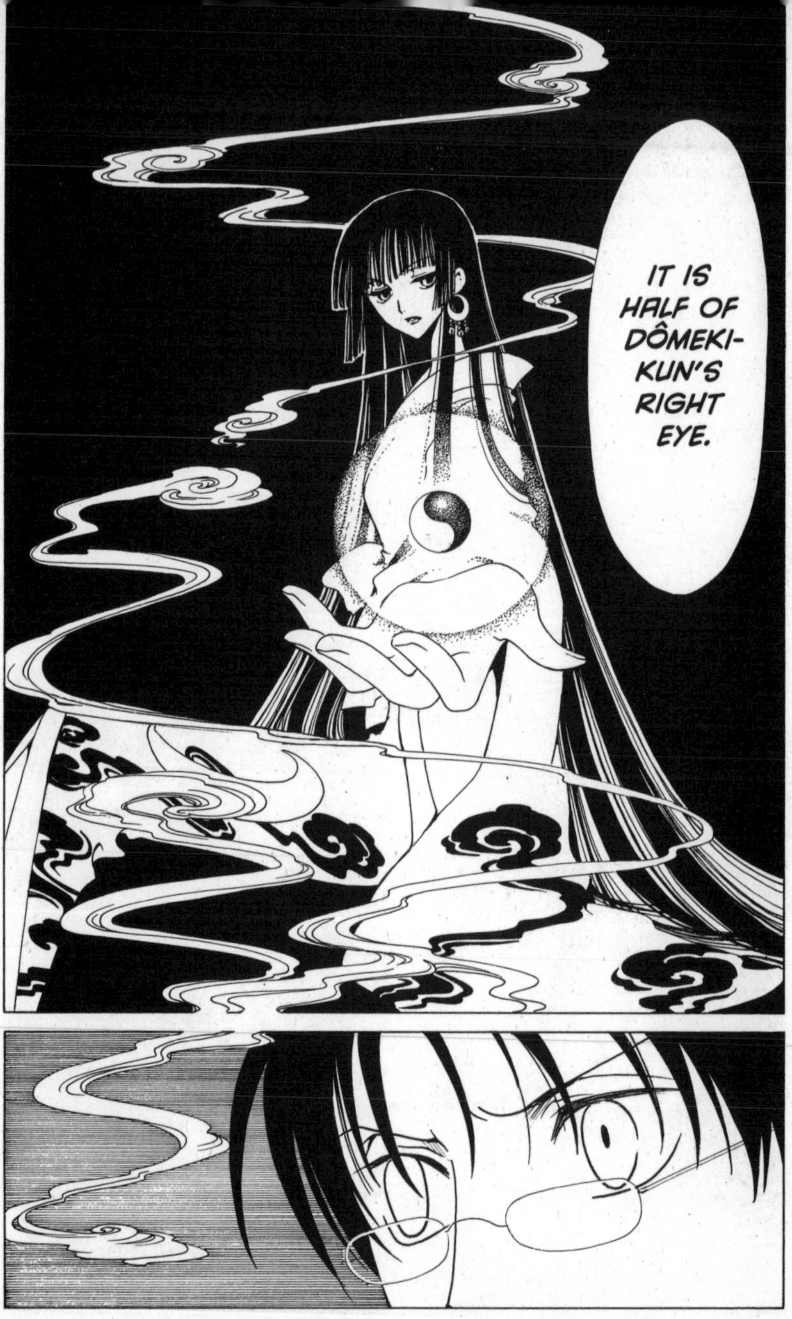
IT IS HALF OF DÔMEKI-KUN'S RIGHT EYE.

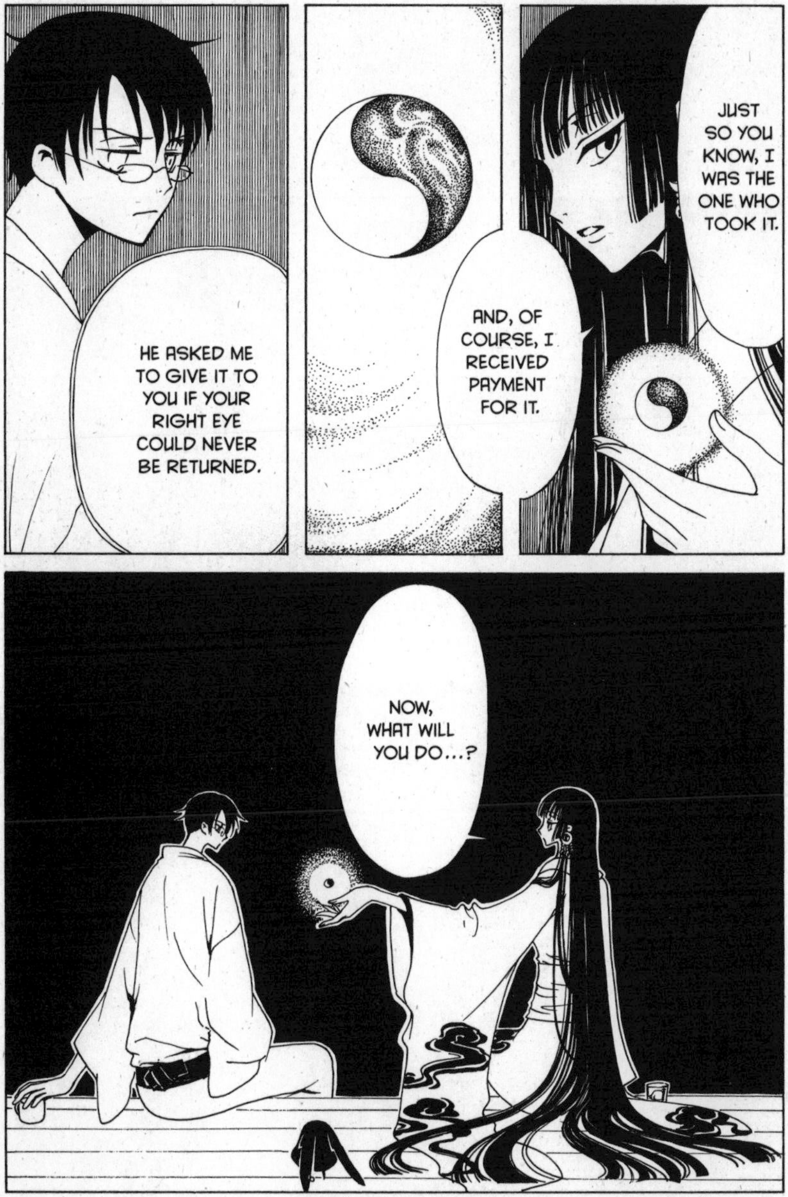
JUST SO YOU KNOW, I WAS THE ONE WHO TOOK IT.
AND, OF COURSE, I RECEIVED PAYMENT FOR IT.
HE ASKED ME TO GIVE IT TO YOU IF YOUR RIGHT EYE COULD NEVER BE RETURNED.
NOW, WHAT WILL YOU DO...?

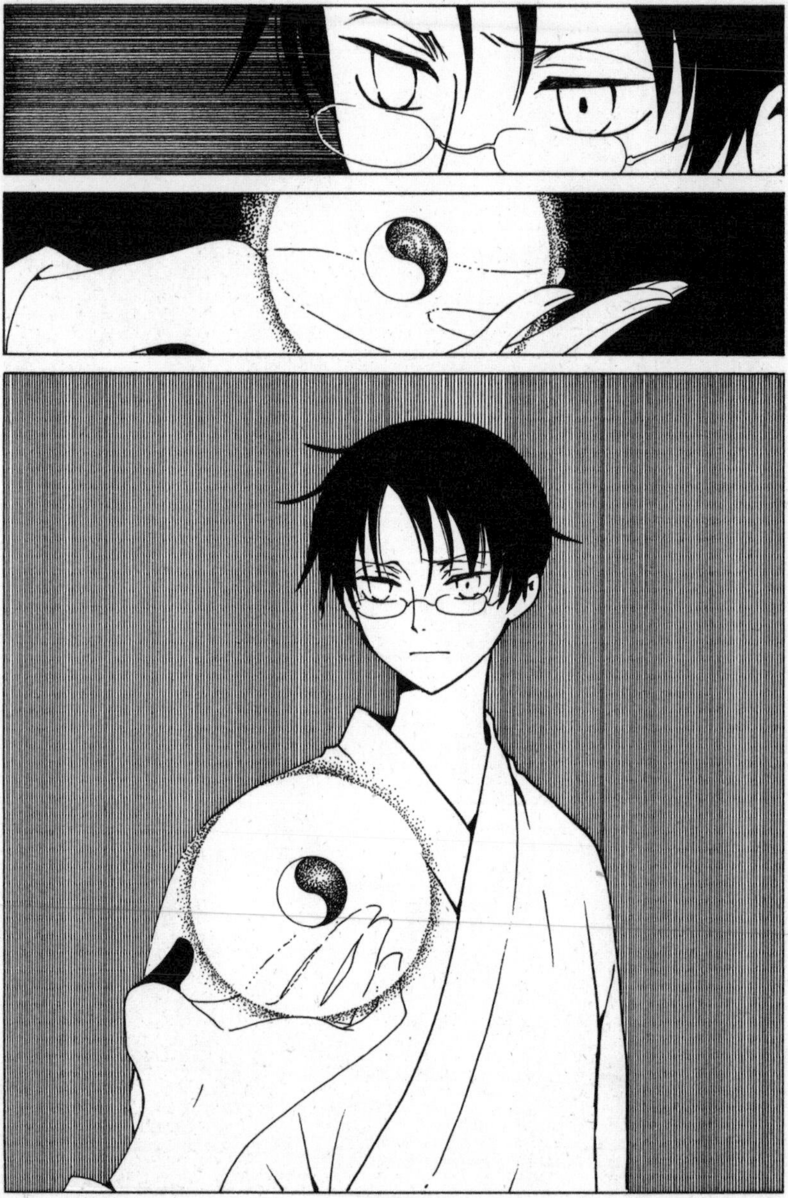

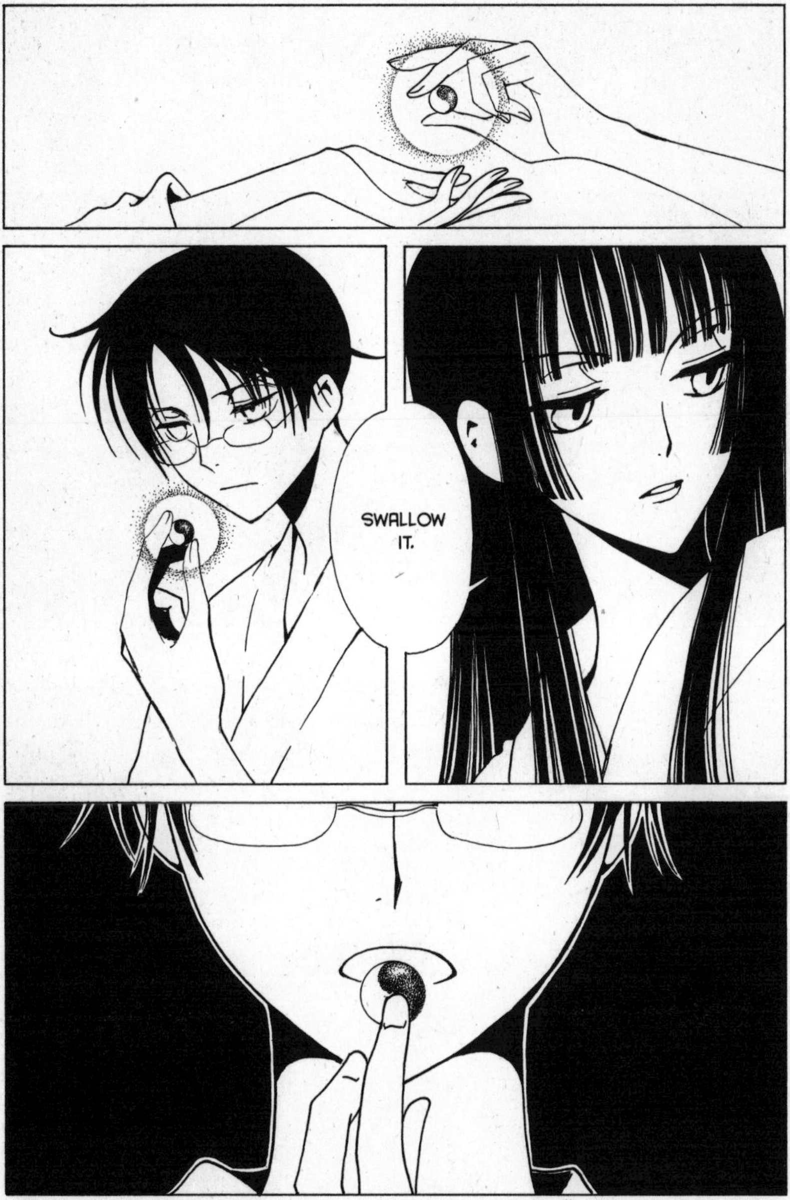
SWALLOW IT.

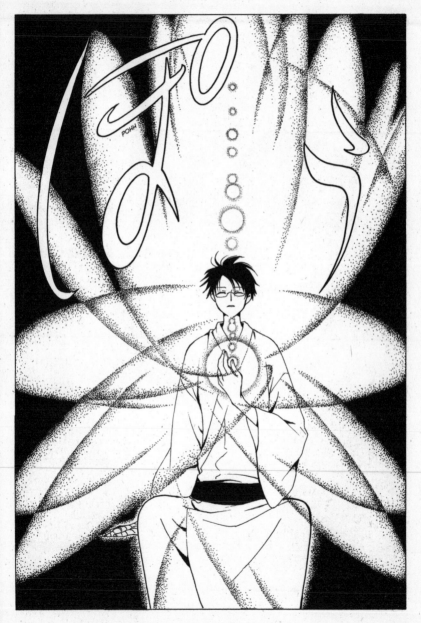

POHH

110

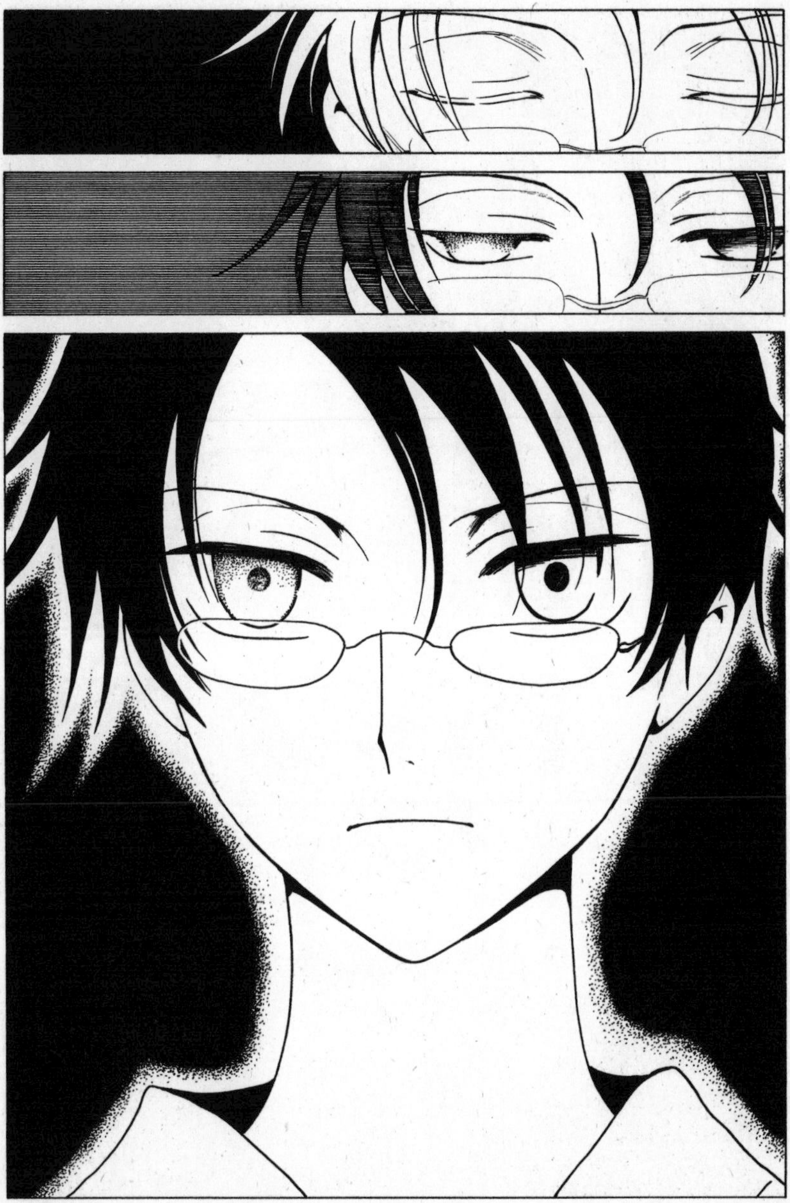

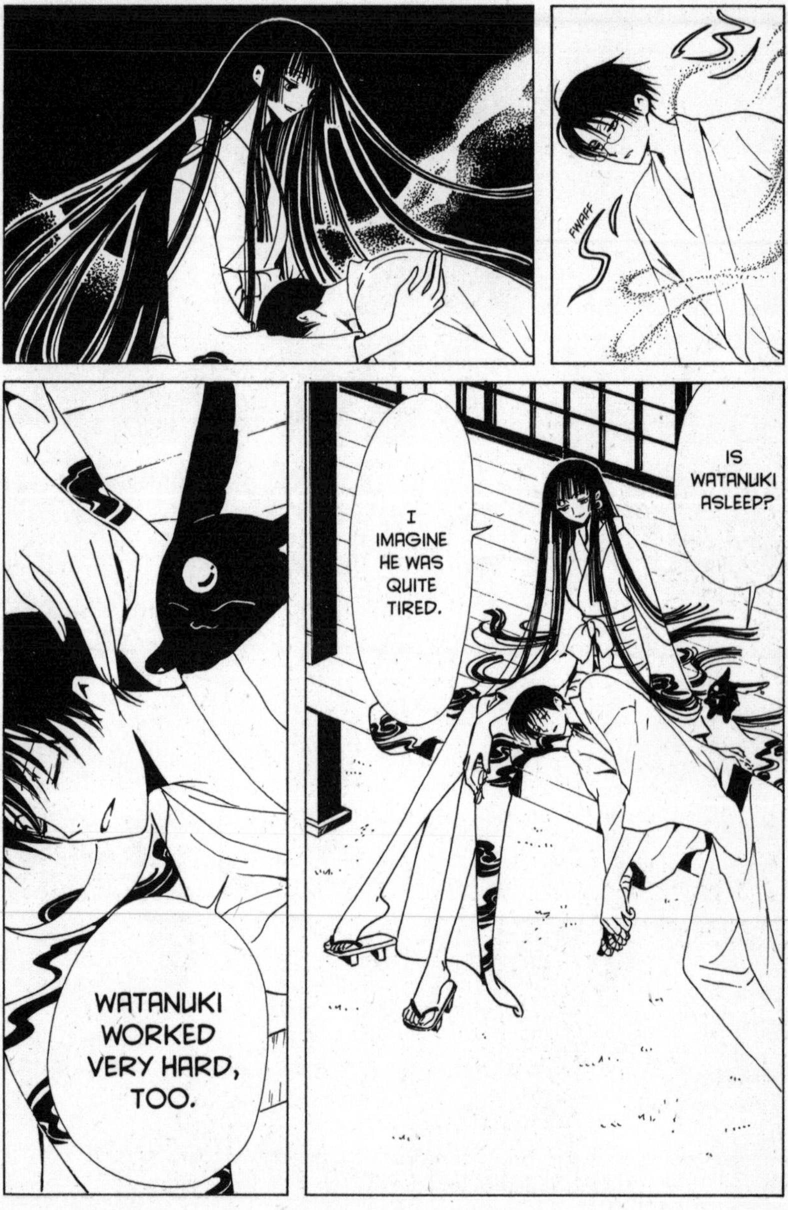
FWAFF
IS WATANUKI ASLEEP?
I IMAGINE HE WAS QUITE TIRED.
WATANUKI WORKED VERY HARD, TOO.

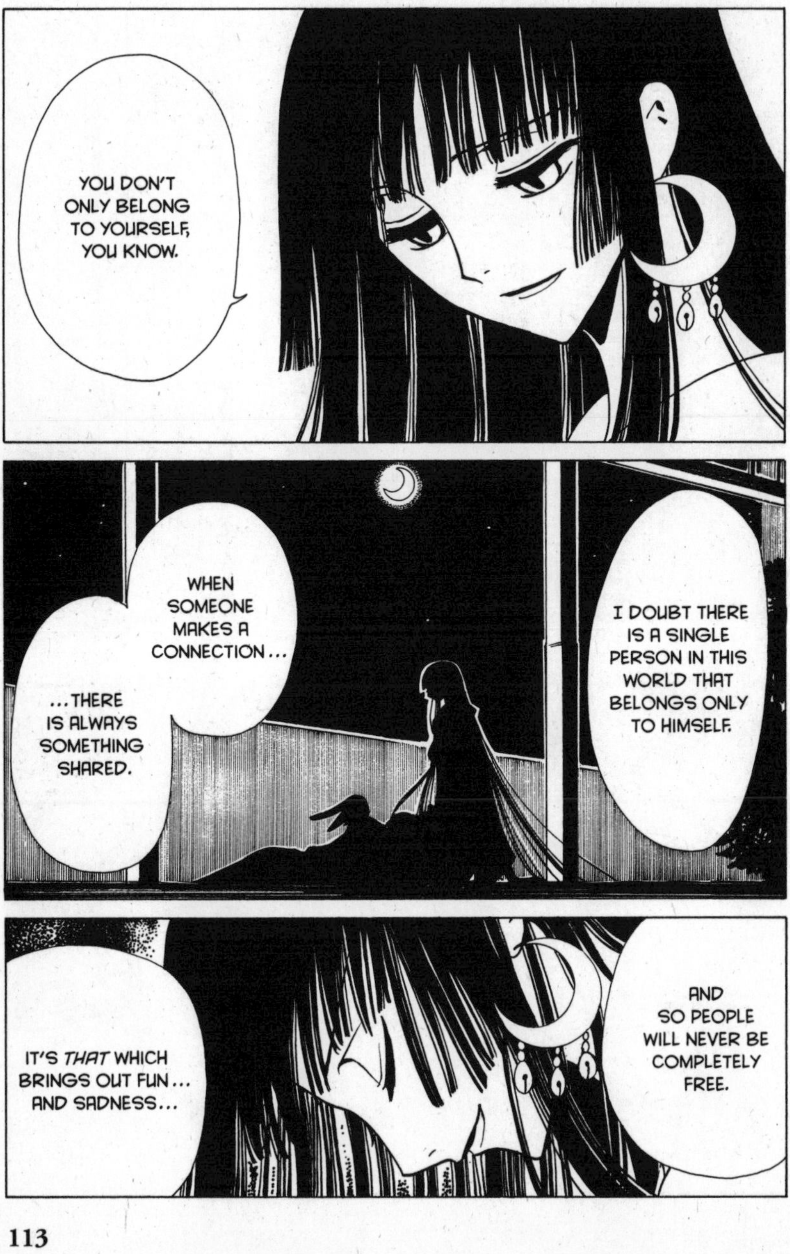
YOU DON'T ONLY BELONG TO YOURSELF, YOU KNOW.
I DOUBT THERE IS A SINGLE PERSON IN THIS WORLD THAT BELONGS ONLY TO HIMSELF.
WHEN SOMEONE MAKES A CONNECTION...
...THERE IS ALWAYS SOMETHING SHARED.
AND SO PEOPLE WILL NEVER BE COMPLETELY FREE.
IT'S *THAT* WHICH BRINGS OUT FUN... AND SADNESS...

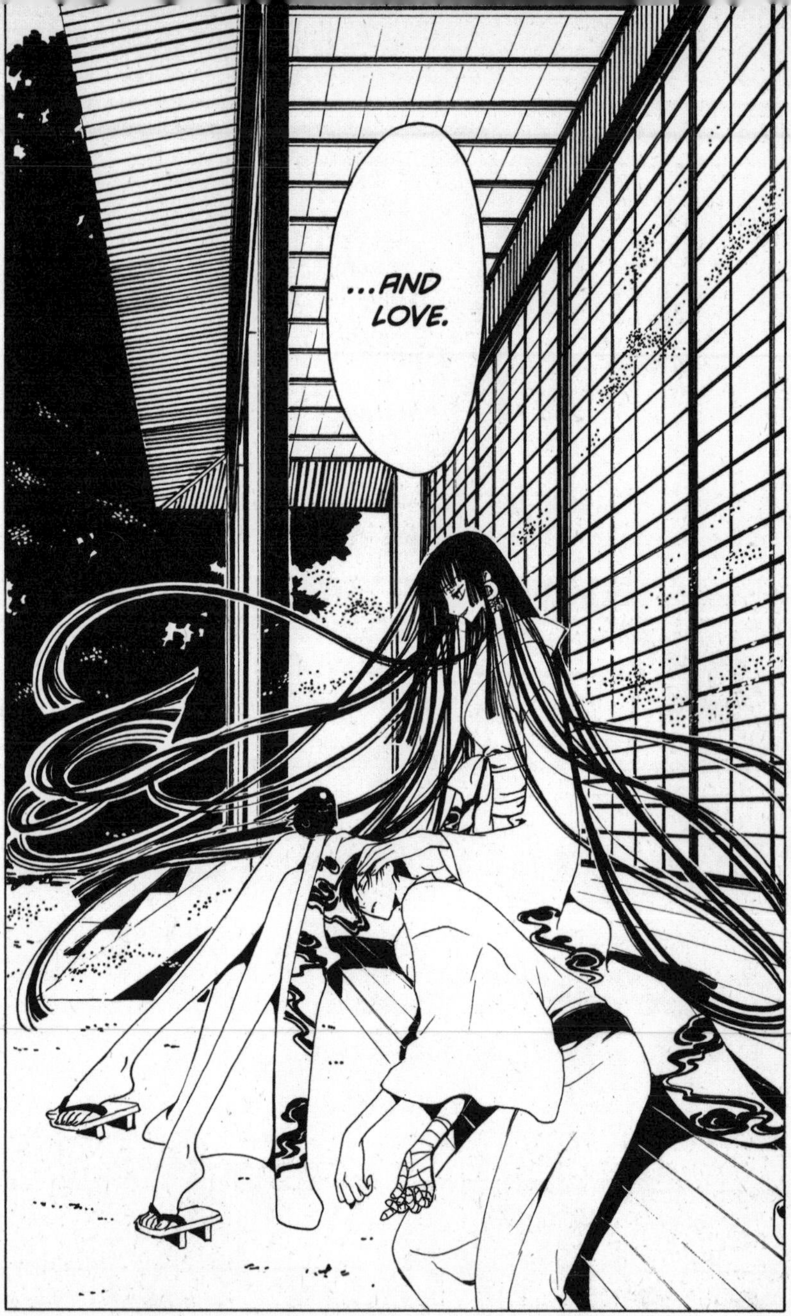
...AND LOVE.

ZWIPP

115

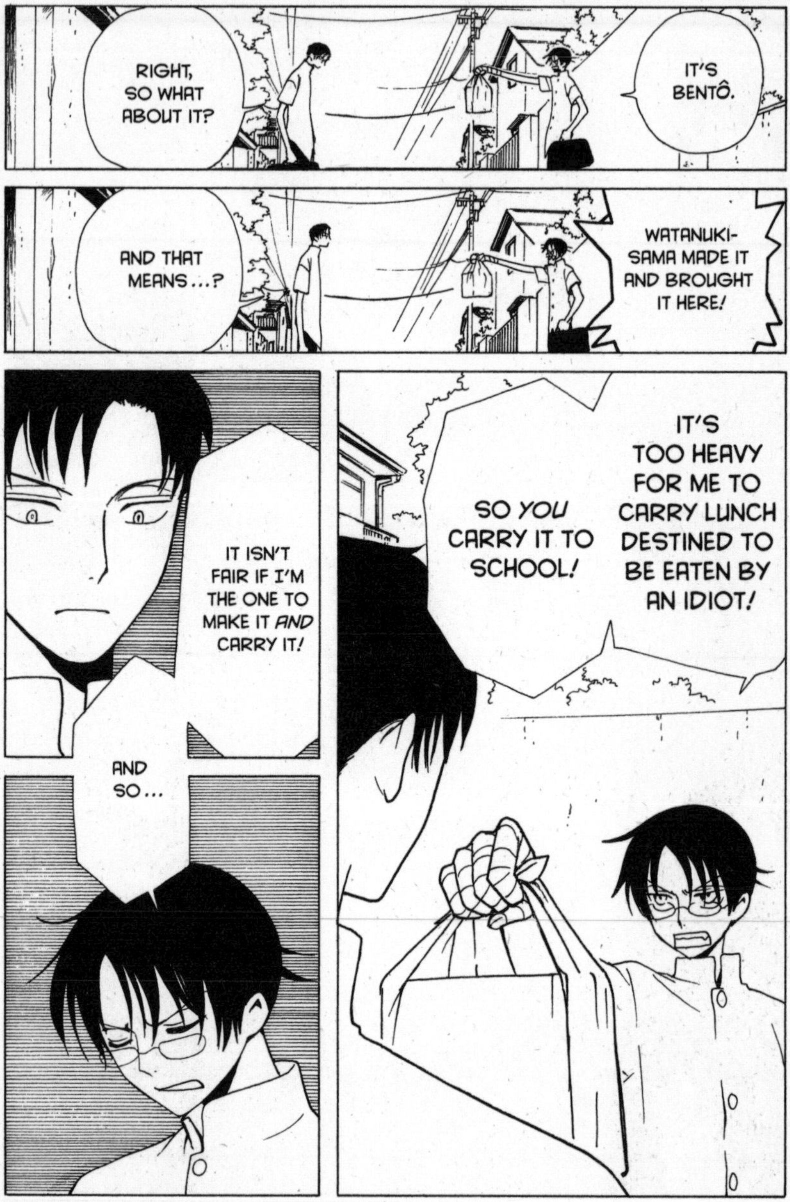
IT'S BENTÔ.
RIGHT, SO WHAT ABOUT IT?
WATANUKI-SAMA MADE IT AND BROUGHT IT HERE!
AND THAT MEANS ...?
IT'S TOO HEAVY FOR ME TO CARRY LUNCH DESTINED TO BE EATEN BY AN IDIOT!
SO *YOU* CARRY IT TO SCHOOL!
IT ISN'T FAIR IF I'M THE ONE TO MAKE IT *AND* CARRY IT!
AND SO ...

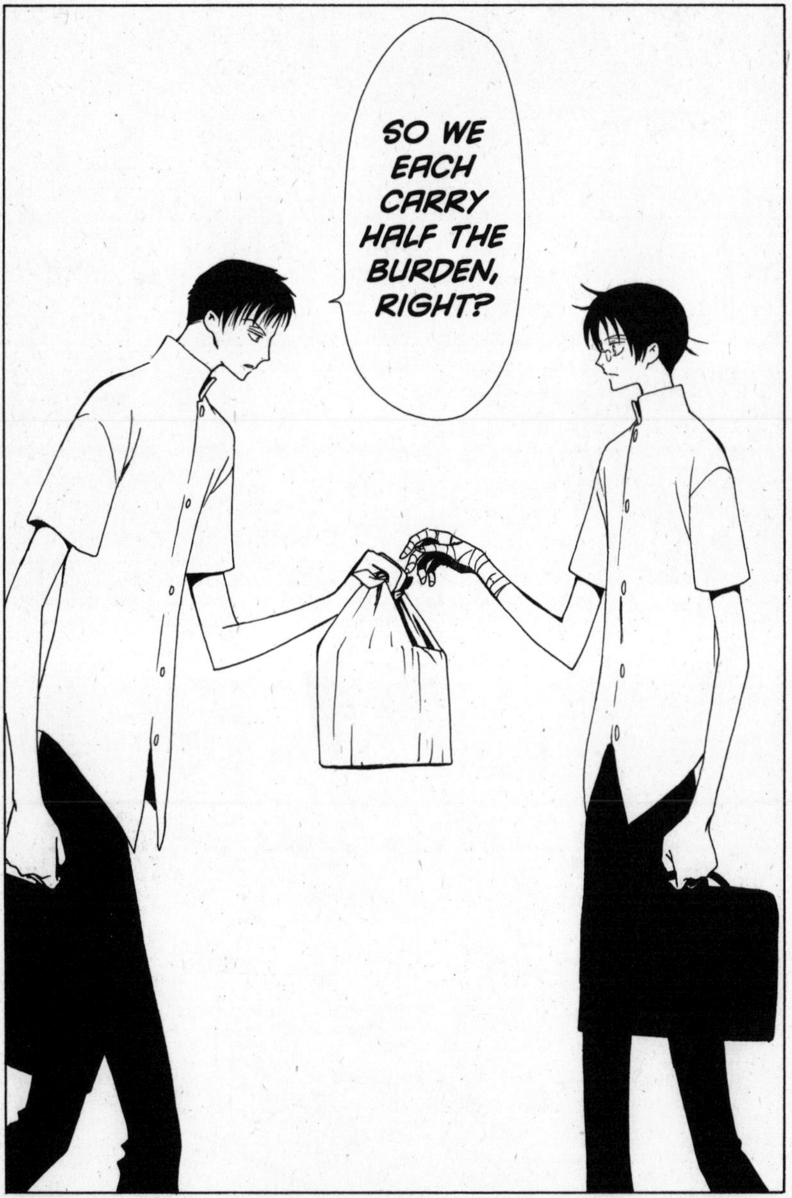
SO WE EACH CARRY HALF THE BURDEN, RIGHT?

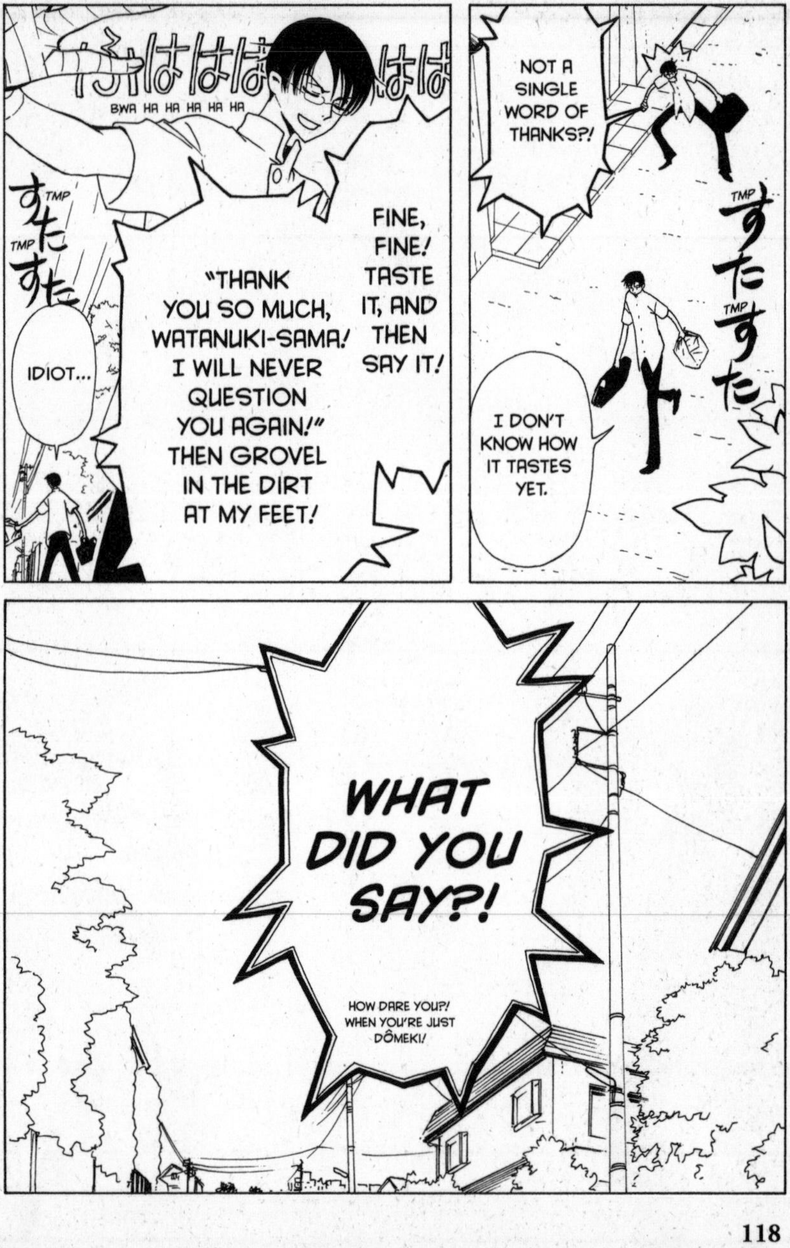
NOT A SINGLE WORD OF THANKS?!
TMP すた TMP すた
I DON'T KNOW HOW IT TASTES YET.
BWA HA HA HA HA HA
FINE, FINE! TASTE IT, AND THEN SAY IT!
"THANK YOU SO MUCH, WATANUKI-SAMA! I WILL NEVER QUESTION YOU AGAIN!" THEN GROVEL IN THE DIRT AT MY FEET!
TMP すた TMP すた
IDIOT...
WHAT DID YOU SAY?!
HOW DARE YOU?! WHEN YOU'RE JUST DÔMEKI!

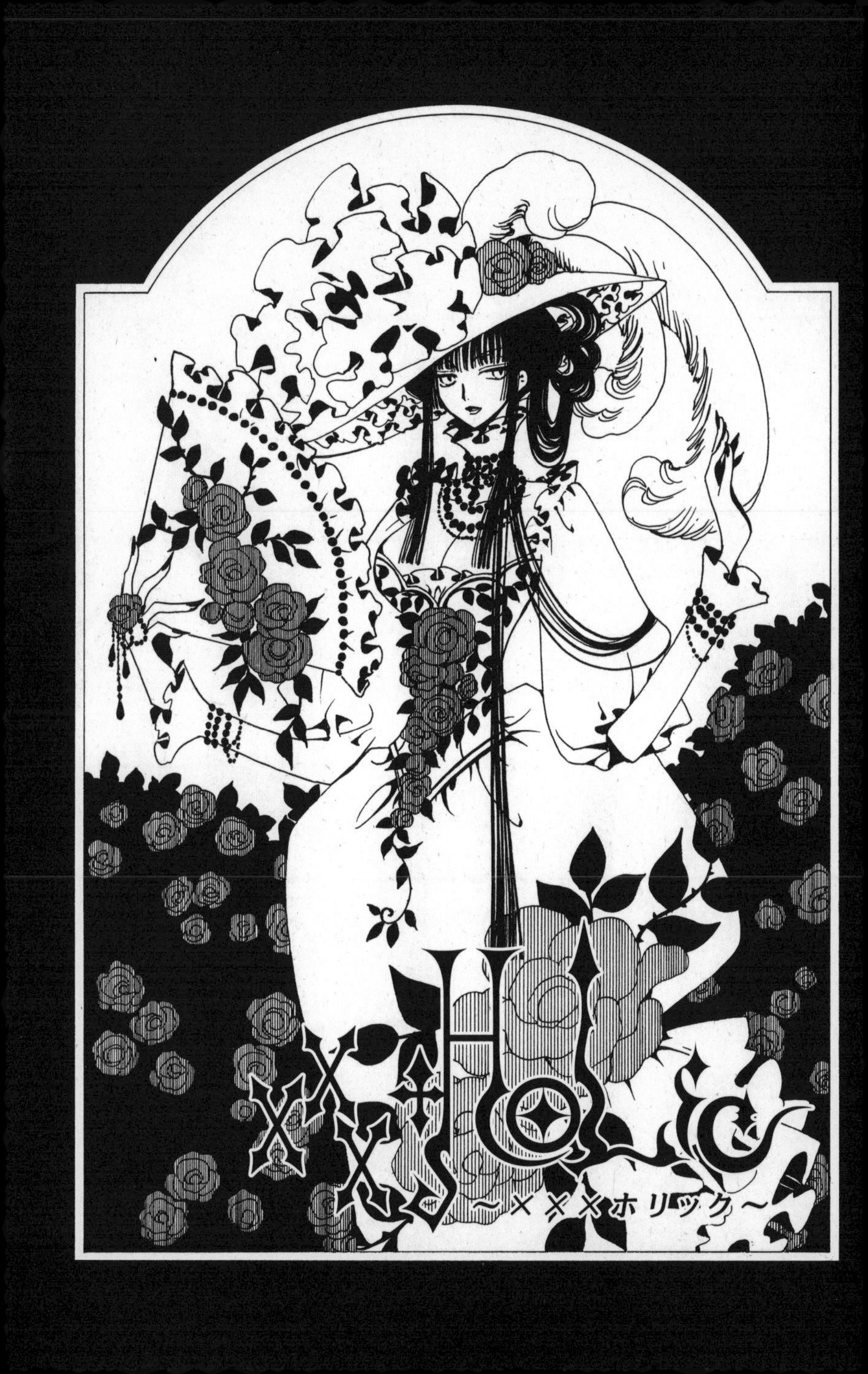
xxxHOLiC
～×××ホリック～

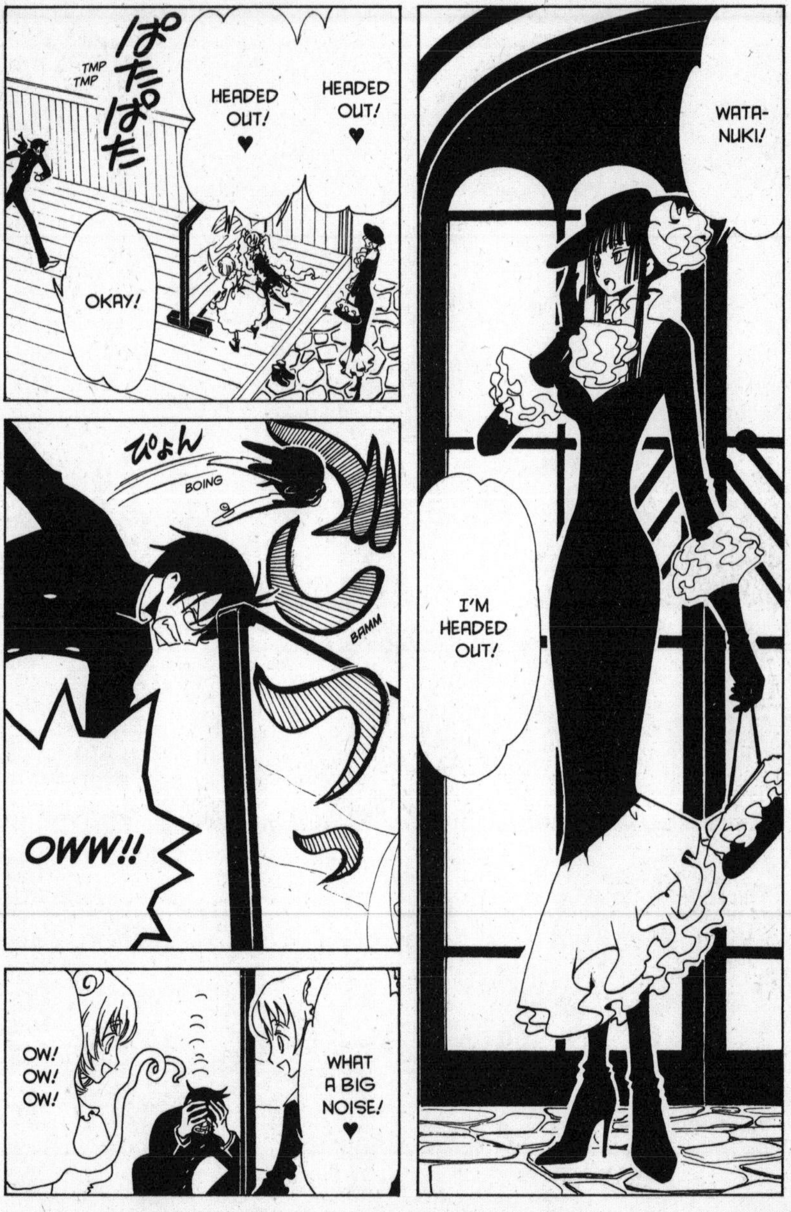
WATA-NUKI!
I'M HEADED OUT!
HEADED OUT! ♥
HEADED OUT! ♥
ぱたぱた
TMP TMP
OKAY!
ぴょん
BOING
BAMM
OWW!!
WHAT A BIG NOISE! ♥
OW! OW! OW!

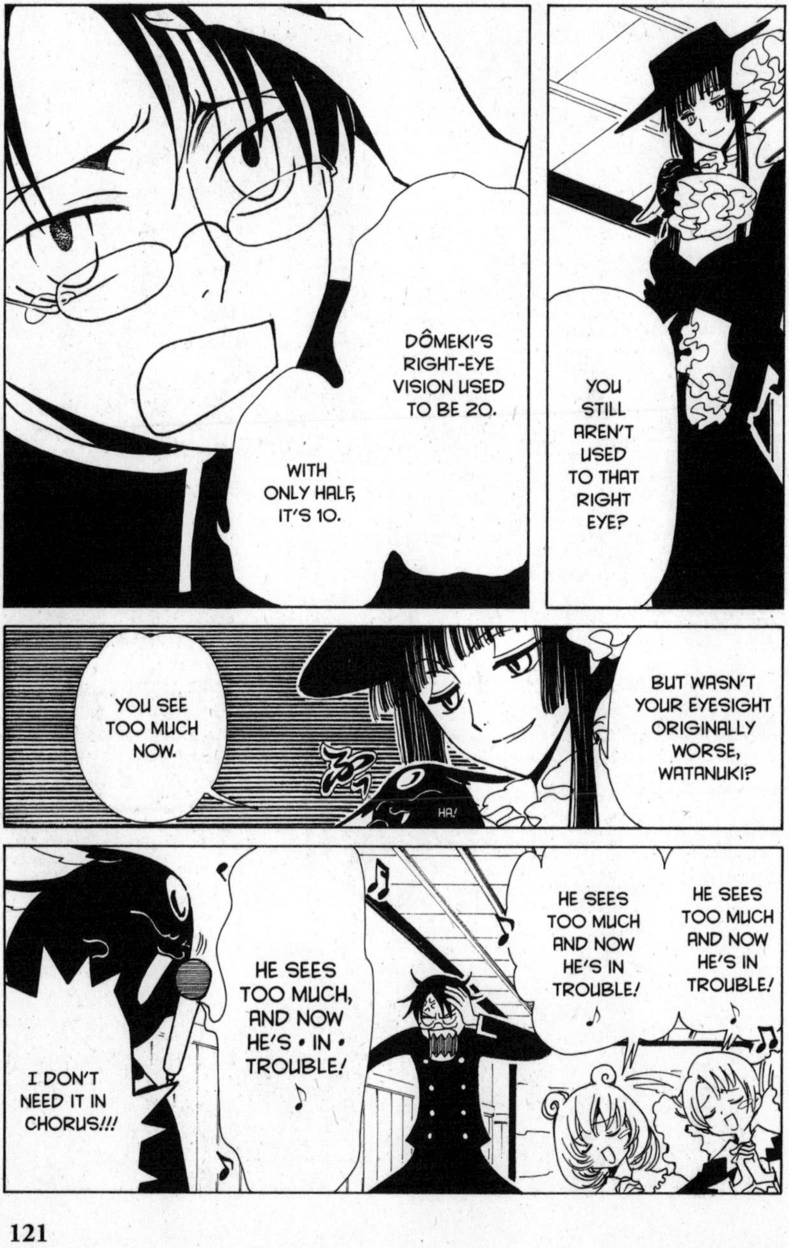
YOU STILL AREN'T USED TO THAT RIGHT EYE?
DÔMEKI'S RIGHT-EYE VISION USED TO BE 20.
WITH ONLY HALF, IT'S 10.
BUT WASN'T YOUR EYESIGHT ORIGINALLY WORSE, WATANUKI?
HA!
YOU SEE TOO MUCH NOW.
HE SEES TOO MUCH AND NOW HE'S IN TROUBLE!
HE SEES TOO MUCH AND NOW HE'S IN TROUBLE!
HE SEES TOO MUCH, AND NOW HE'S • IN • TROUBLE!
I DON'T NEED IT IN CHORUS!!!

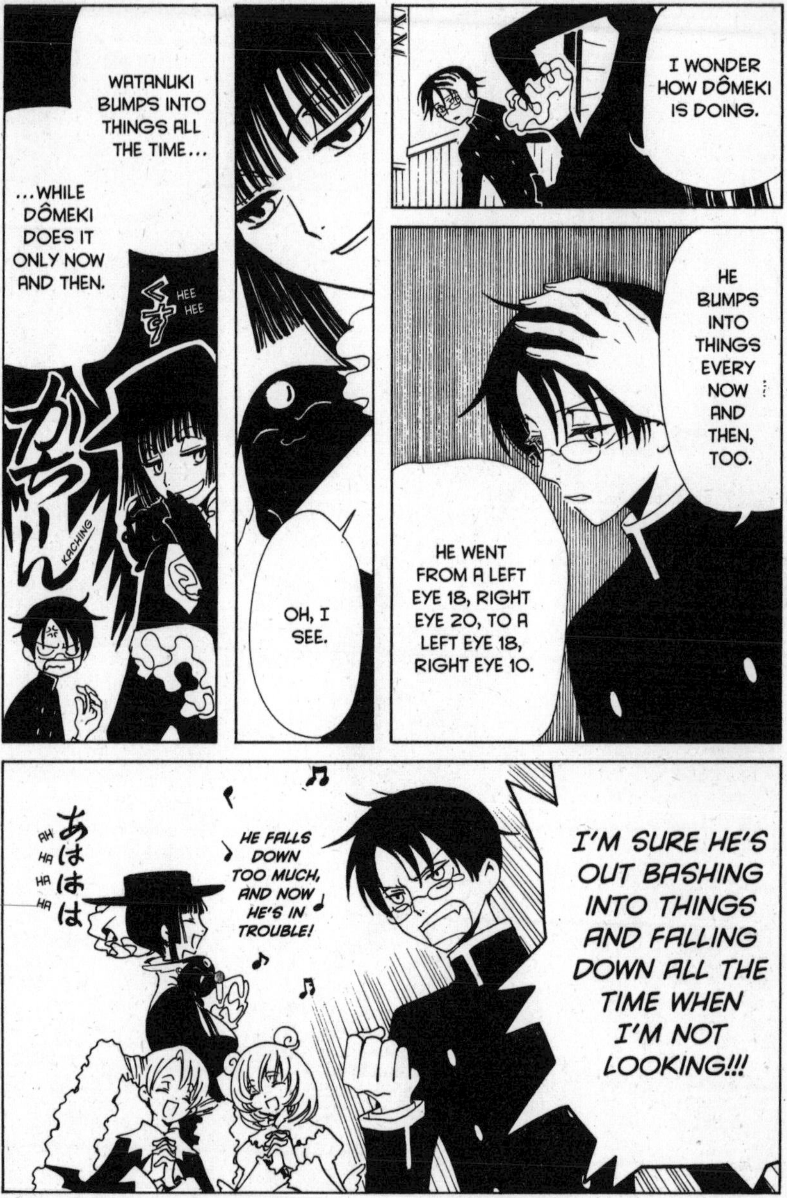
I WONDER HOW DÔMEKI IS DOING.
HE BUMPS INTO THINGS EVERY NOW AND THEN, TOO.
HE WENT FROM A LEFT EYE 18, RIGHT EYE 20, TO A LEFT EYE 18, RIGHT EYE 10.
OH, I SEE.
WATANUKI BUMPS INTO THINGS ALL THE TIME...
...WHILE DÔMEKI DOES IT ONLY NOW AND THEN.
くす
HEE HEE
かちーん
KACHING
I'M SURE HE'S OUT BASHING INTO THINGS AND FALLING DOWN ALL THE TIME WHEN I'M NOT LOOKING!!!
HE FALLS DOWN TOO MUCH, AND NOW HE'S IN TROUBLE!
あははは
AH HA HA HA

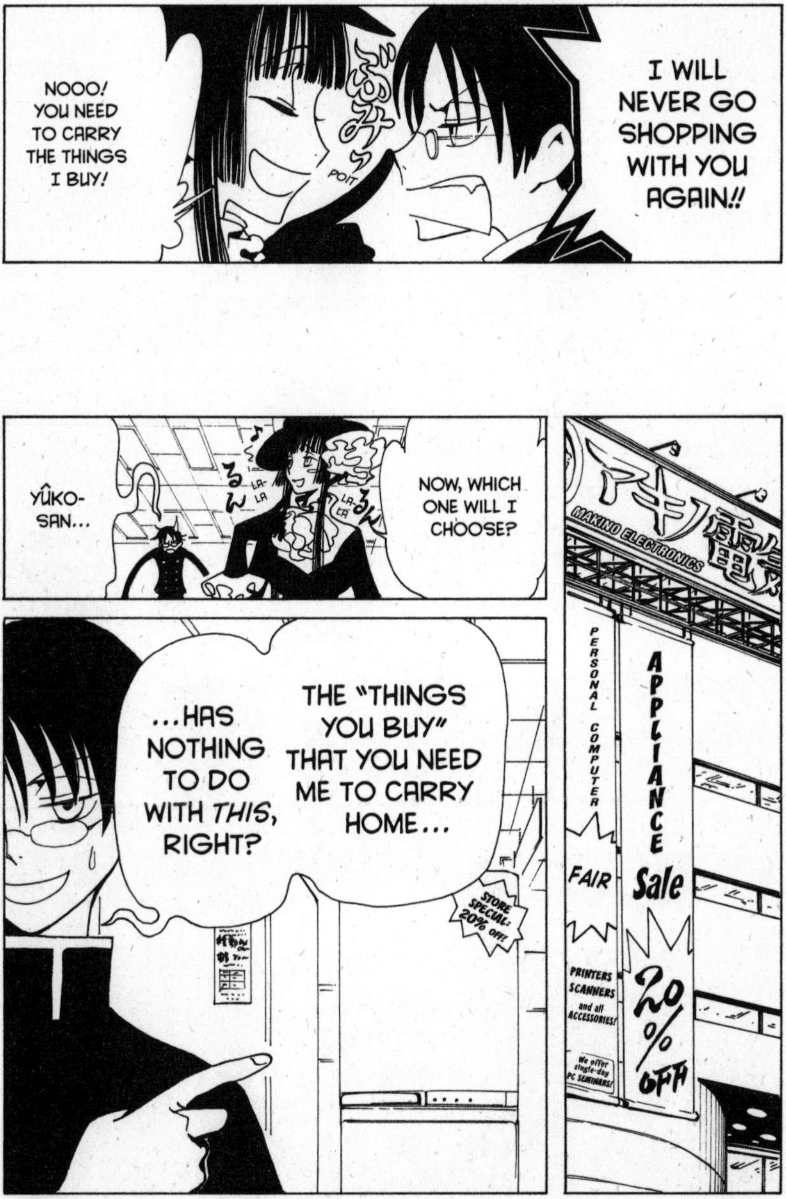
I WILL NEVER GO SHOPPING WITH YOU AGAIN!!
POIT
NOOO! YOU NEED TO CARRY THE THINGS I BUY!
MAKINO ELECTRONICS
PERSONAL COMPUTER FAIR
APPLIANCE Sale
20% OFF
PRINTERS SCANNERS and all ACCESSORIES!
We offer single-day PC SEMINARS!
NOW, WHICH ONE WILL I CHOOSE?
LA-LA
LA-LA
YÛKO-SAN...
THE "THINGS YOU BUY" THAT YOU NEED ME TO CARRY HOME...
...HAS NOTHING TO DO WITH *THIS*, RIGHT?
STORE SPECIAL: 20% OFF!

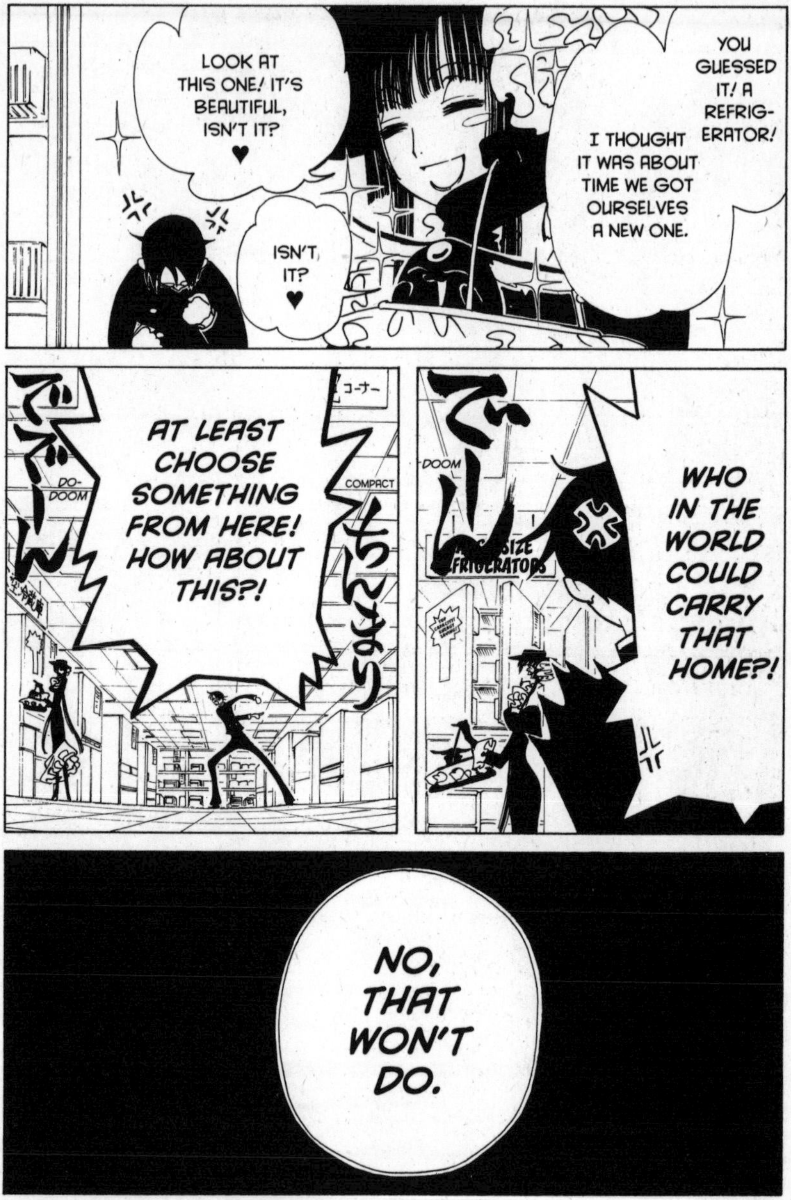
YOU GUESSED IT! A REFRIGERATOR!
I THOUGHT IT WAS ABOUT TIME WE GOT OURSELVES A NEW ONE.
LOOK AT THIS ONE! IT'S BEAUTIFUL, ISN'T IT? ♥
ISN'T IT? ♥
DOOM
WHO IN THE WORLD COULD CARRY THAT HOME?!
AT LEAST CHOOSE SOMETHING FROM HERE! HOW ABOUT THIS?!
COMPACT
ちんまり
DO-DOOM
NO, THAT WON'T DO.

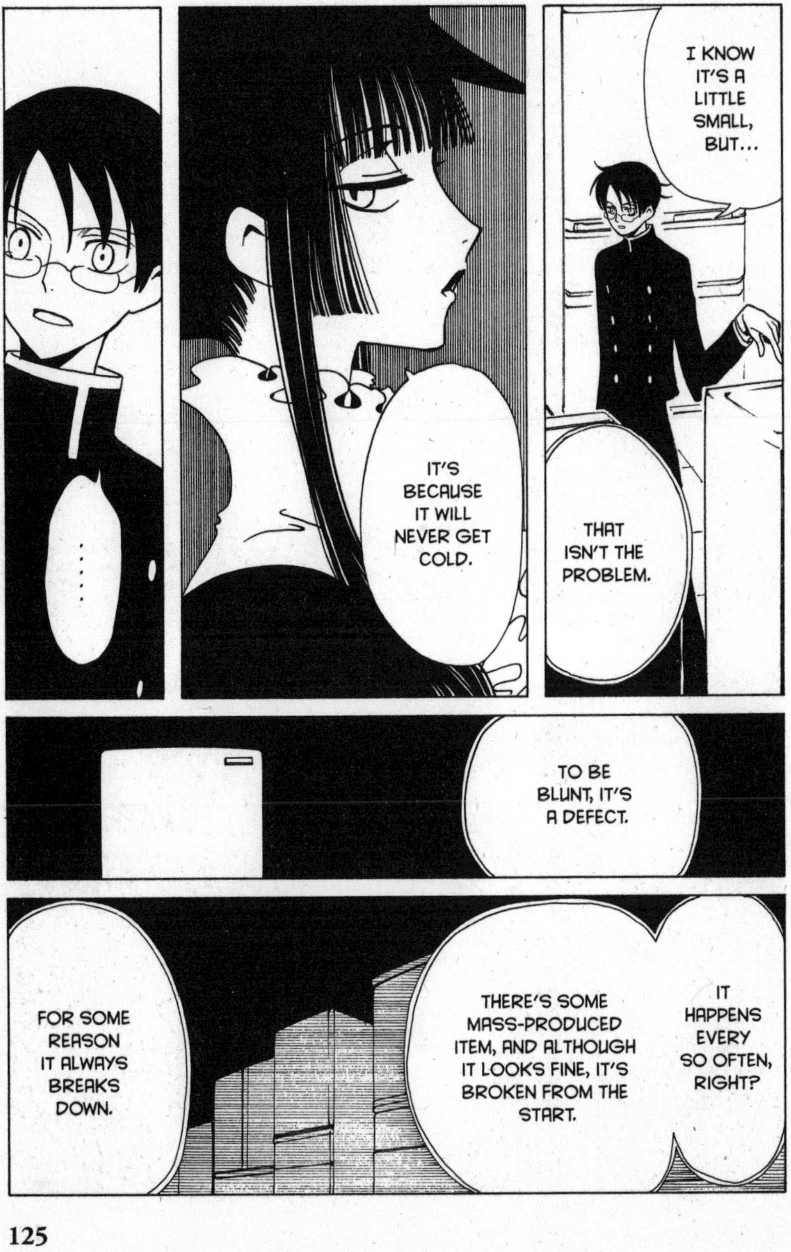
I KNOW IT'S A LITTLE SMALL, BUT...
THAT ISN'T THE PROBLEM.
IT'S BECAUSE IT WILL NEVER GET COLD.
.....
TO BE BLUNT, IT'S A DEFECT.
IT HAPPENS EVERY SO OFTEN, RIGHT?
THERE'S SOME MASS-PRODUCED ITEM, AND ALTHOUGH IT LOOKS FINE, IT'S BROKEN FROM THE START.
FOR SOME REASON IT ALWAYS BREAKS DOWN.

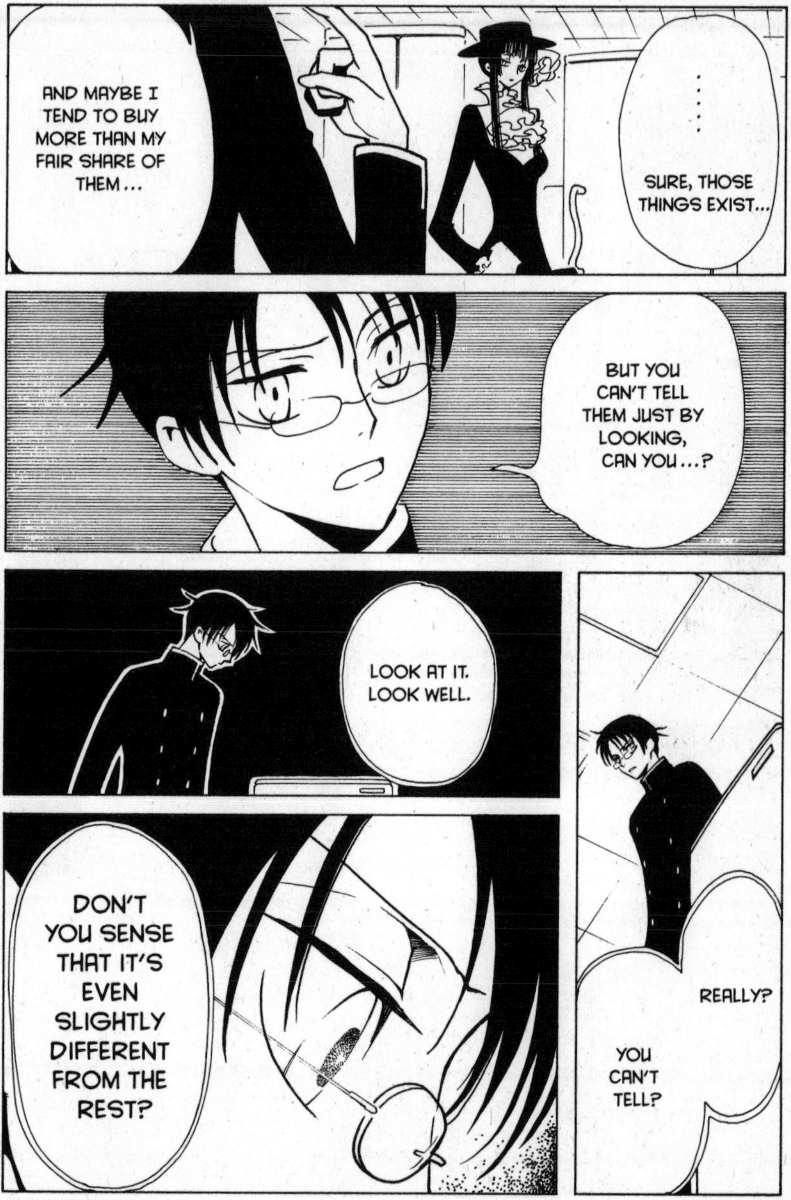

......
SURE, THOSE THINGS EXIST...
AND MAYBE I TEND TO BUY MORE THAN MY FAIR SHARE OF THEM...
BUT YOU CAN'T TELL THEM JUST BY LOOKING, CAN YOU...?
REALLY? YOU CAN'T TELL?
LOOK AT IT. LOOK WELL.
DON'T YOU SENSE THAT IT'S EVEN SLIGHTLY DIFFERENT FROM THE REST?

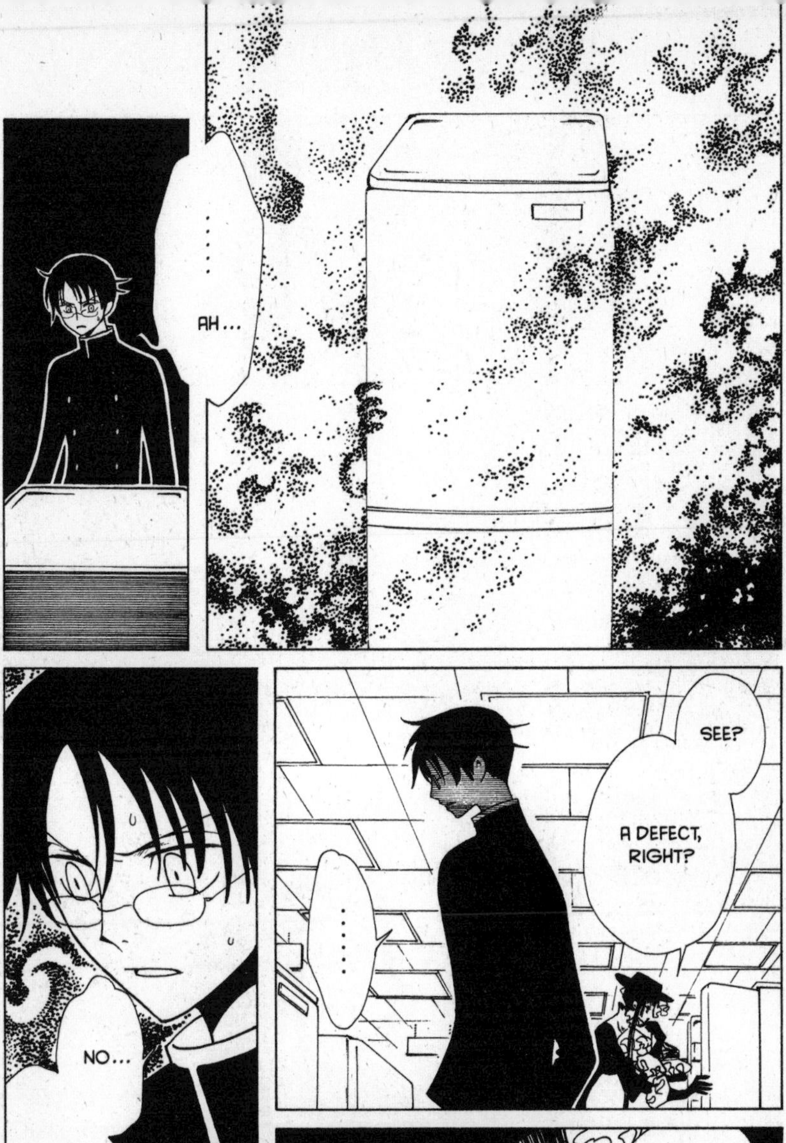
……
AH…
SEE?
A DEFECT, RIGHT?
……
DO YOU STILL WANT ME TO BUY IT?
NO…
…I'D HAVE YOU PASS ON THIS ONE.

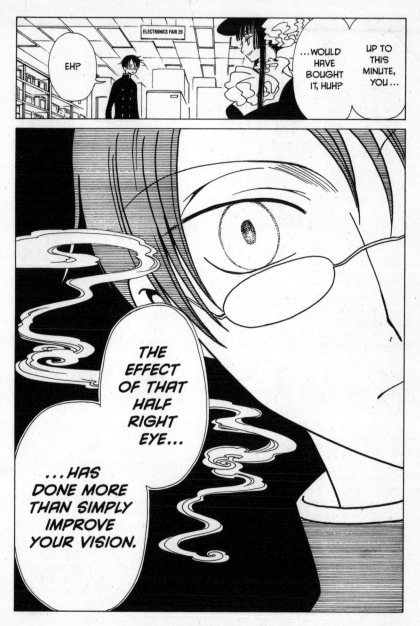

UP TO THIS MINUTE, YOU...
...WOULD HAVE BOUGHT IT, HUH?
ELECTRONICS FAIR 20
EH?
THE EFFECT OF THAT HALF RIGHT EYE...
...HAS DONE MORE THAN SIMPLY IMPROVE YOUR VISION.

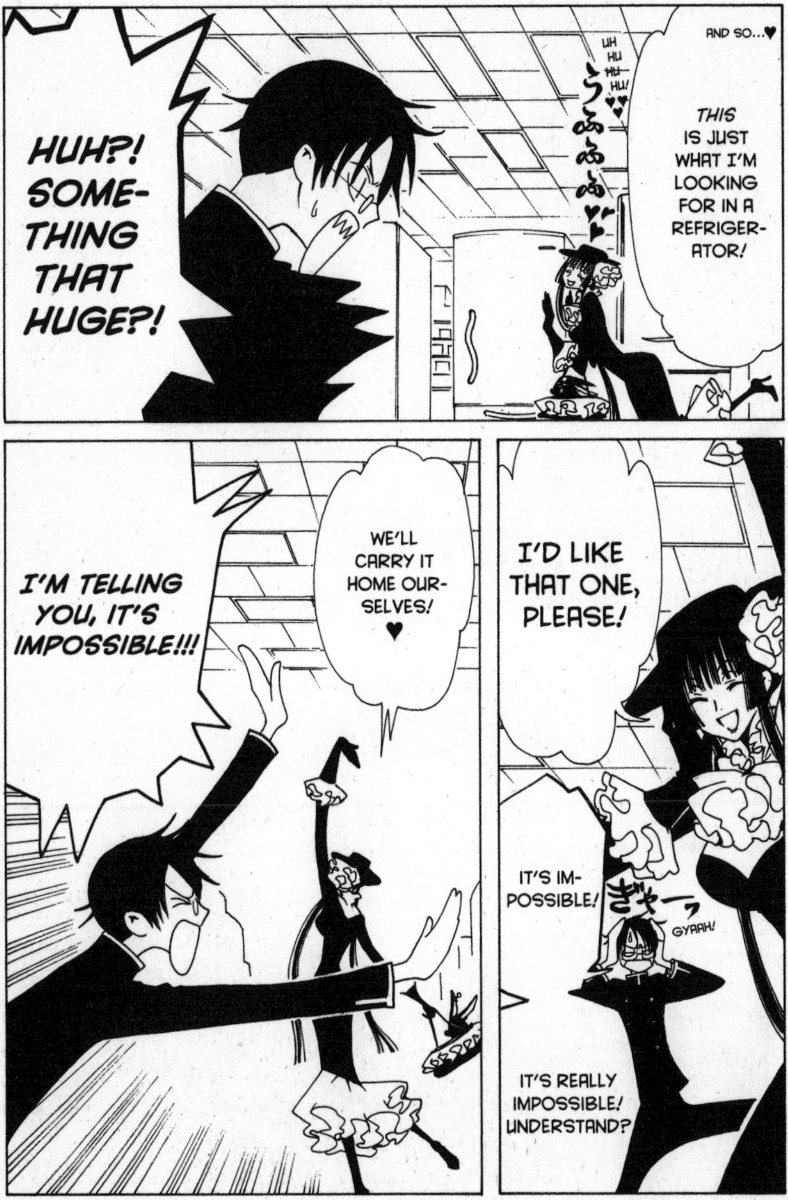
AND SO...♥
THIS IS JUST WHAT I'M LOOKING FOR IN A REFRIGERATOR!
うふふふ♥♥
UH HU HU HU! ♥♥
HUH?! SOMETHING THAT HUGE?!
I'D LIKE THAT ONE, PLEASE!
IT'S IMPOSSIBLE!
ぎゃーッ
GYAAH!
IT'S REALLY IMPOSSIBLE! UNDERSTAND?
WE'LL CARRY IT HOME OURSELVES! ♥
I'M TELLING YOU, IT'S IMPOSSIBLE!!!

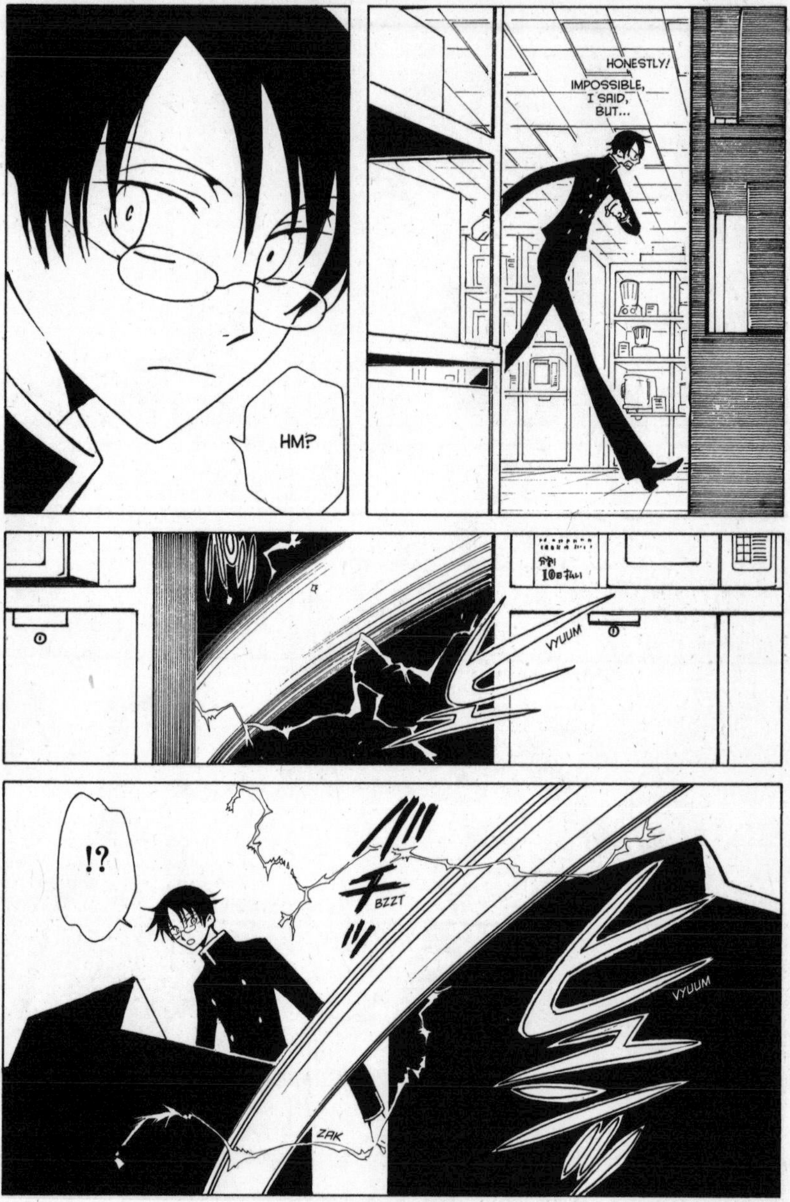
HONESTLY!
IMPOSSIBLE, I SAID, BUT...
HM?
VYUUM
BZZT
VYUUM
!?
ZAK

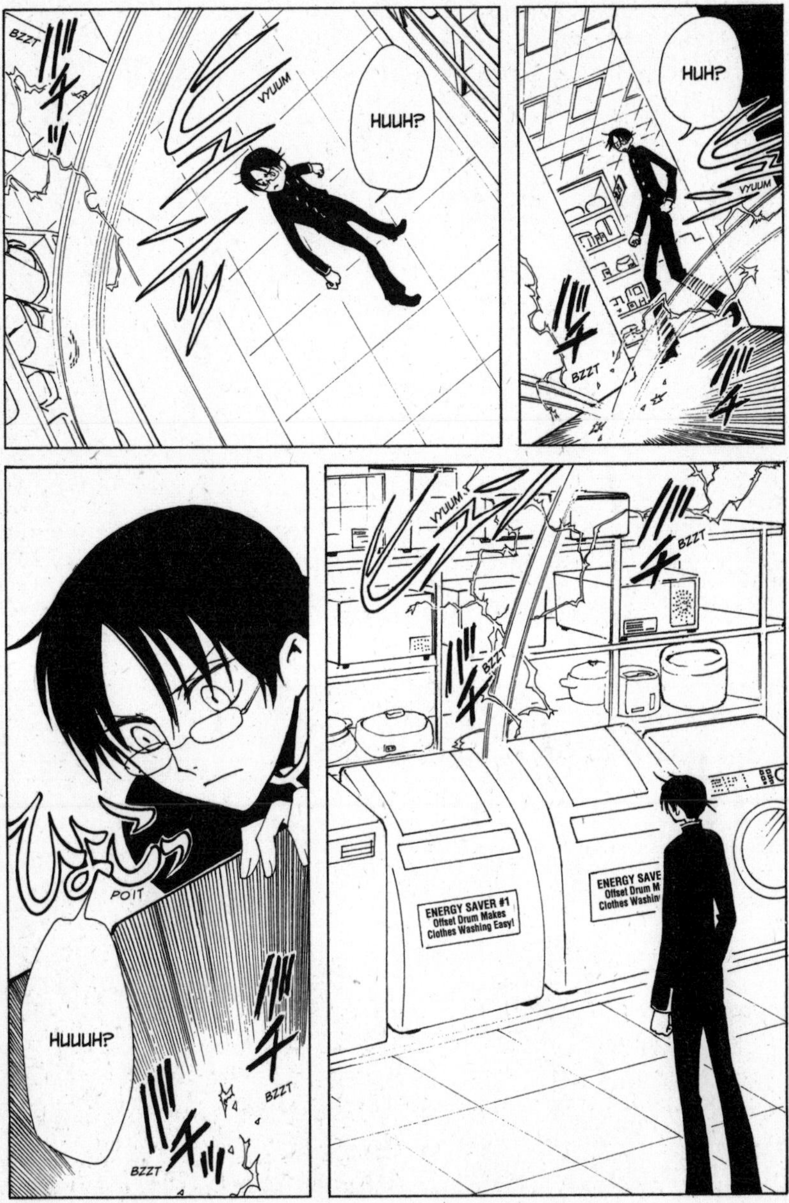
HUH?
VYUUM
BZZT
HUUH?
VYUUM
BZZT
VYUUM
BZZT
BZZT
ENERGY SAVER #1
Offset Drum Makes
Clothes Washing Easy!
POIT
HUUUH?
BZZT
BZZT

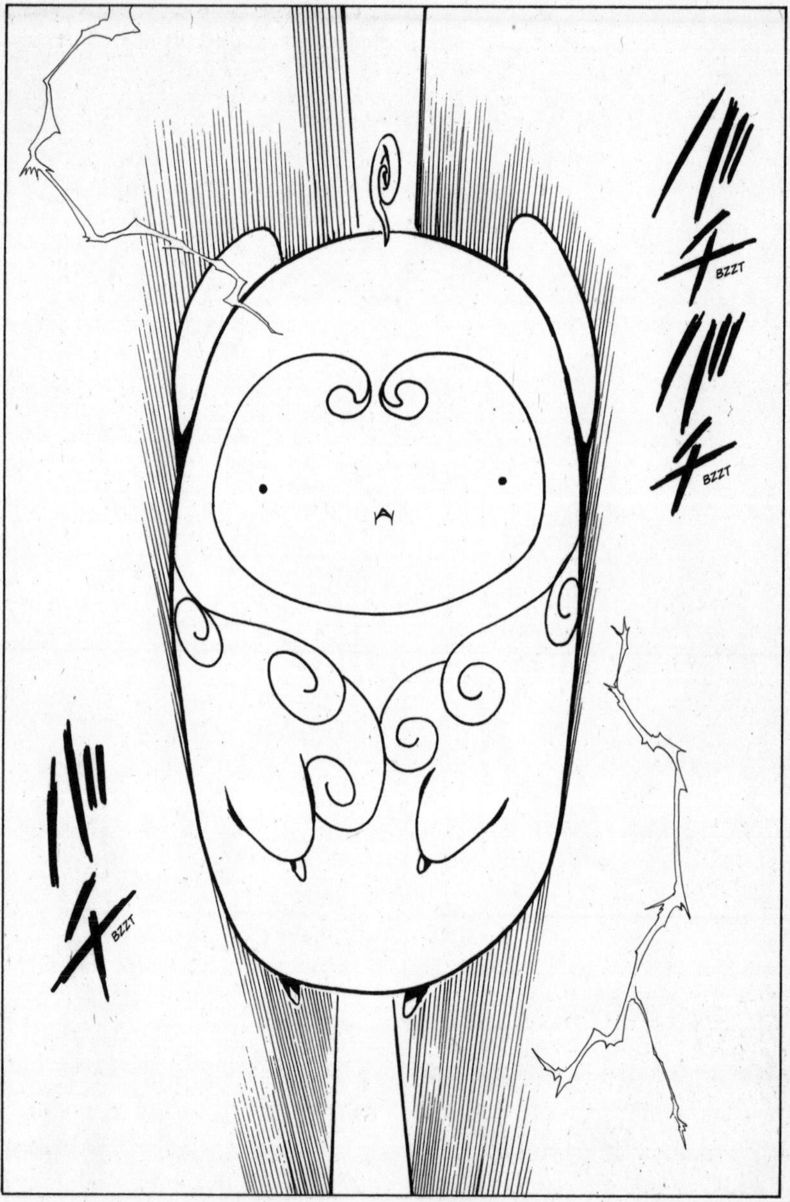

バチ
BZZT
バチ
BZZT
バチ
BZZT

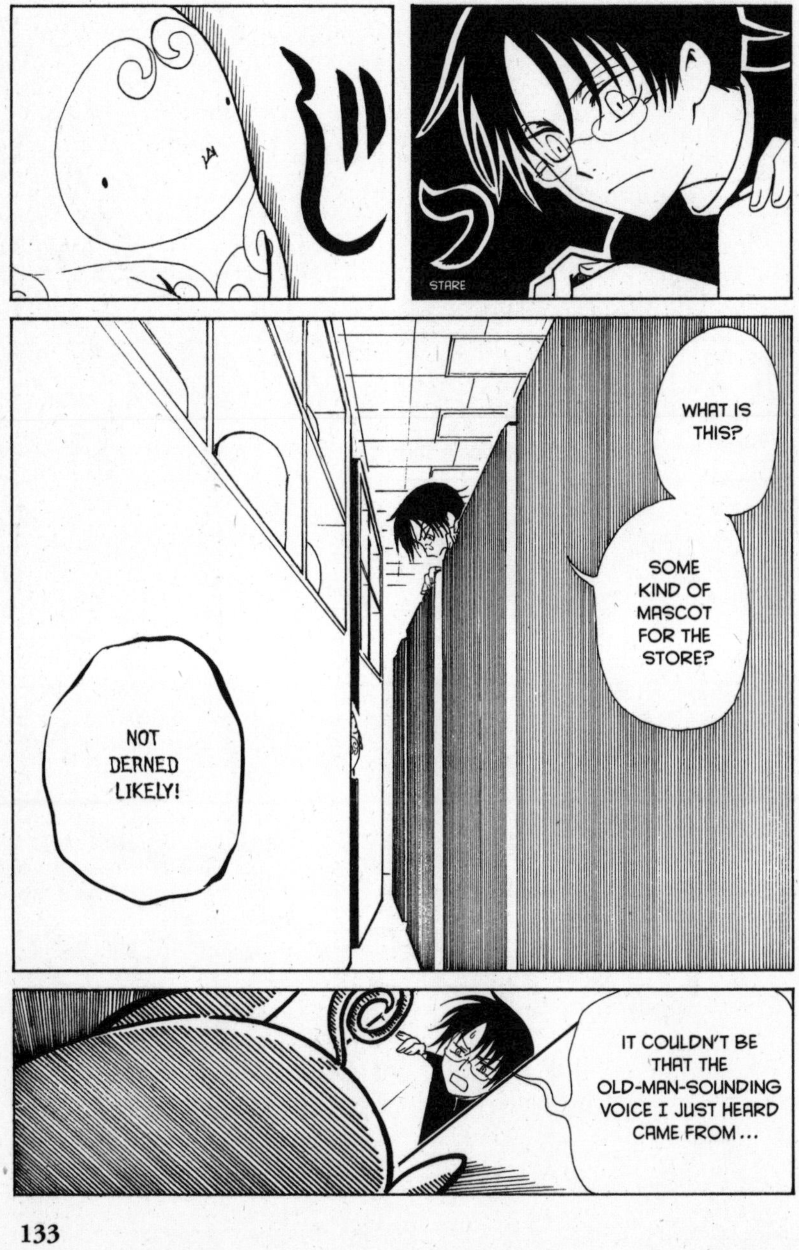
STARE
WHAT IS THIS?
SOME KIND OF MASCOT FOR THE STORE?
NOT DERNED LIKELY!
IT COULDN'T BE THAT THE OLD-MAN-SOUNDING VOICE I JUST HEARD CAME FROM...

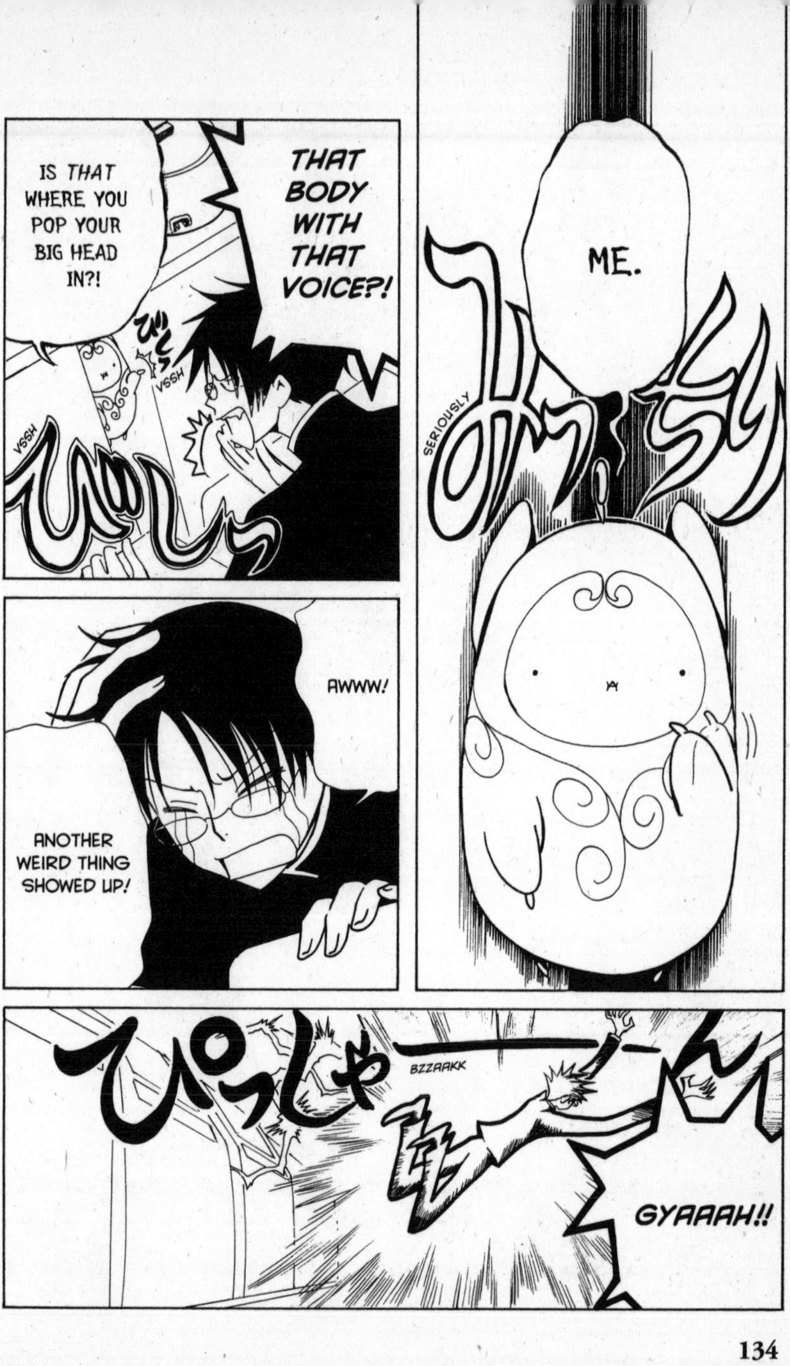
ME.
SERIOUSLY
THAT BODY WITH THAT VOICE?!
IS THAT WHERE YOU POP YOUR BIG HEAD IN?!
VSSH
VSSH
AWWW!
ANOTHER WEIRD THING SHOWED UP!
BZZAAKK
GYAAAH!!

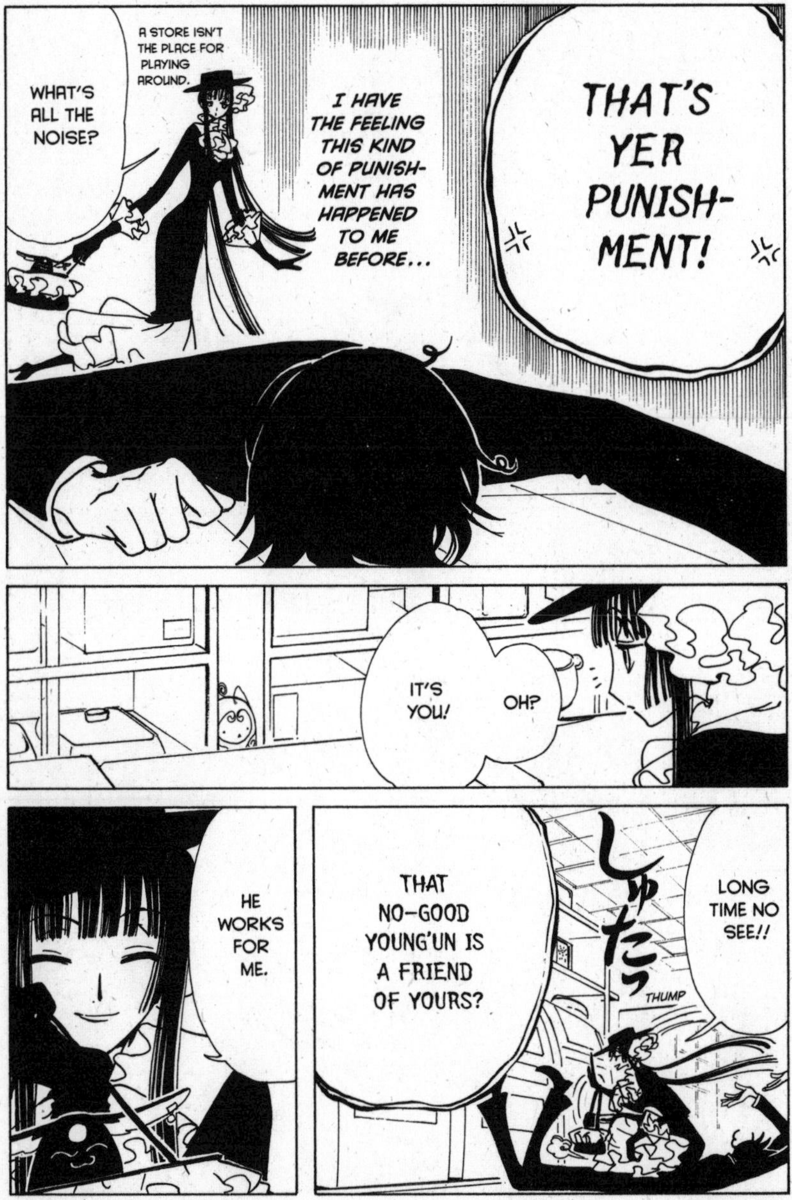
THAT'S YER PUNISHMENT!
I HAVE THE FEELING THIS KIND OF PUNISHMENT HAS HAPPENED TO ME BEFORE...
A STORE ISN'T THE PLACE FOR PLAYING AROUND.
WHAT'S ALL THE NOISE?
OH?
IT'S YOU!
LONG TIME NO SEE!!
しゅたっ
THUMP
THAT NO-GOOD YOUNG'UN IS A FRIEND OF YOURS?
HE WORKS FOR ME.

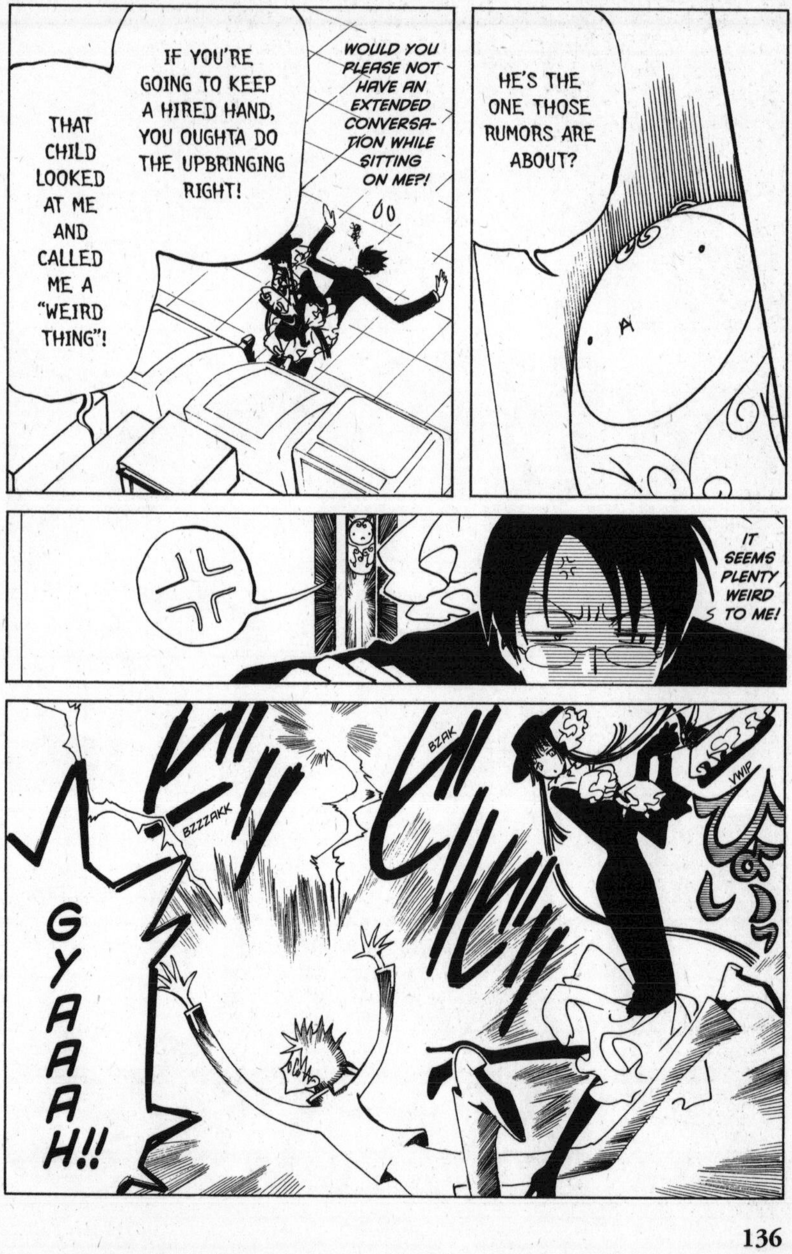
HE'S THE ONE THOSE RUMORS ARE ABOUT?
WOULD YOU PLEASE NOT HAVE AN EXTENDED CONVERSATION WHILE SITTING ON ME?!
IF YOU'RE GOING TO KEEP A HIRED HAND, YOU OUGHTA DO THE UPBRINGING RIGHT!
THAT CHILD LOOKED AT ME AND CALLED ME A "WEIRD THING"!
IT SEEMS PLENTY WEIRD TO ME!
VWIP
BZAK
BZZZAKK
GYAAAAH!!

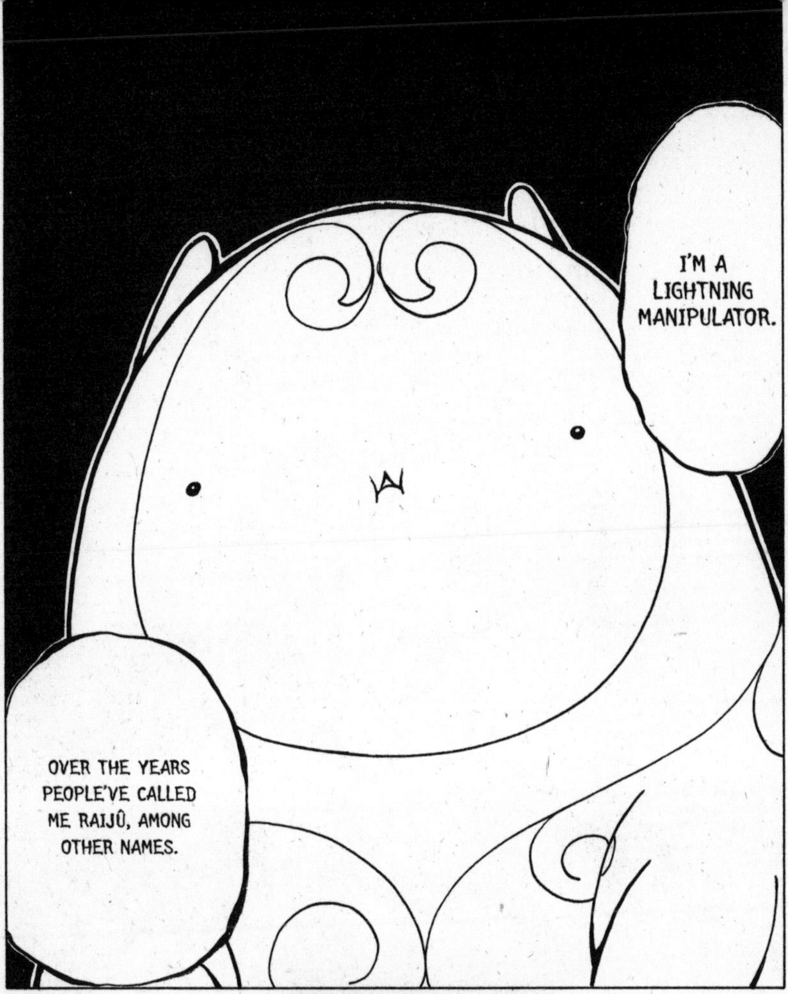
I'M A LIGHTNING MANIPULATOR.
OVER THE YEARS PEOPLE'VE CALLED ME RAIJÛ, AMONG OTHER NAMES.

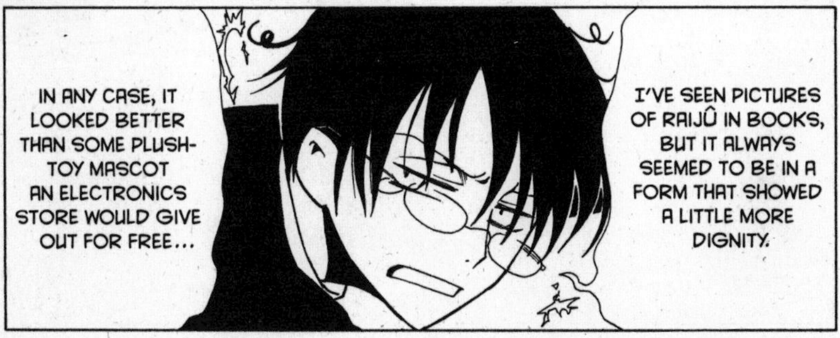
I'VE SEEN PICTURES OF RAIJÛ IN BOOKS, BUT IT ALWAYS SEEMED TO BE IN A FORM THAT SHOWED A LITTLE MORE DIGNITY.
IN ANY CASE, IT LOOKED BETTER THAN SOME PLUSH-TOY MASCOT AN ELECTRONICS STORE WOULD GIVE OUT FOR FREE...

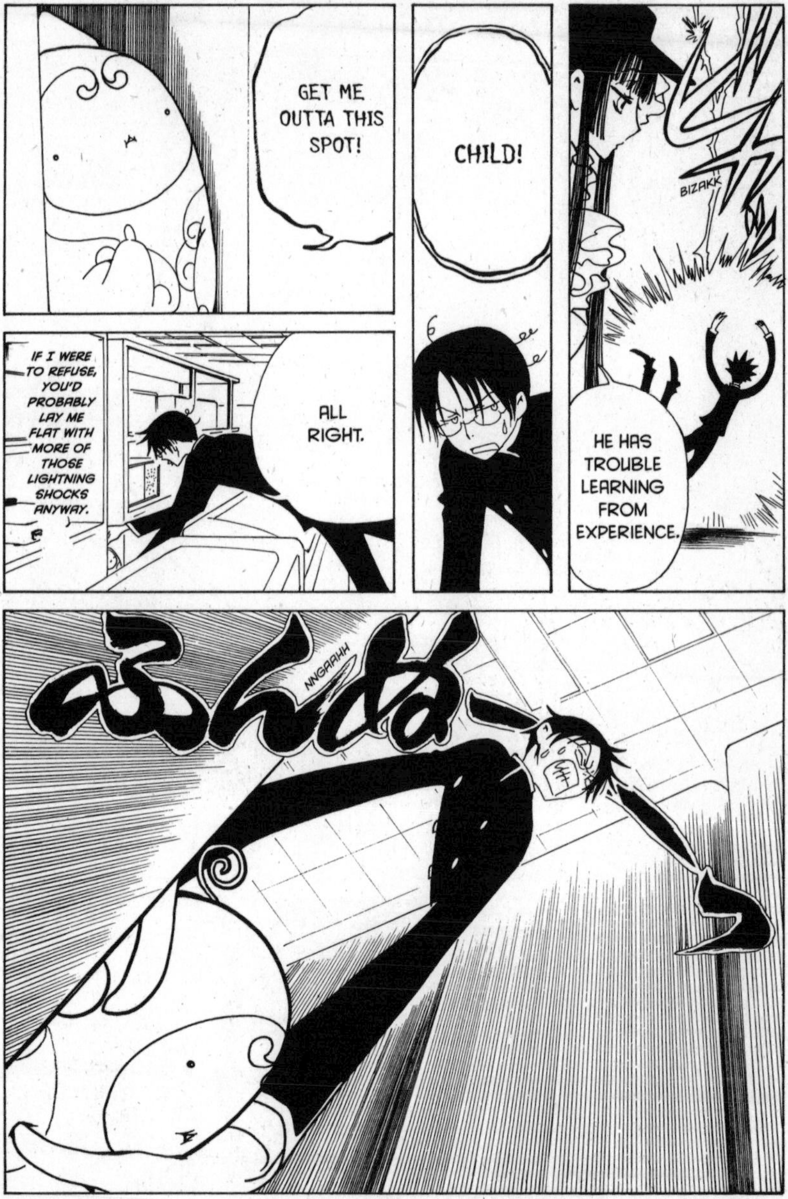
BIZAKK
HE HAS TROUBLE LEARNING FROM EXPERIENCE.
CHILD!
GET ME OUTTA THIS SPOT!
ALL RIGHT.
IF I WERE TO REFUSE, YOU'D PROBABLY LAY ME FLAT WITH MORE OF THOSE LIGHTNING SHOCKS ANYWAY.
ふんぬー
NNGAAHH

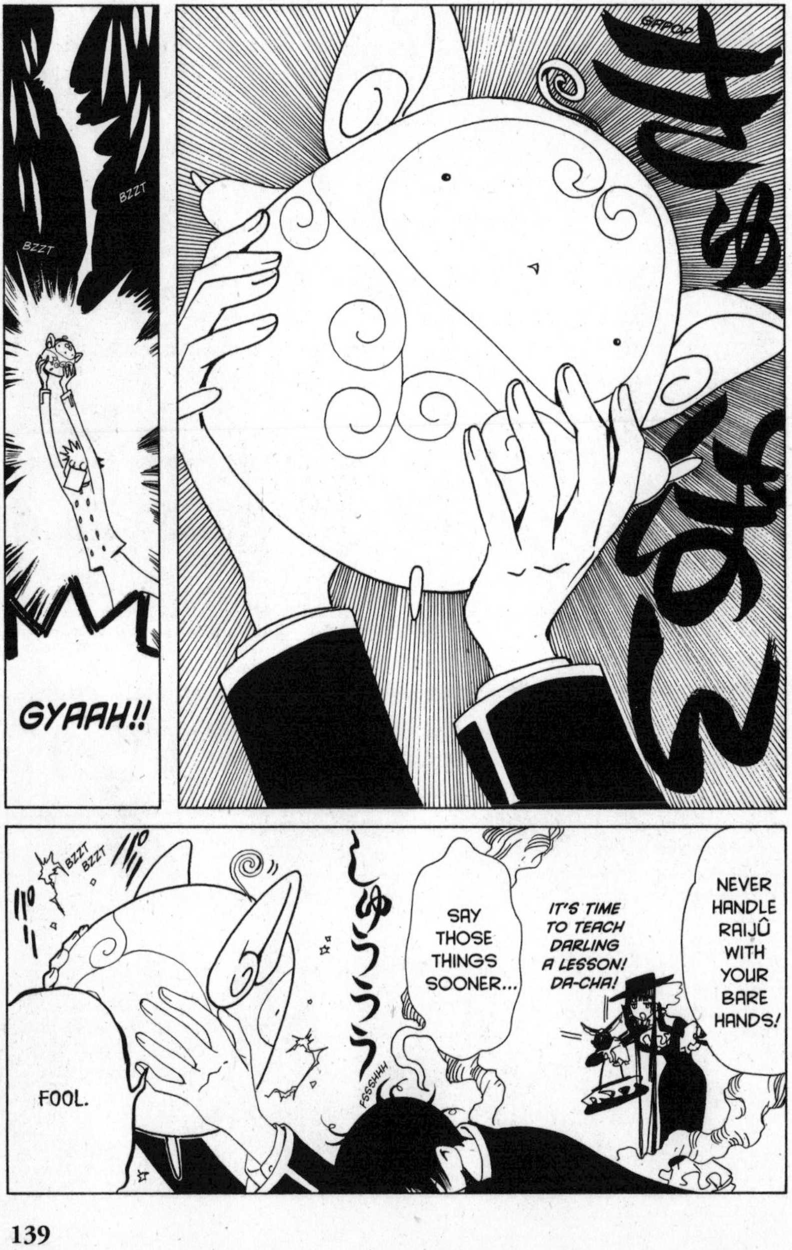
GAPOP
きゅぽん
BZZT
BZZT
GYAAH!!
NEVER HANDLE RAIJÛ WITH YOUR BARE HANDS!
IT'S TIME TO TEACH DARLING A LESSON! DA-CHA!
SAY THOSE THINGS SOONER...
しゅううう
FSSSHHH
BZZT BZZT
FOOL.

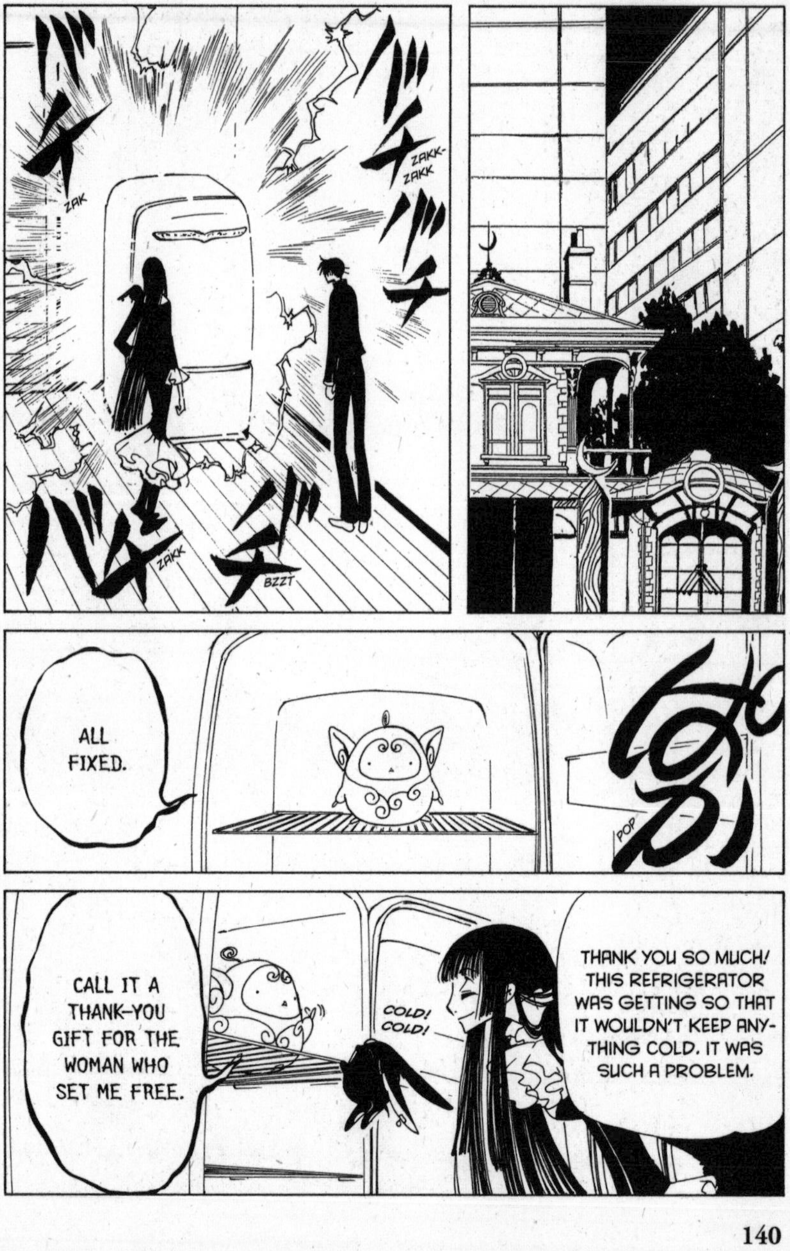
ZAKK-ZAKK
ZAK
BZZT
ZAKK
POP
ALL FIXED.
THANK YOU SO MUCH! THIS REFRIGERATOR WAS GETTING SO THAT IT WOULDN'T KEEP ANY-THING COLD. IT WAS SUCH A PROBLEM.
COLD! COLD!
CALL IT A THANK-YOU GIFT FOR THE WOMAN WHO SET ME FREE.

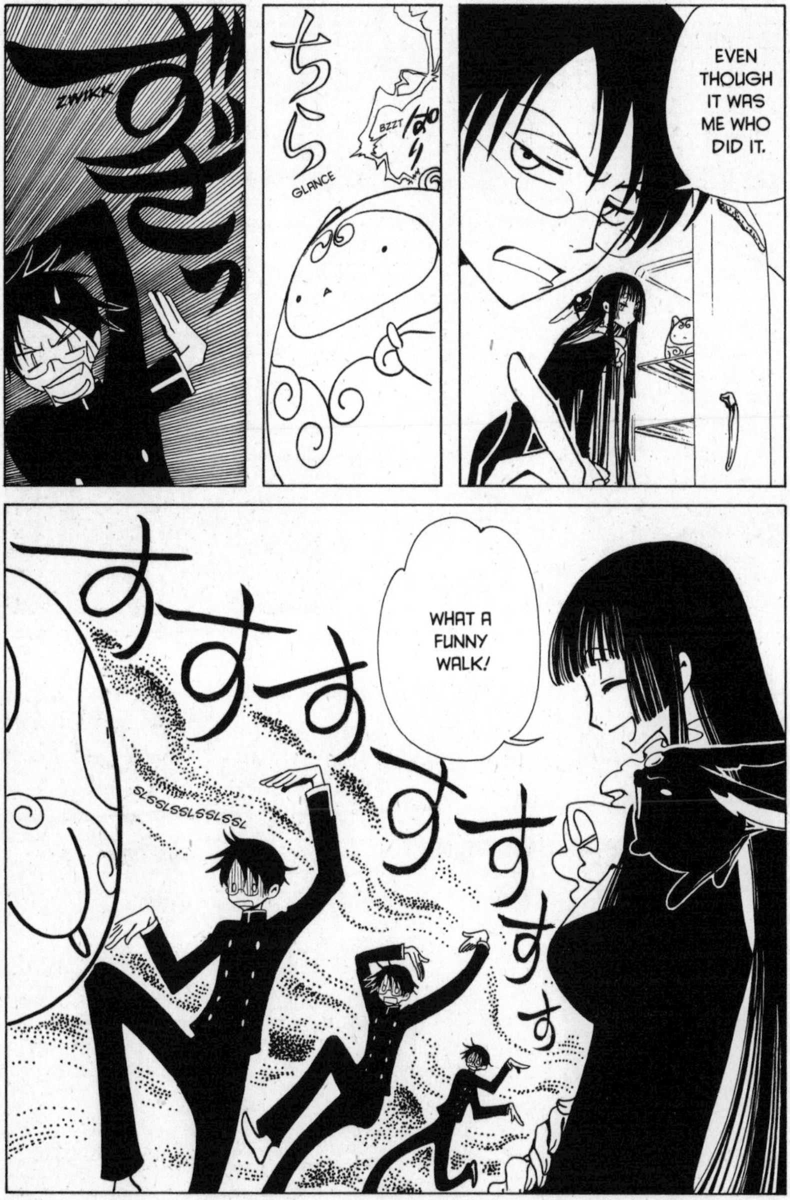
EVEN THOUGH IT WAS ME WHO DID IT.
ちら
GLANCE
BZZT
ZWIKK
WHAT A FUNNY WALK!

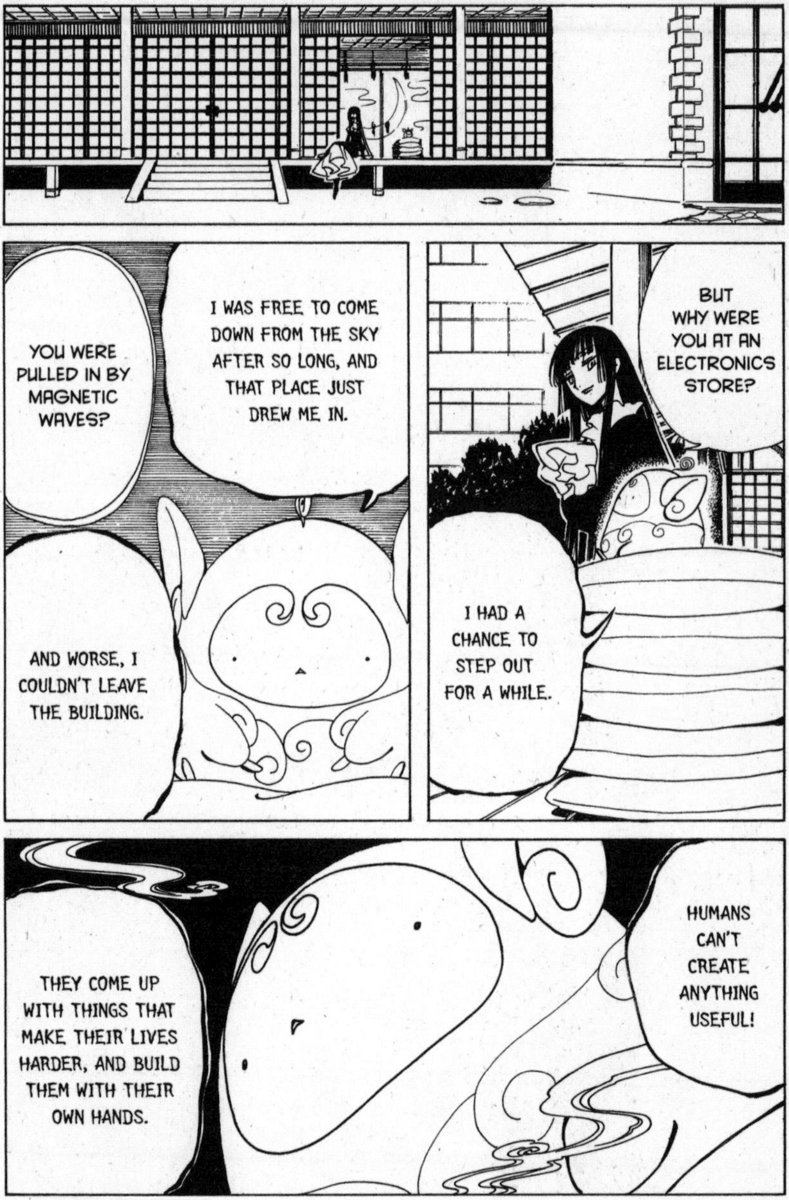
BUT WHY WERE YOU AT AN ELECTRONICS STORE?
I HAD A CHANCE TO STEP OUT FOR A WHILE.
I WAS FREE TO COME DOWN FROM THE SKY AFTER SO LONG, AND THAT PLACE JUST DREW ME IN.
YOU WERE PULLED IN BY MAGNETIC WAVES?
AND WORSE, I COULDN'T LEAVE THE BUILDING.
HUMANS CAN'T CREATE ANYTHING USEFUL!
THEY COME UP WITH THINGS THAT MAKE THEIR LIVES HARDER, AND BUILD THEM WITH THEIR OWN HANDS.

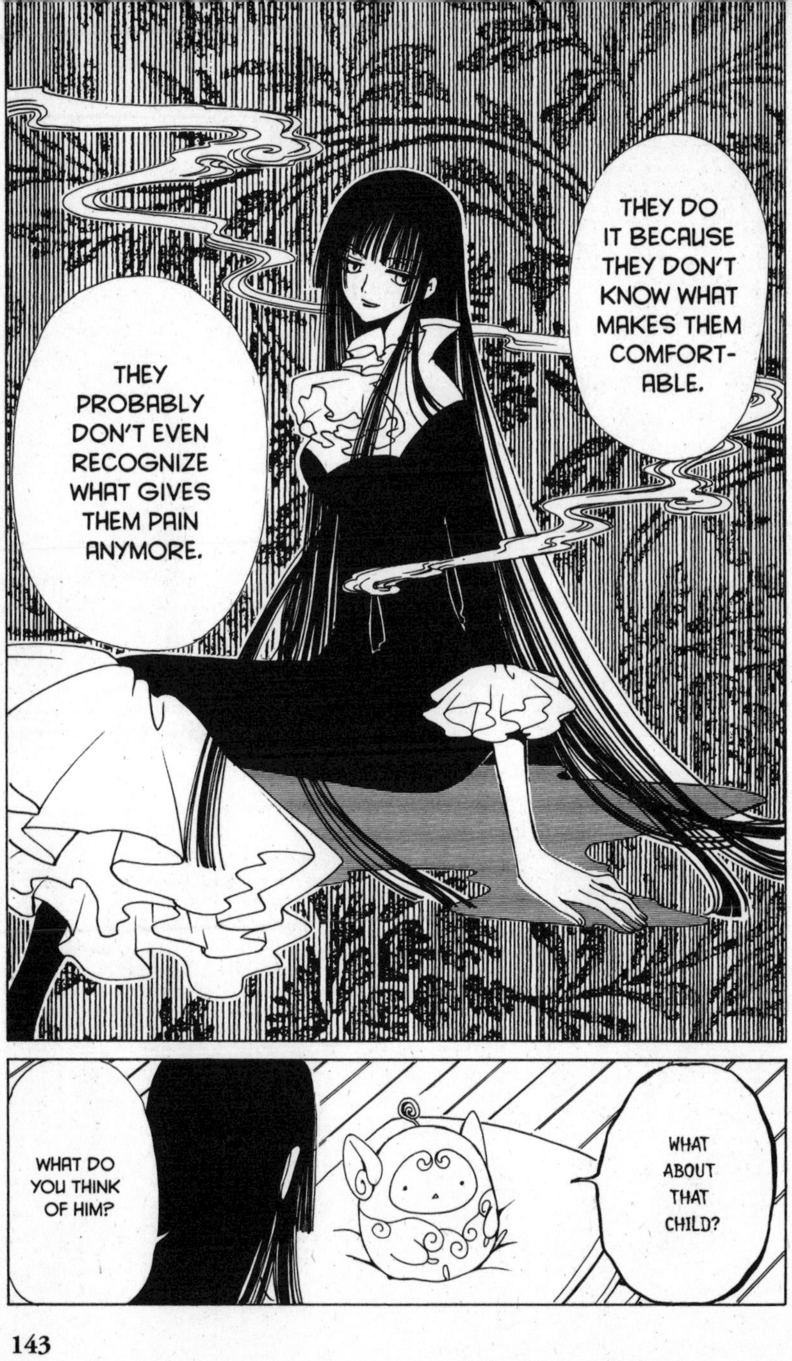
THEY DO IT BECAUSE THEY DON'T KNOW WHAT MAKES THEM COMFORT-ABLE.
THEY PROBABLY DON'T EVEN RECOGNIZE WHAT GIVES THEM PAIN ANYMORE.
WHAT ABOUT THAT CHILD?
WHAT DO YOU THINK OF HIM?

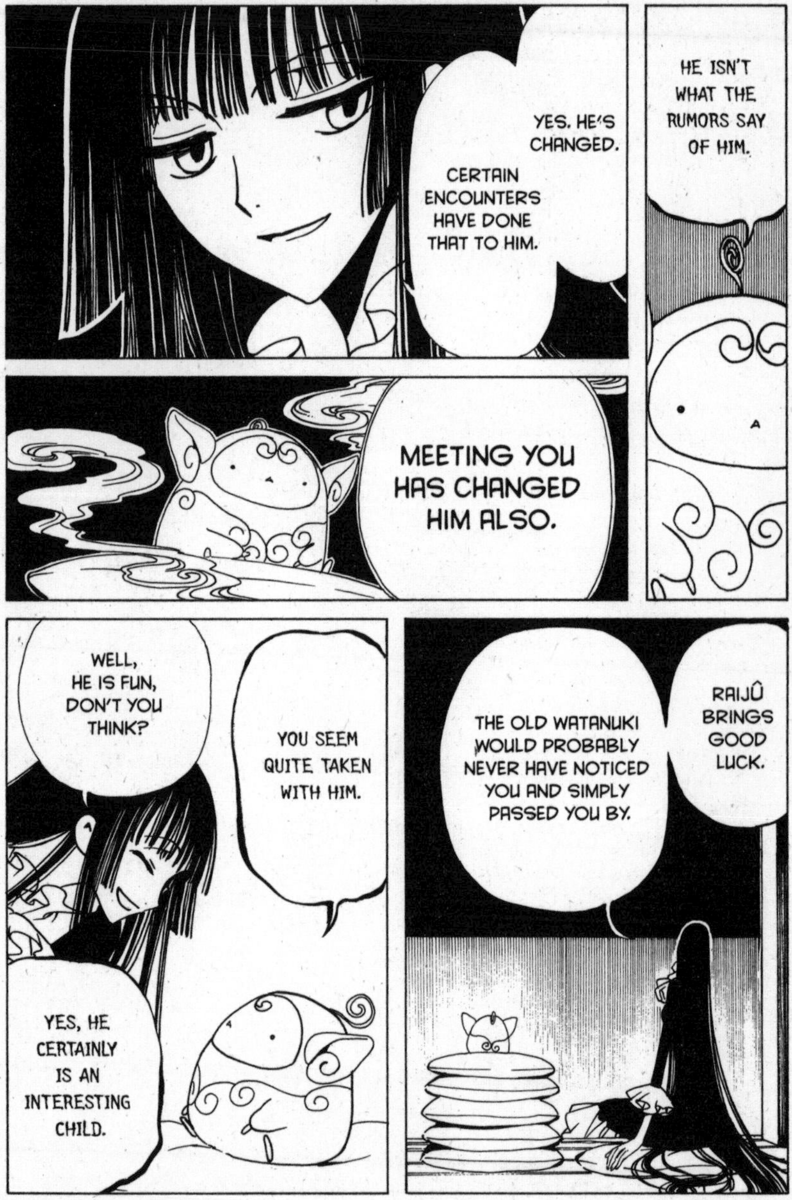
HE ISN'T WHAT THE RUMORS SAY OF HIM.
YES. HE'S CHANGED.
CERTAIN ENCOUNTERS HAVE DONE THAT TO HIM.
MEETING YOU HAS CHANGED HIM ALSO.
RAIJÛ BRINGS GOOD LUCK.
THE OLD WATANUKI WOULD PROBABLY NEVER HAVE NOTICED YOU AND SIMPLY PASSED YOU BY.
YOU SEEM QUITE TAKEN WITH HIM.
WELL, HE IS FUN, DON'T YOU THINK?
YES, HE CERTAINLY IS AN INTERESTING CHILD.

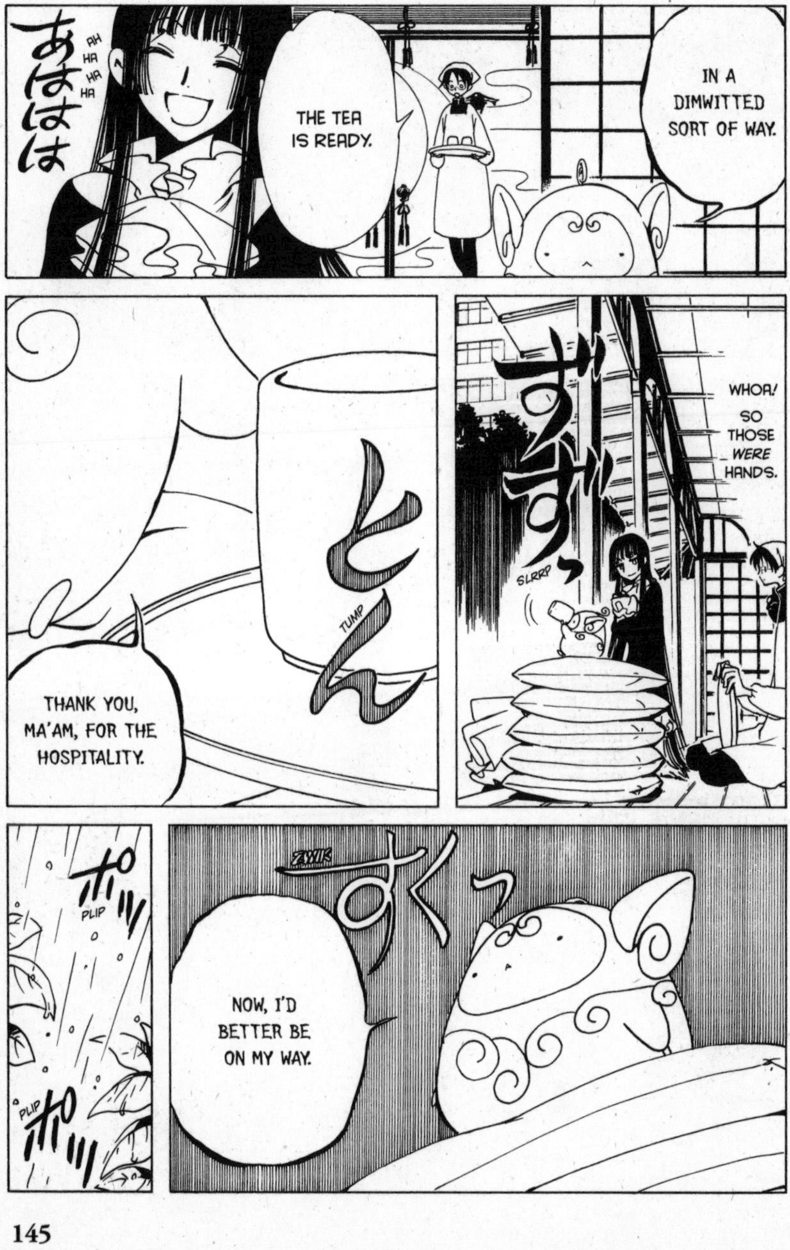
IN A DIMWITTED SORT OF WAY.
THE TEA IS READY.
あははは
AH HA HA HA
WHOA! SO THOSE WERE HANDS.
ずずっ
SLRRP
とん
TUMP
THANK YOU, MA'AM, FOR THE HOSPITALITY.
すくっ
ZWIK
NOW, I'D BETTER BE ON MY WAY.
ポツ
PLIP
ポツ
PLIP

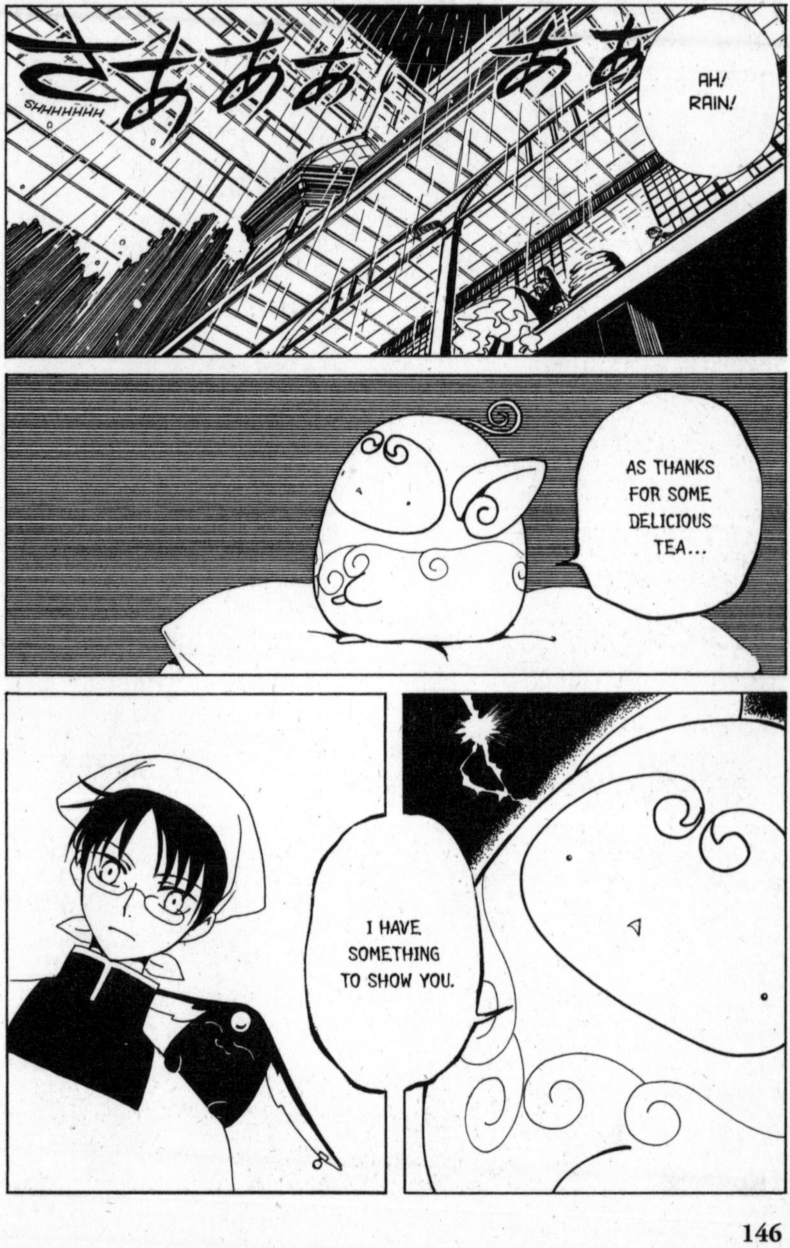
AH! RAIN!
さあああああ
SHHHHHHH
AS THANKS FOR SOME DELICIOUS TEA...
I HAVE SOMETHING TO SHOW YOU.

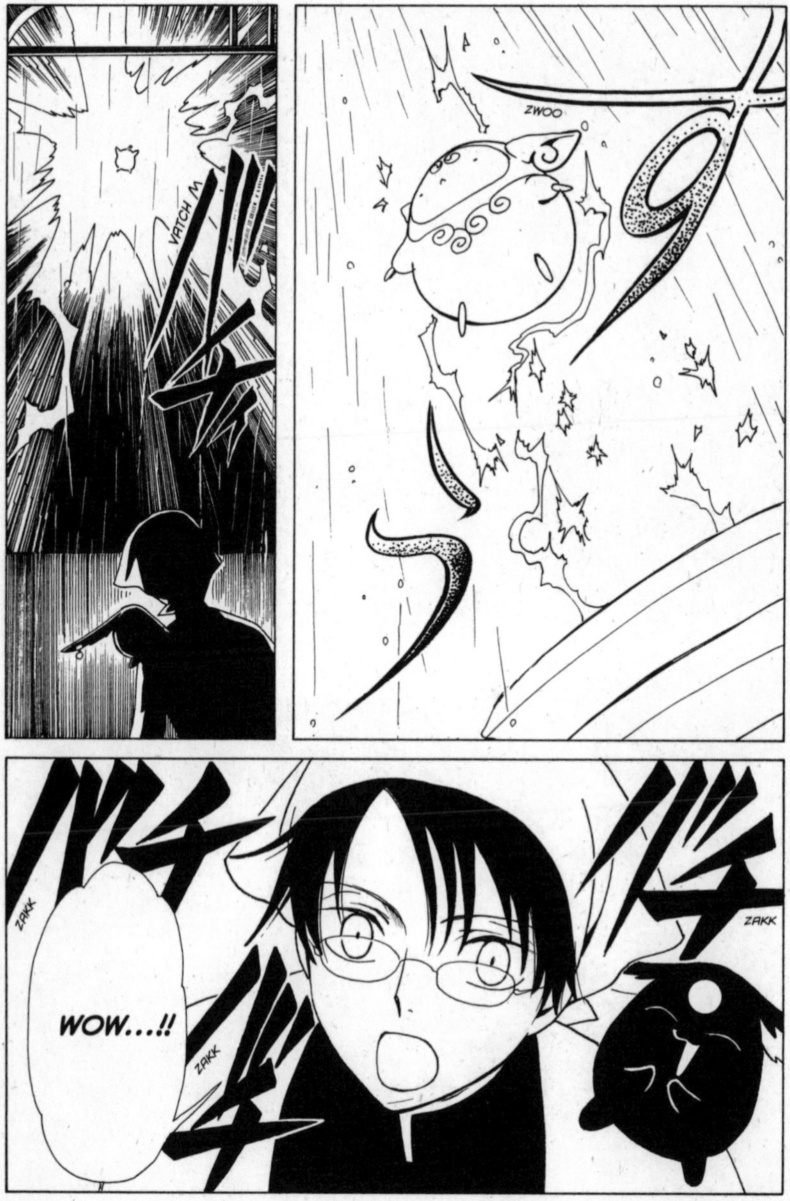
ZWOO
VATCH M
ZAKK
ZAKK
WOW...!!
ZAKK

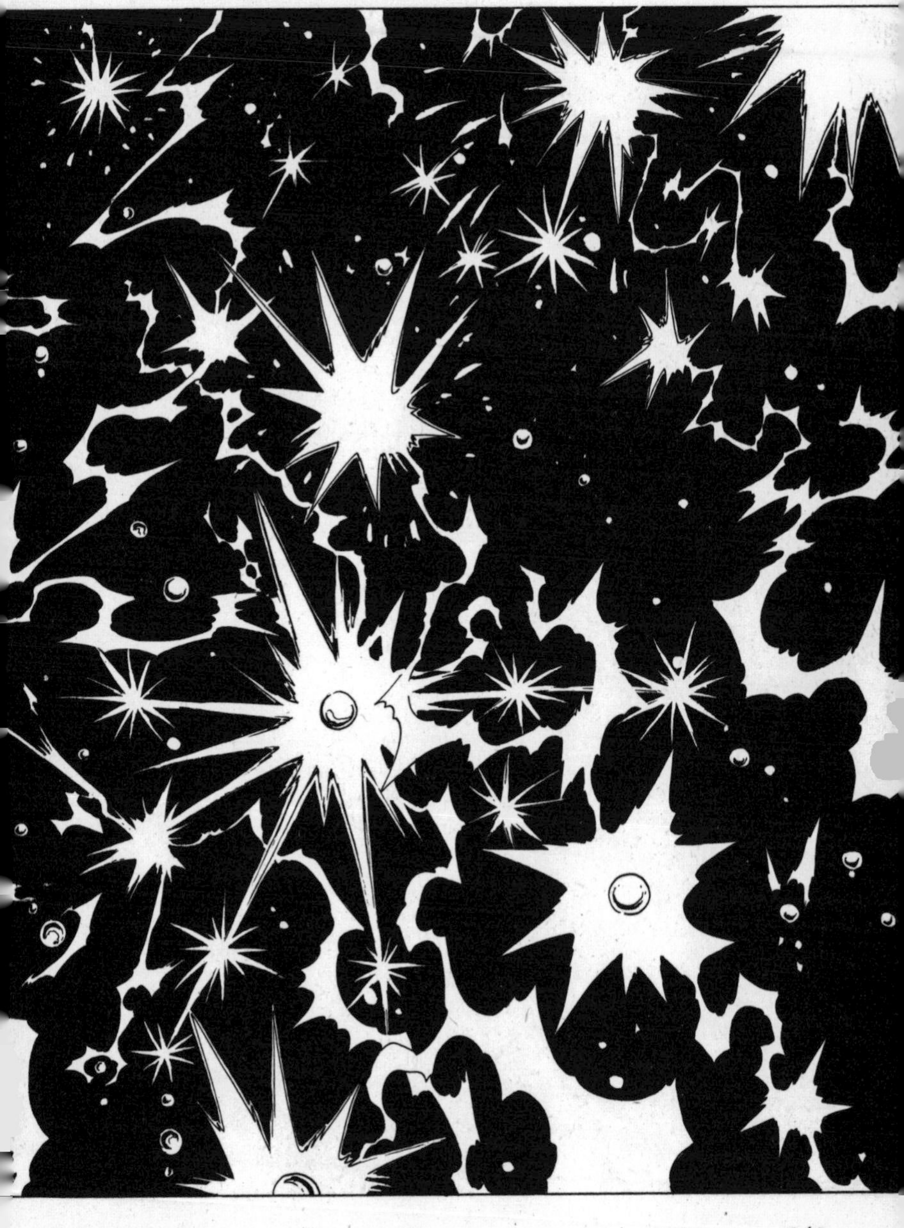

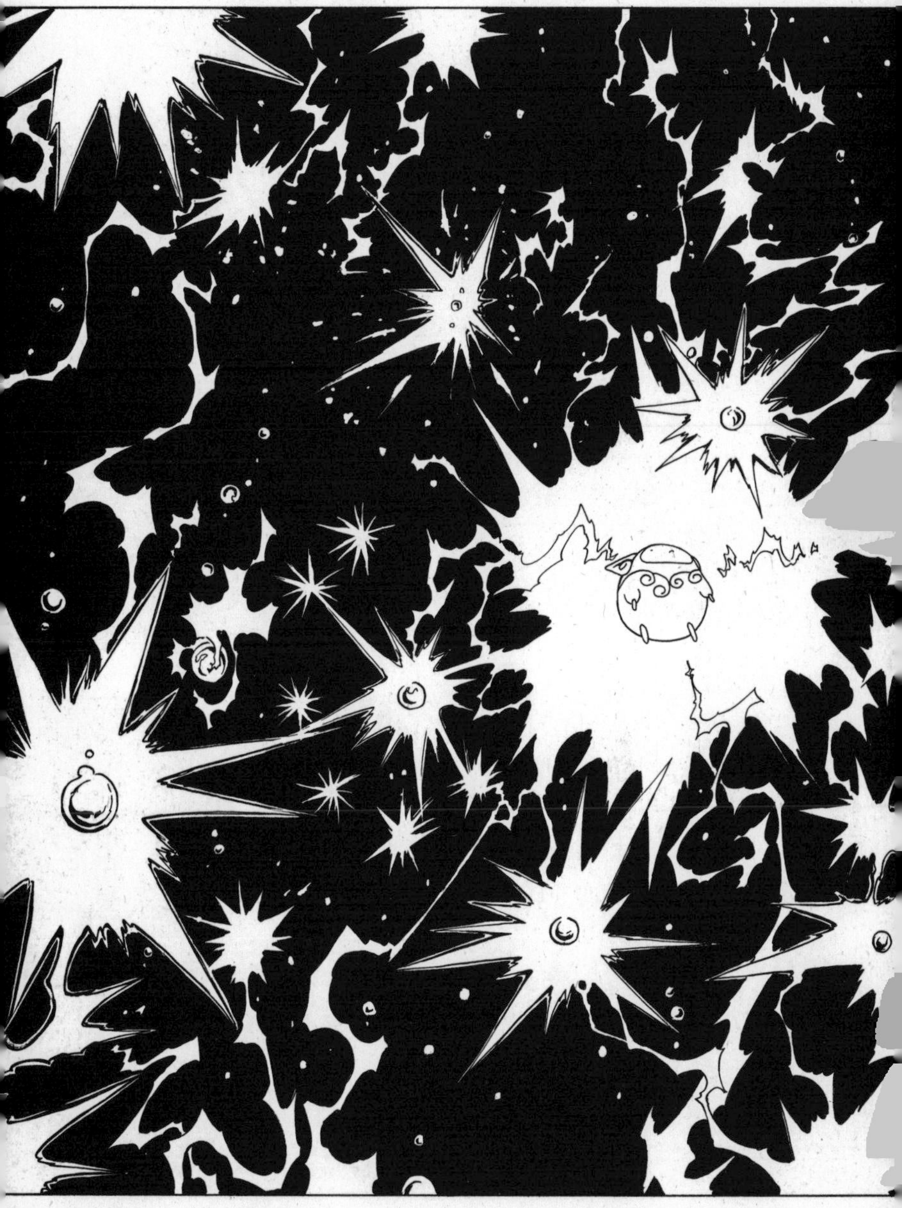

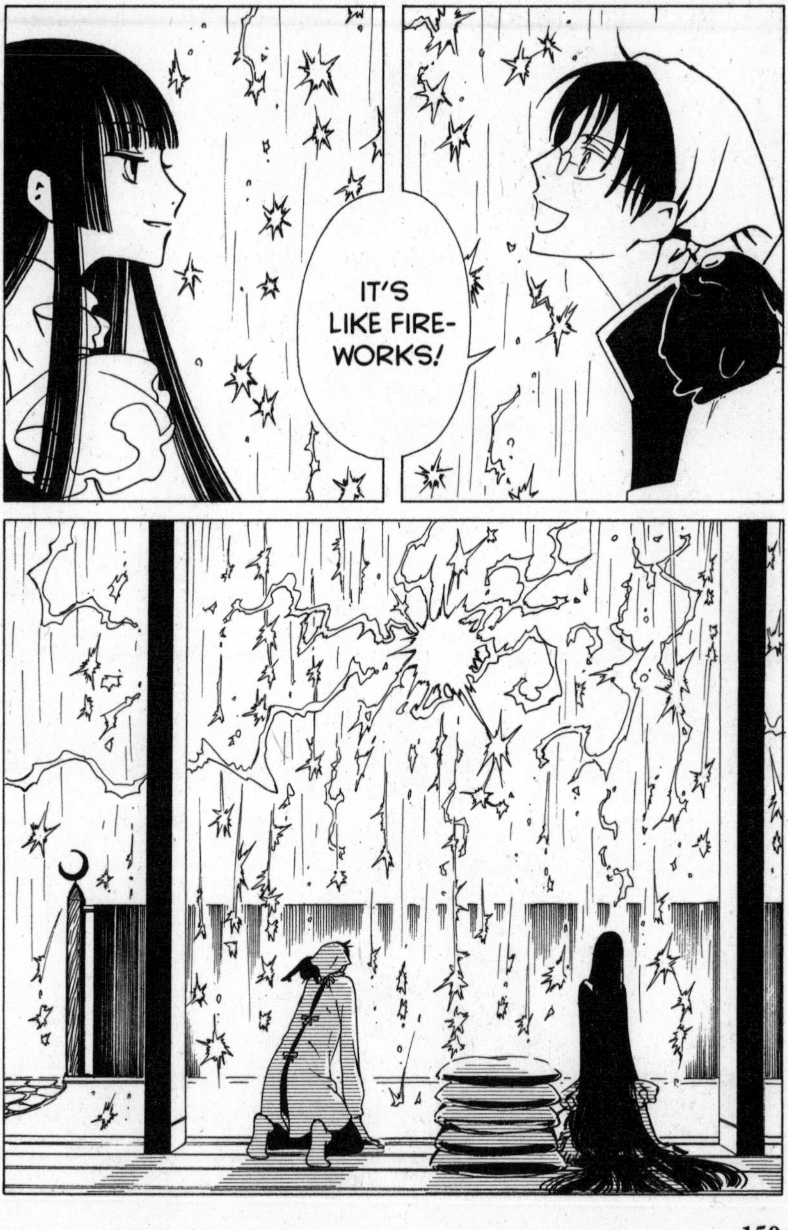
IT'S LIKE FIRE-WORKS!

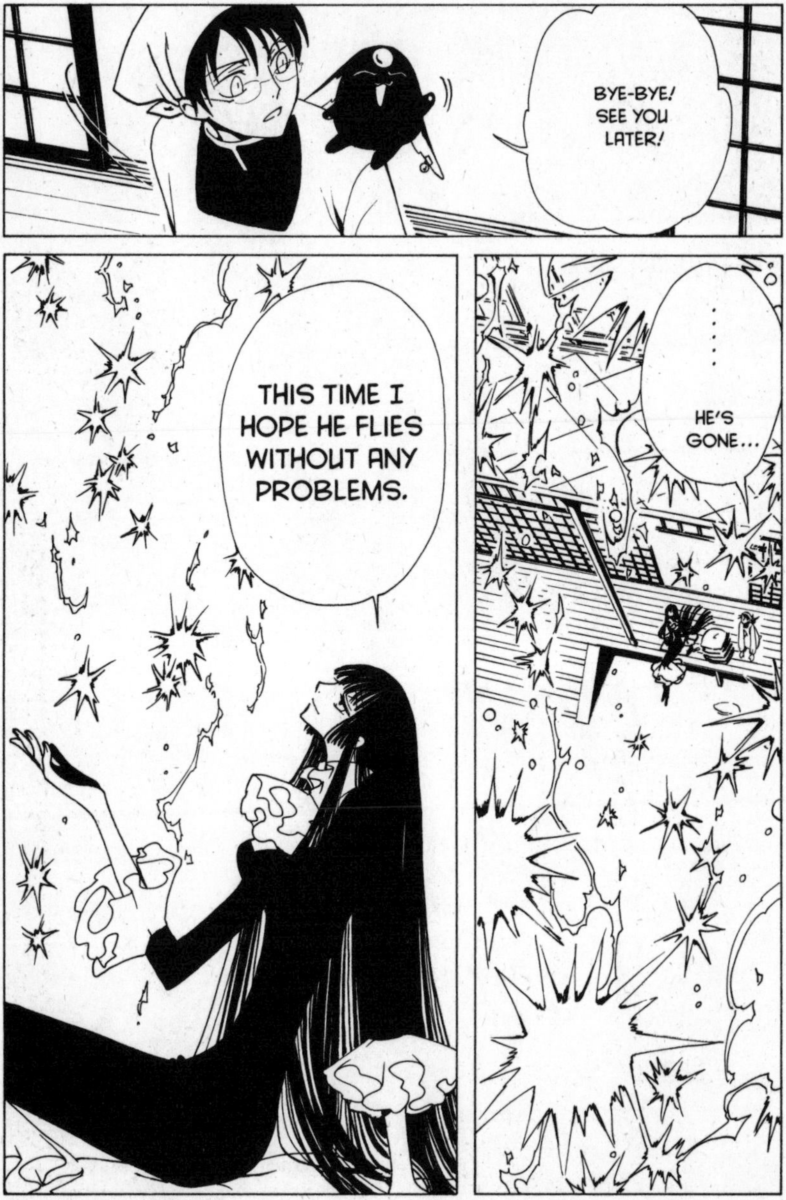
BYE-BYE! SEE YOU LATER!
.....
HE'S GONE...
THIS TIME I HOPE HE FLIES WITHOUT ANY PROBLEMS.

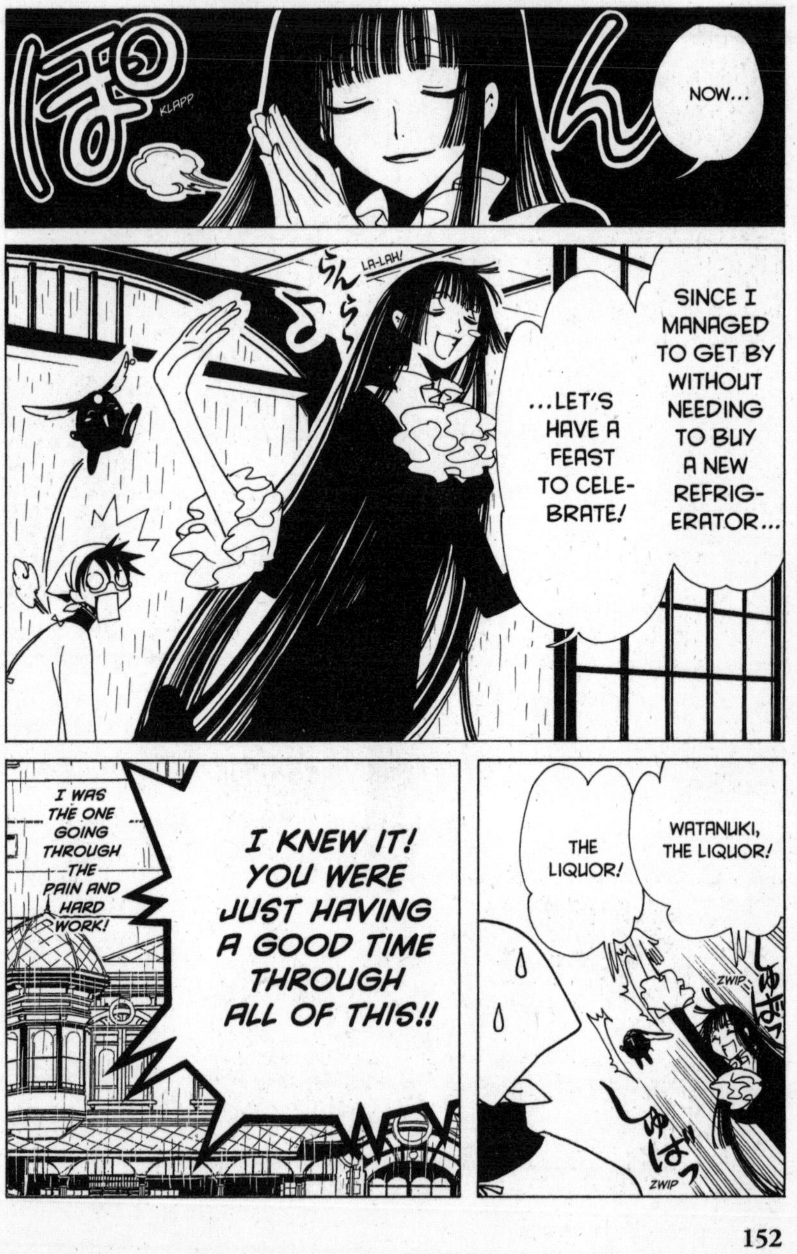
NOW...
ぽん
KLAPP
SINCE I MANAGED TO GET BY WITHOUT NEEDING TO BUY A NEW REFRIGERATOR...
...LET'S HAVE A FEAST TO CELEBRATE!
らんらら
LA-LAH!
WATANUKI, THE LIQUOR!
THE LIQUOR!
しゅばっ
ZWIP
しゅばっ
ZWIP
I KNEW IT! YOU WERE JUST HAVING A GOOD TIME THROUGH ALL OF THIS!!
I WAS THE ONE GOING THROUGH THE PAIN AND HARD WORK!

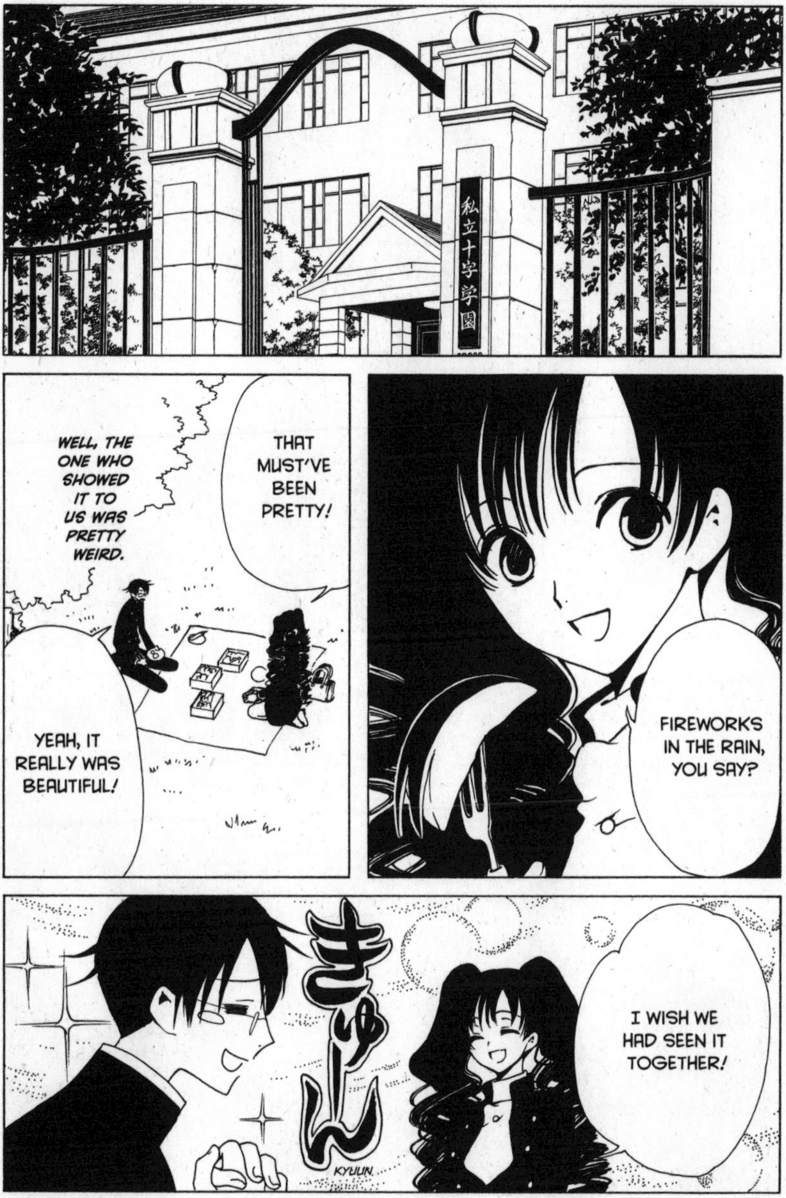
私立十字学園
FIREWORKS IN THE RAIN, YOU SAY?
THAT MUST'VE BEEN PRETTY!
WELL, THE ONE WHO SHOWED IT TO US WAS PRETTY WEIRD.
YEAH, IT REALLY WAS BEAUTIFUL!
I WISH WE HAD SEEN IT TOGETHER!
きゅーん
KYUUN

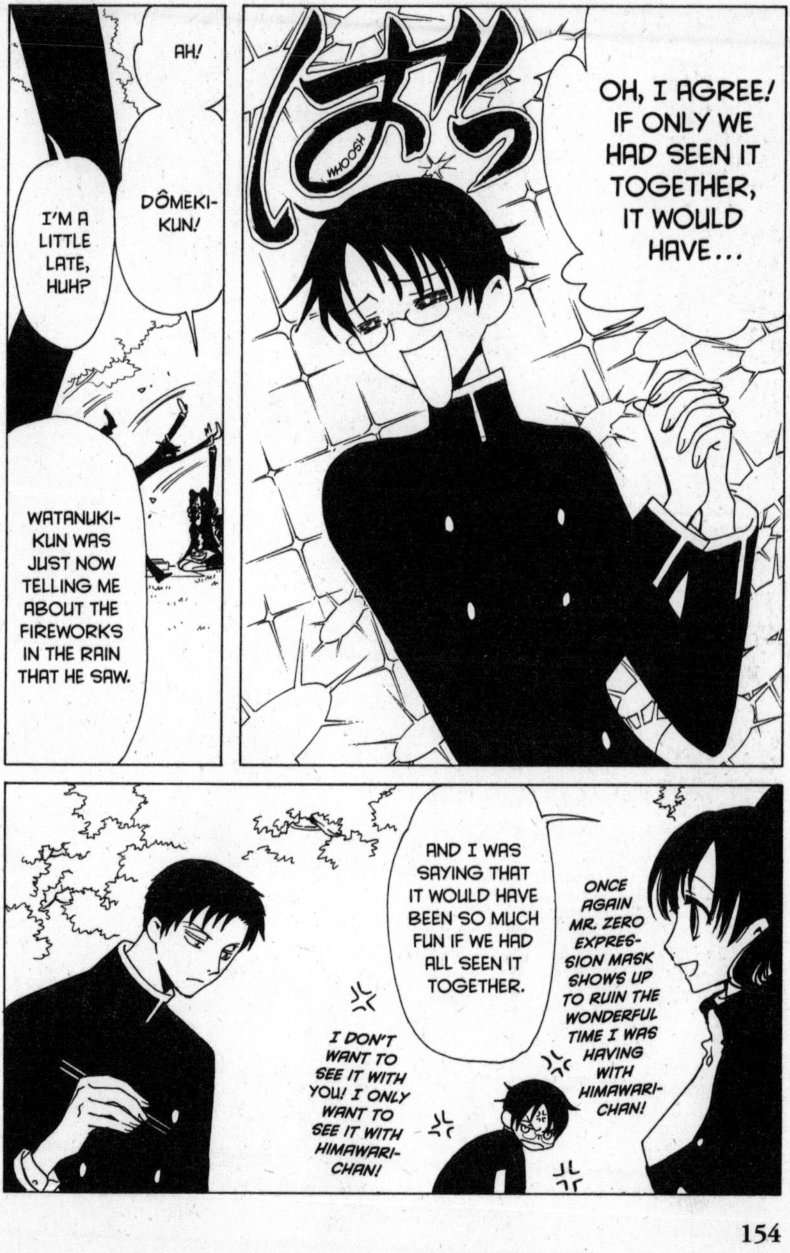
WHOOSH
OH, I AGREE! IF ONLY WE HAD SEEN IT TOGETHER, IT WOULD HAVE...
AH!
DÔMEKI-KUN!
I'M A LITTLE LATE, HUH?
WATANUKI-KUN WAS JUST NOW TELLING ME ABOUT THE FIREWORKS IN THE RAIN THAT HE SAW.
ONCE AGAIN MR. ZERO EXPRESSION MASK SHOWS UP TO RUIN THE WONDERFUL TIME I WAS HAVING WITH HIMAWARI-CHAN!
AND I WAS SAYING THAT IT WOULD HAVE BEEN SO MUCH FUN IF WE HAD ALL SEEN IT TOGETHER.
I DON'T WANT TO SEE IT WITH YOU! I ONLY WANT TO SEE IT WITH HIMAWARI-CHAN!

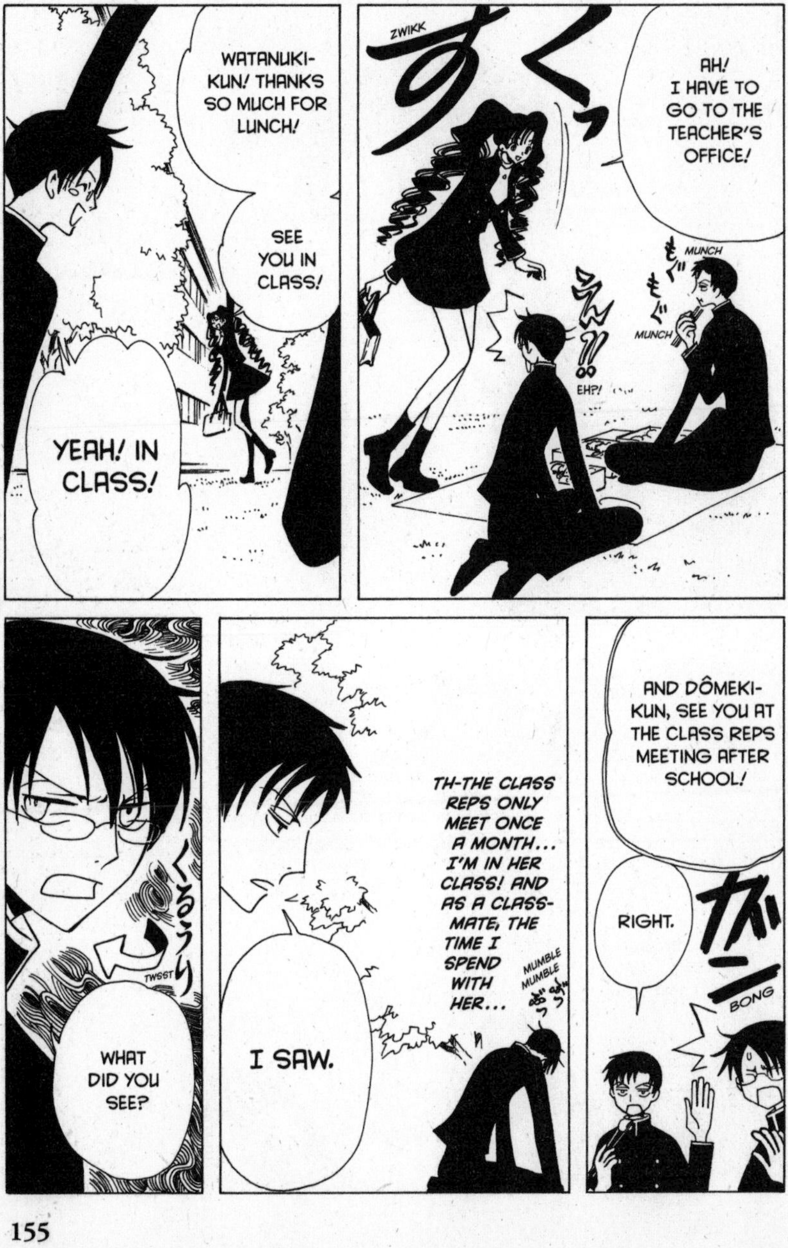
ZWIKK
AH! I HAVE TO GO TO THE TEACHER'S OFFICE!
MUNCH
MUNCH
EH?!
WATANUKI-KUN! THANKS SO MUCH FOR LUNCH!
SEE YOU IN CLASS!
YEAH! IN CLASS!
AND DÔMEKI-KUN, SEE YOU AT THE CLASS REPS MEETING AFTER SCHOOL!
RIGHT.
BONG
TH-THE CLASS REPS ONLY MEET ONCE A MONTH... I'M IN HER CLASS! AND AS A CLASS-MATE, THE TIME I SPEND WITH HER...
MUMBLE MUMBLE
I SAW.
TWSST
WHAT DID YOU SEE?

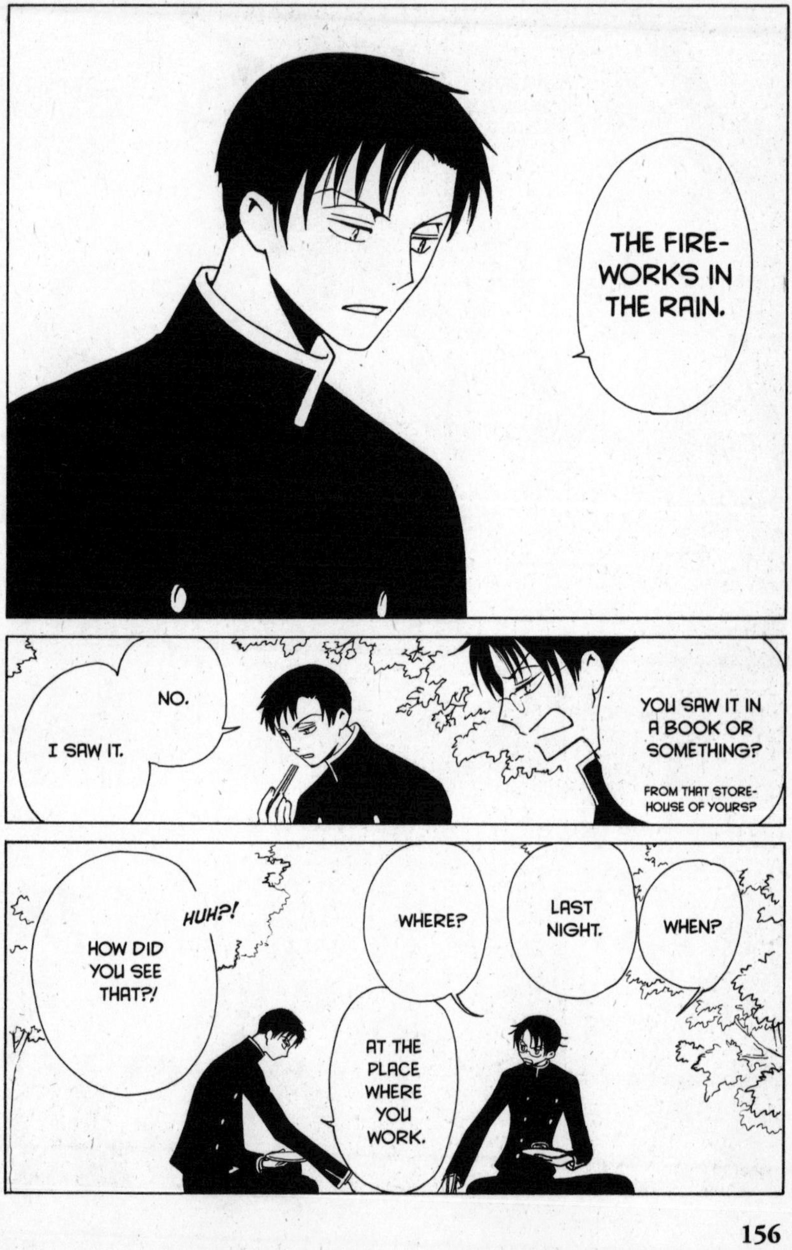
THE FIRE-WORKS IN THE RAIN.
YOU SAW IT IN A BOOK OR SOMETHING?
FROM THAT STORE-HOUSE OF YOURS?
NO. I SAW IT.
WHEN?
LAST NIGHT.
WHERE?
AT THE PLACE WHERE YOU WORK.
HUH?!
HOW DID YOU SEE THAT?!

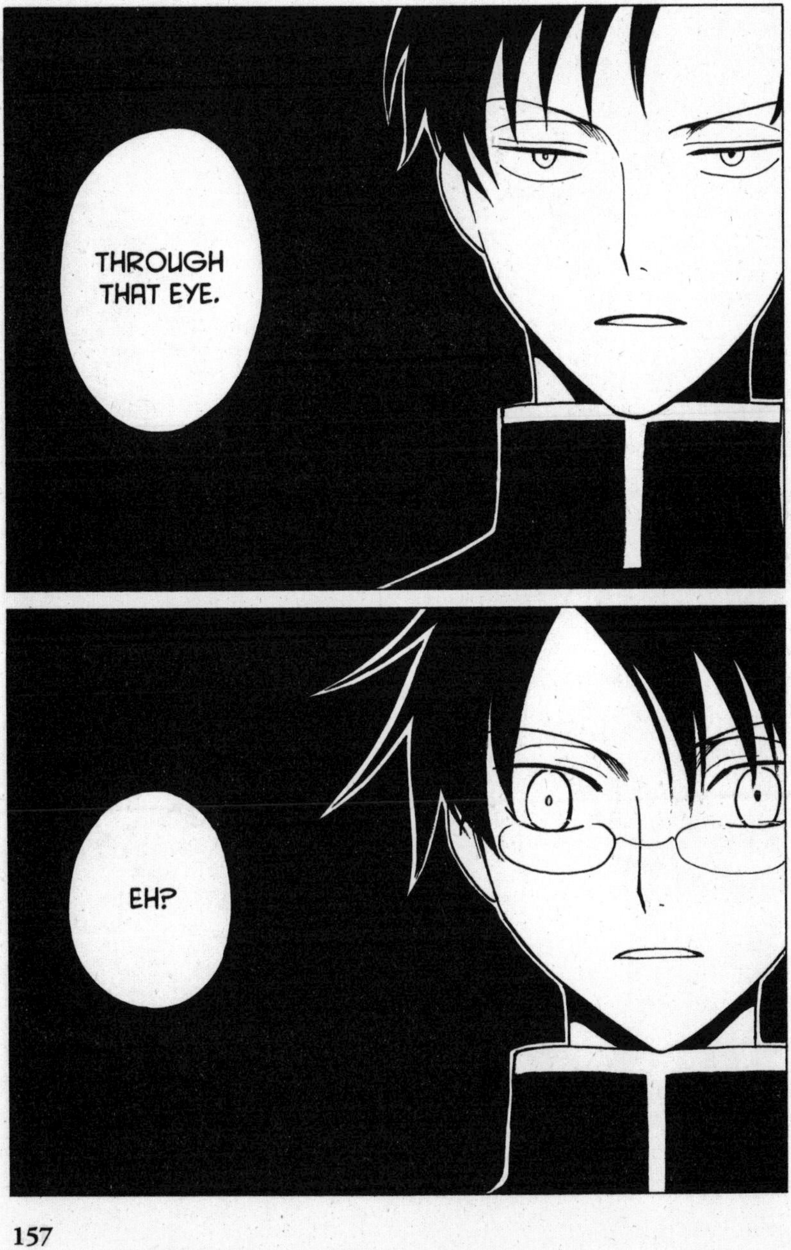
THROUGH THAT EYE.
EH?

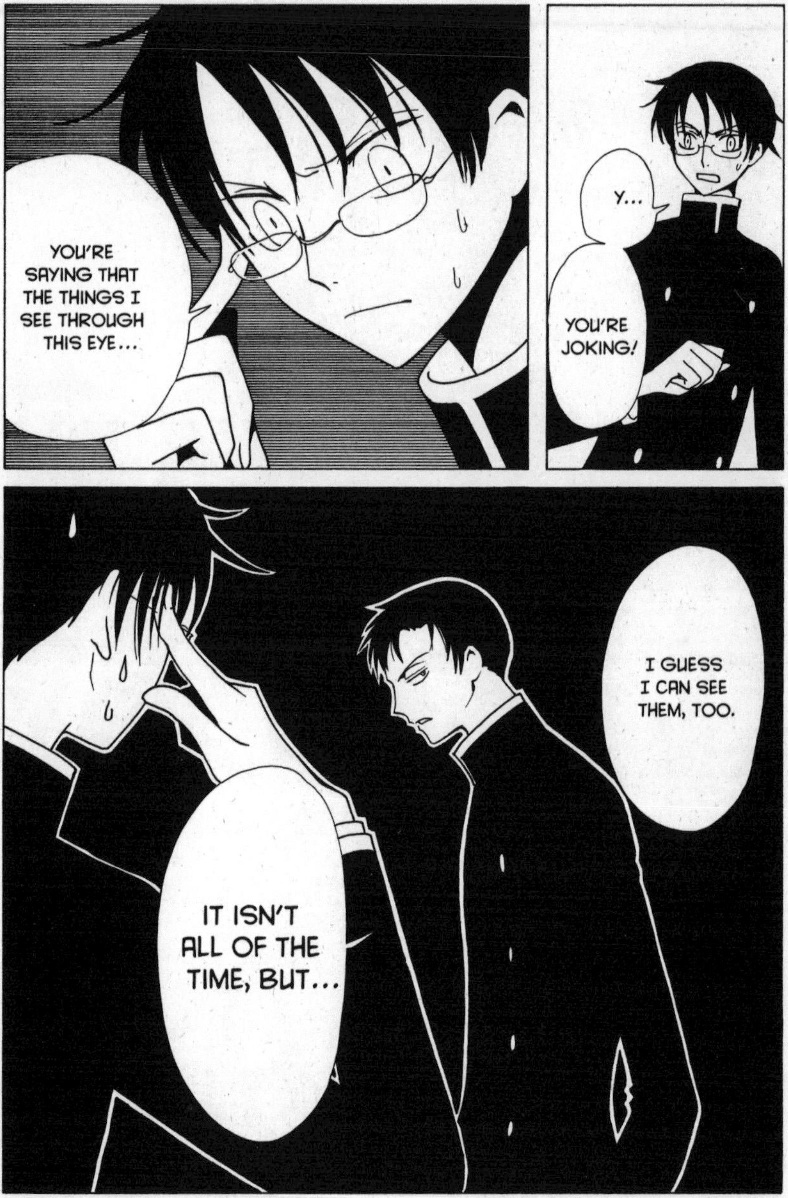
Y...
YOU'RE JOKING!
YOU'RE SAYING THAT THE THINGS I SEE THROUGH THIS EYE...
I GUESS I CAN SEE THEM, TOO.
IT ISN'T ALL OF THE TIME, BUT...

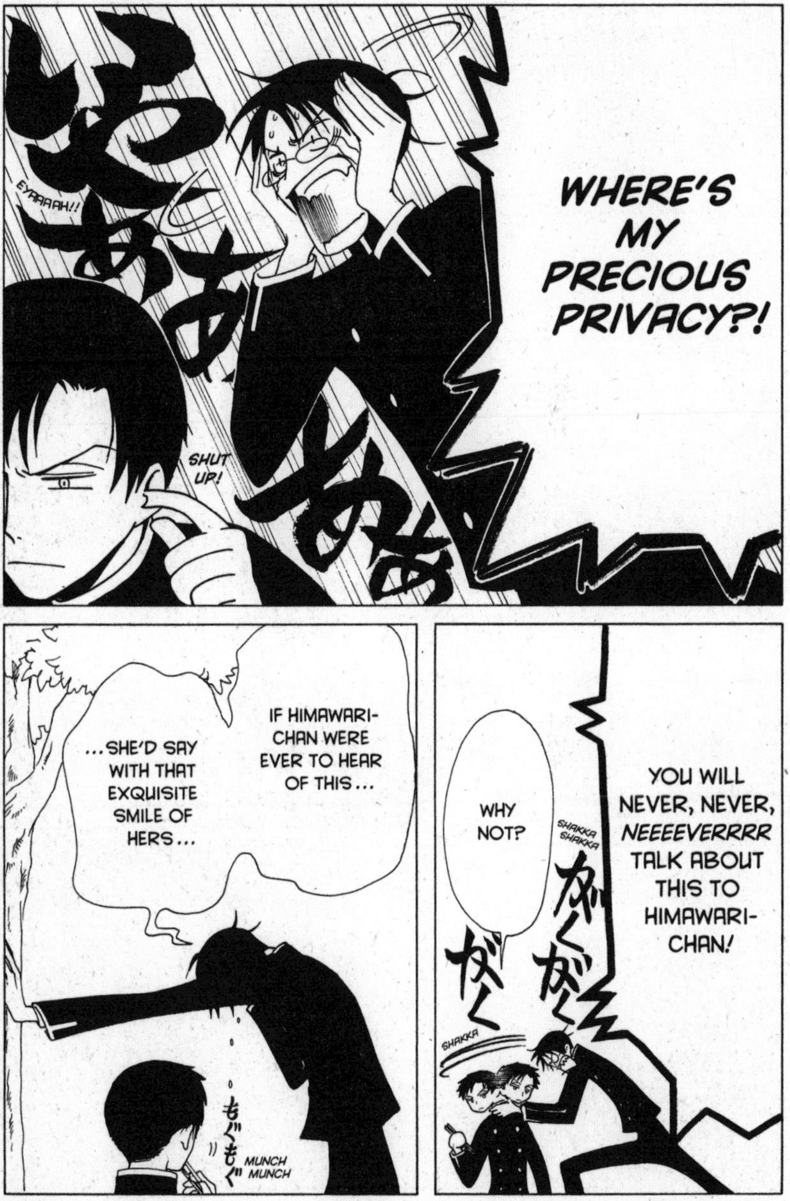
EYAAAAH!!
WHERE'S MY PRECIOUS PRIVACY?!
SHUT UP!
YOU WILL NEVER, NEVER, NEEEEVERRRR TALK ABOUT THIS TO HIMAWARI-CHAN!
WHY NOT?
SHAKKA SHAKKA
がくがくがく
SHAKKA
IF HIMAWARI-CHAN WERE EVER TO HEAR OF THIS...
...SHE'D SAY WITH THAT EXQUISITE SMILE OF HERS...
もぐもぐ
MUNCH MUNCH

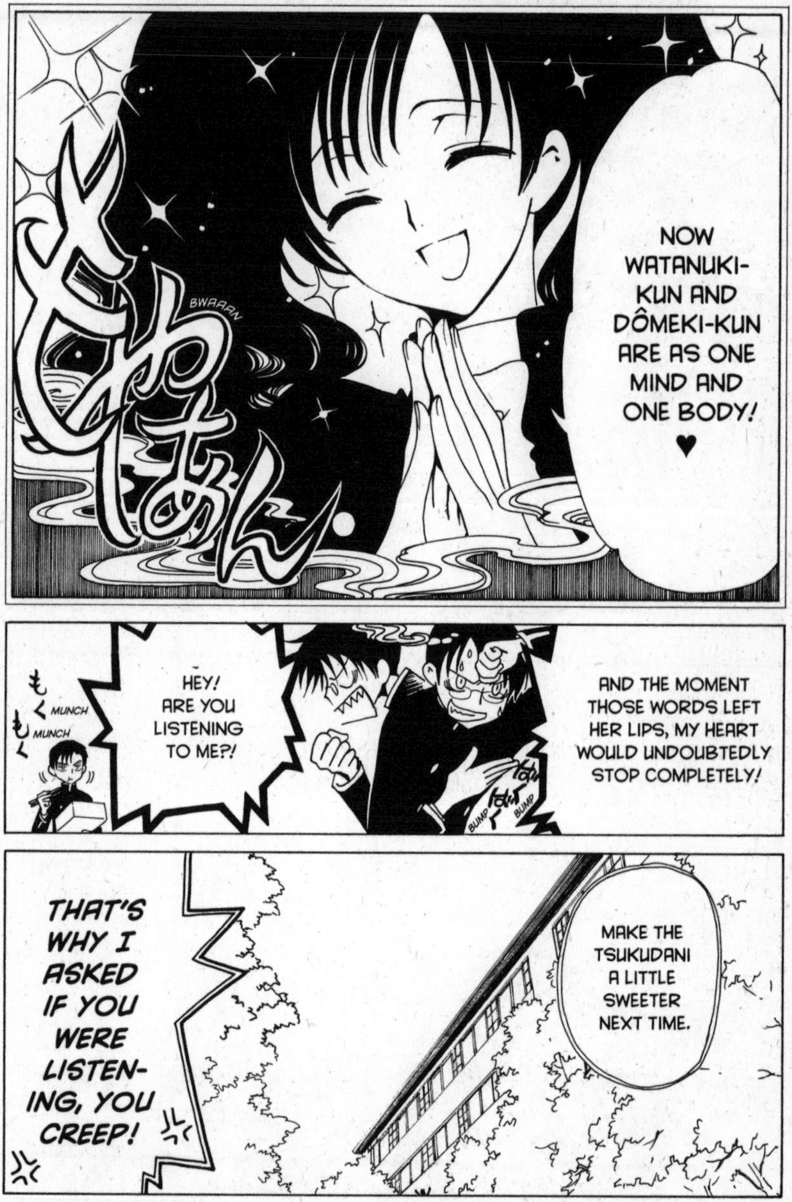
NOW WATANUKI-KUN AND DÔMEKI-KUN ARE AS ONE MIND AND ONE BODY! ♥
BWAAAN
AND THE MOMENT THOSE WORDS LEFT HER LIPS, MY HEART WOULD UNDOUBTEDLY STOP COMPLETELY!
BUMP BUMP
HEY! ARE YOU LISTENING TO ME?!
MUNCH MUNCH
MAKE THE TSUKUDANI A LITTLE SWEETER NEXT TIME.
THAT'S WHY I ASKED IF YOU WERE LISTEN-ING, YOU CREEP!

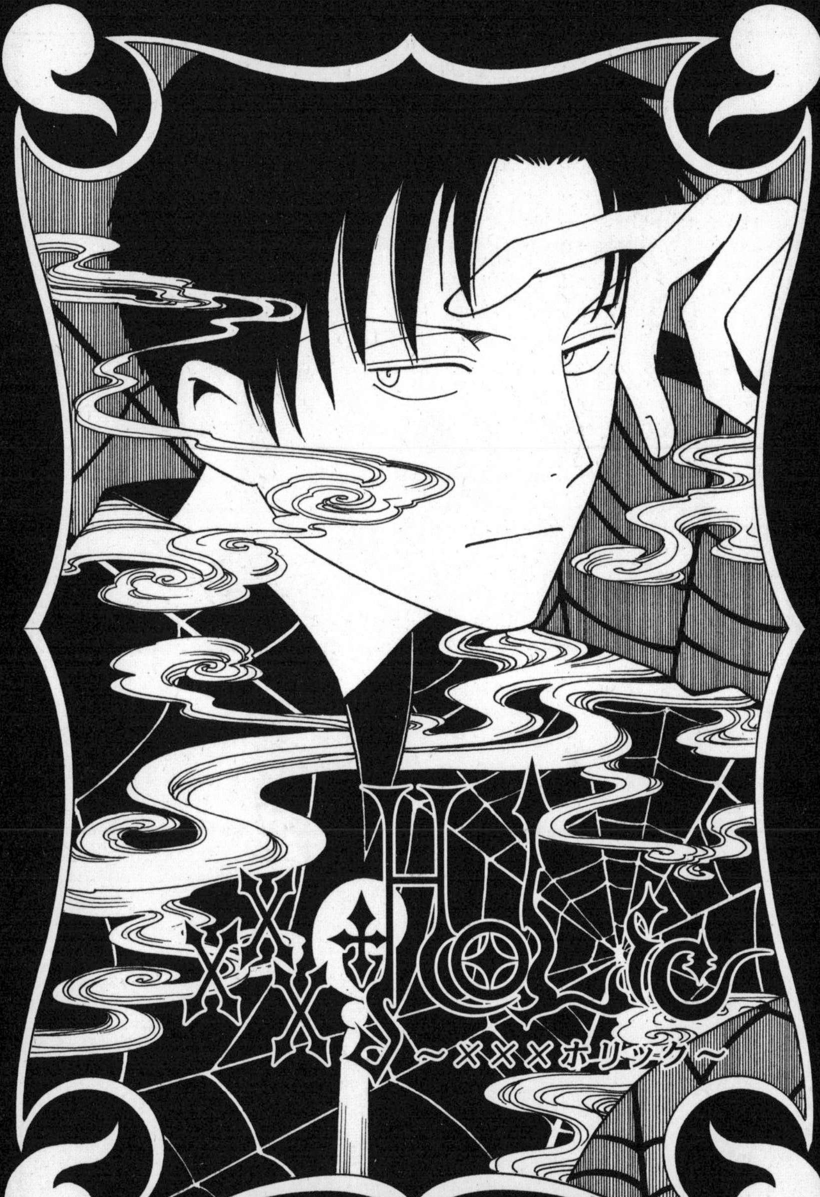
xxxHOLiC
〜×××ホリック〜

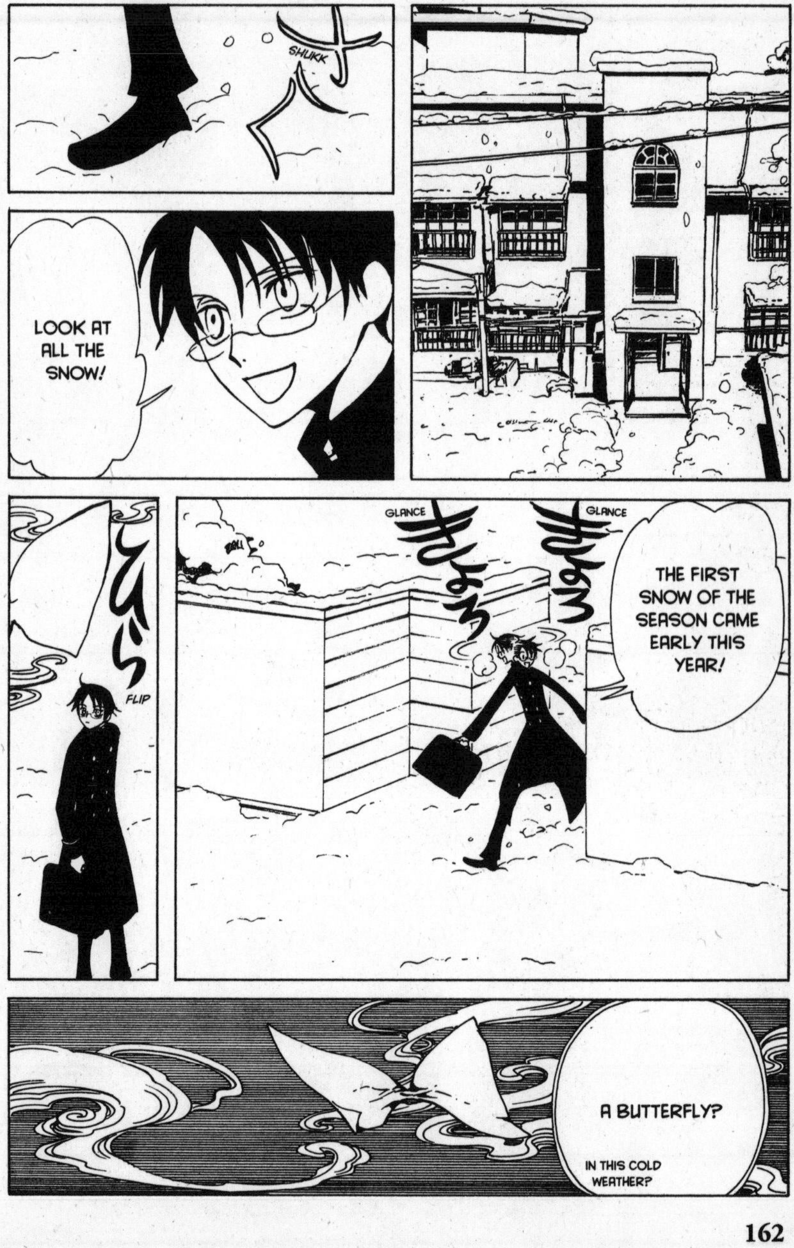
SHUKK
LOOK AT ALL THE SNOW!
THE FIRST SNOW OF THE SEASON CAME EARLY THIS YEAR!
きょろ
GLANCE
きょろ
GLANCE
ひら
FLIP
A BUTTERFLY?
IN THIS COLD WEATHER?

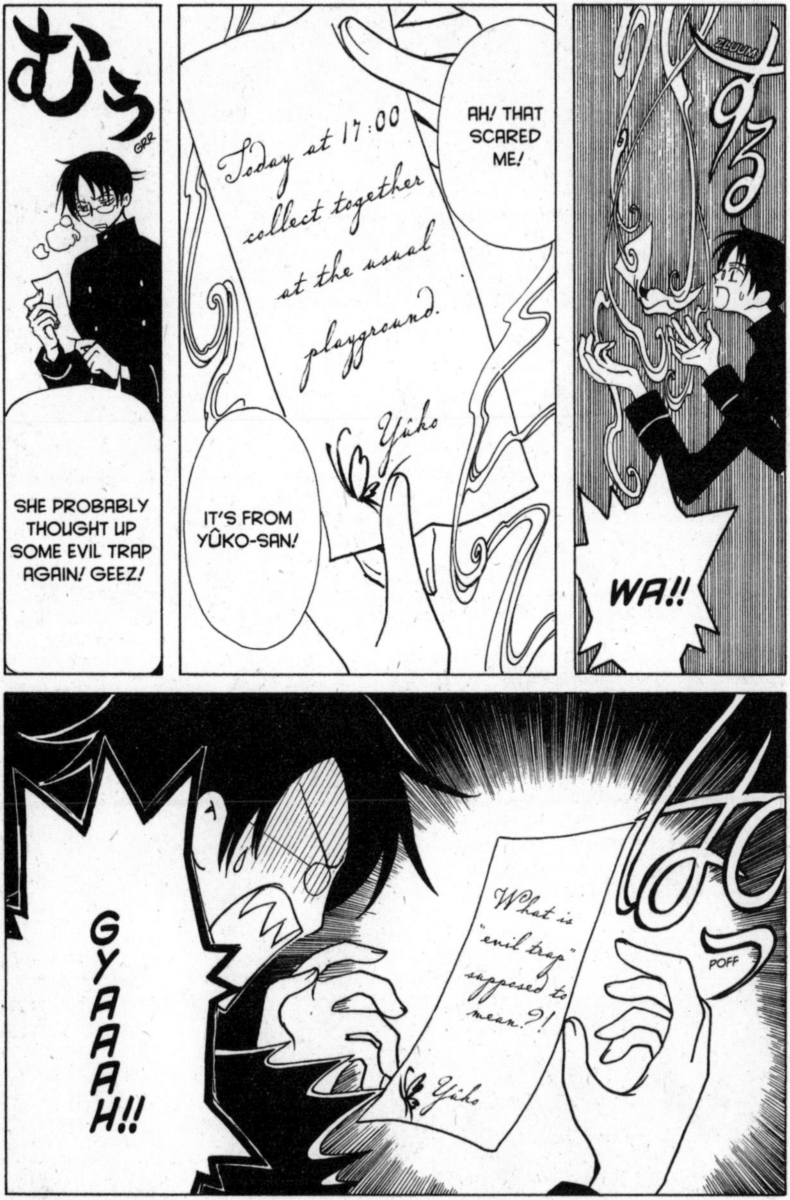
ZLUUM
する
WA!!
AH! THAT SCARED ME!
Today at 17:00 collect together at the usual playground.
Yûko
IT'S FROM YÛKO-SAN!
GRR
SHE PROBABLY THOUGHT UP SOME EVIL TRAP AGAIN! GEEZ!
POFF
What is "evil trap" supposed to mean?!
Yûko
GYAAAAH!!

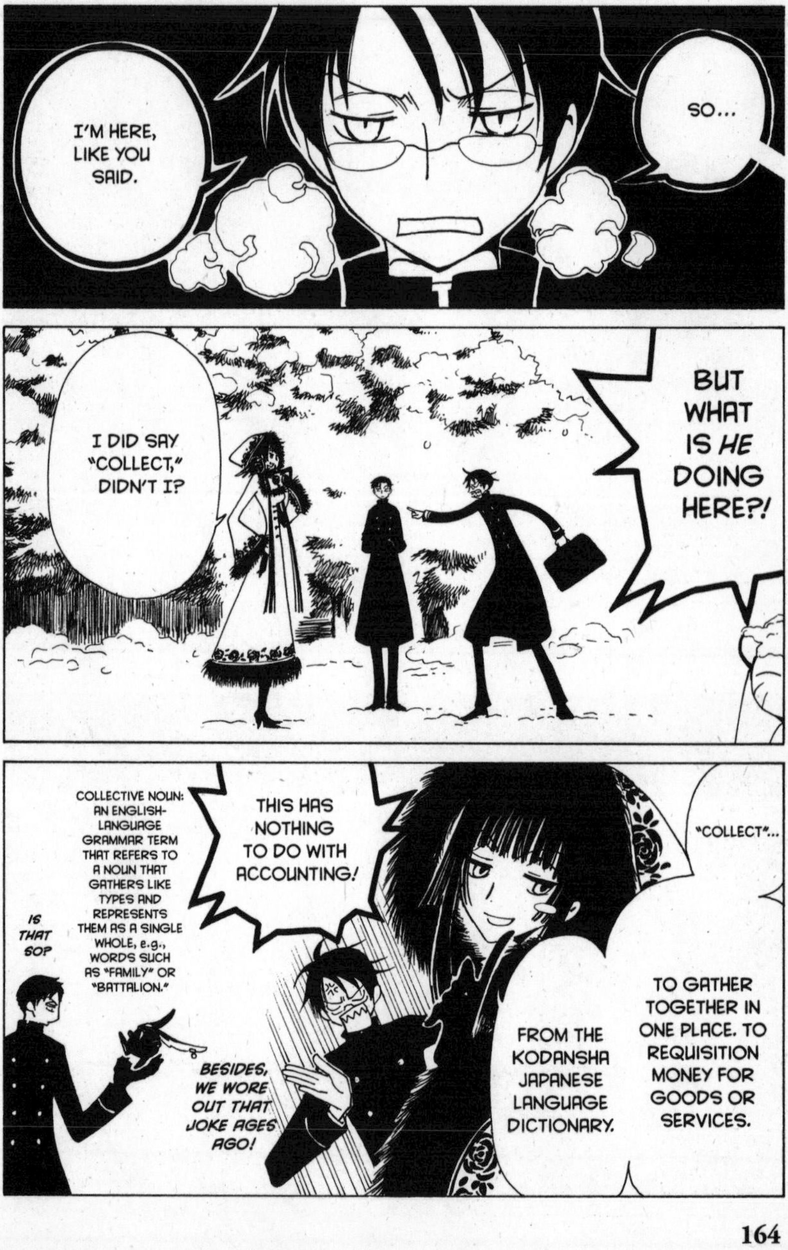
SO...
I'M HERE, LIKE YOU SAID.
BUT WHAT IS *HE* DOING HERE?!
I DID SAY "COLLECT," DIDN'T I?
"COLLECT"...
TO GATHER TOGETHER IN ONE PLACE. TO REQUISITION MONEY FOR GOODS OR SERVICES.
FROM THE KODANSHA JAPANESE LANGUAGE DICTIONARY.
THIS HAS NOTHING TO DO WITH ACCOUNTING!
BESIDES, WE WORE OUT THAT JOKE AGES AGO!
COLLECTIVE NOUN: AN ENGLISH-LANGUAGE GRAMMAR TERM THAT REFERS TO A NOUN THAT GATHERS LIKE TYPES AND REPRESENTS THEM AS A SINGLE WHOLE, e.g., WORDS SUCH AS "FAMILY" OR "BATTALION."
IS THAT SO?

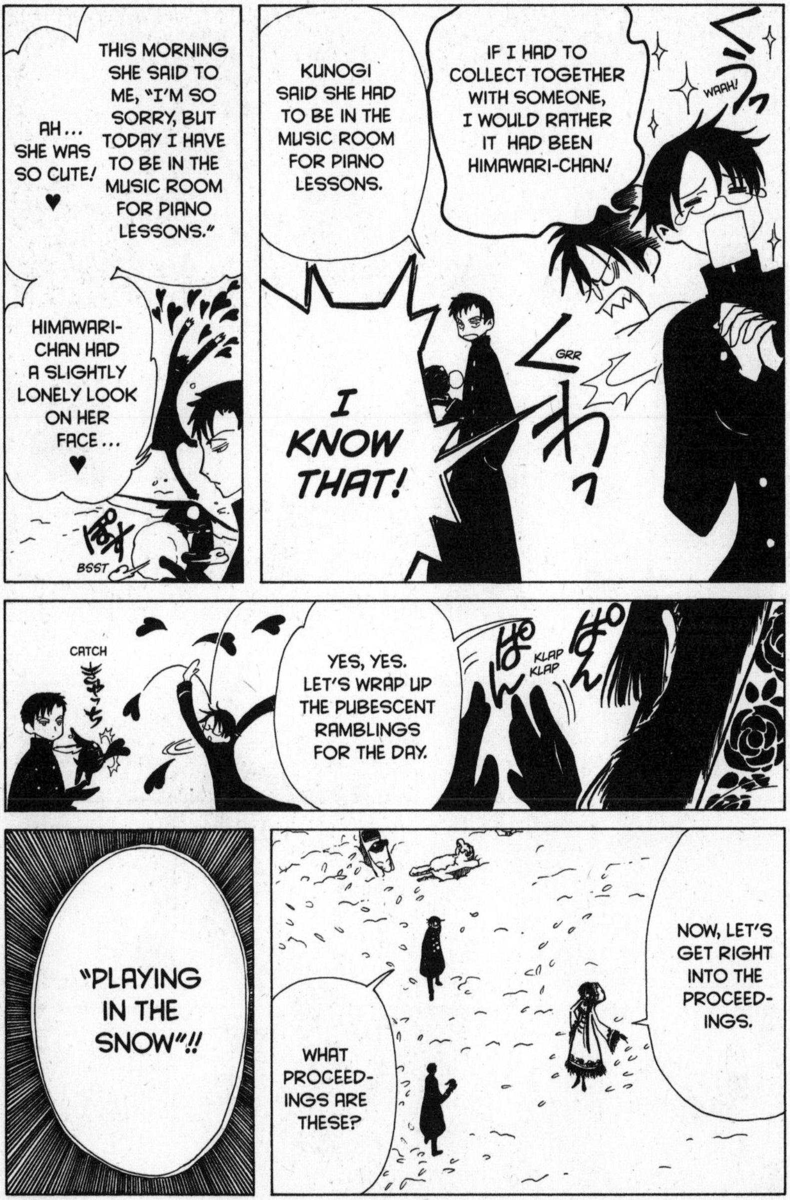
IF I HAD TO COLLECT TOGETHER WITH SOMEONE, I WOULD RATHER IT HAD BEEN HIMAWARI-CHAN!
WAAH!
KUNOGI SAID SHE HAD TO BE IN THE MUSIC ROOM FOR PIANO LESSONS.
GRR
I KNOW THAT!
THIS MORNING SHE SAID TO ME, "I'M SO SORRY, BUT TODAY I HAVE TO BE IN THE MUSIC ROOM FOR PIANO LESSONS."
AH... SHE WAS SO CUTE! ♥
HIMAWARI-CHAN HAD A SLIGHTLY LONELY LOOK ON HER FACE... ♥
BSST
KLAP KLAP
YES, YES. LET'S WRAP UP THE PUBESCENT RAMBLINGS FOR THE DAY.
CATCH
NOW, LET'S GET RIGHT INTO THE PROCEED-INGS.
WHAT PROCEED-INGS ARE THESE?
"PLAYING IN THE SNOW"!!

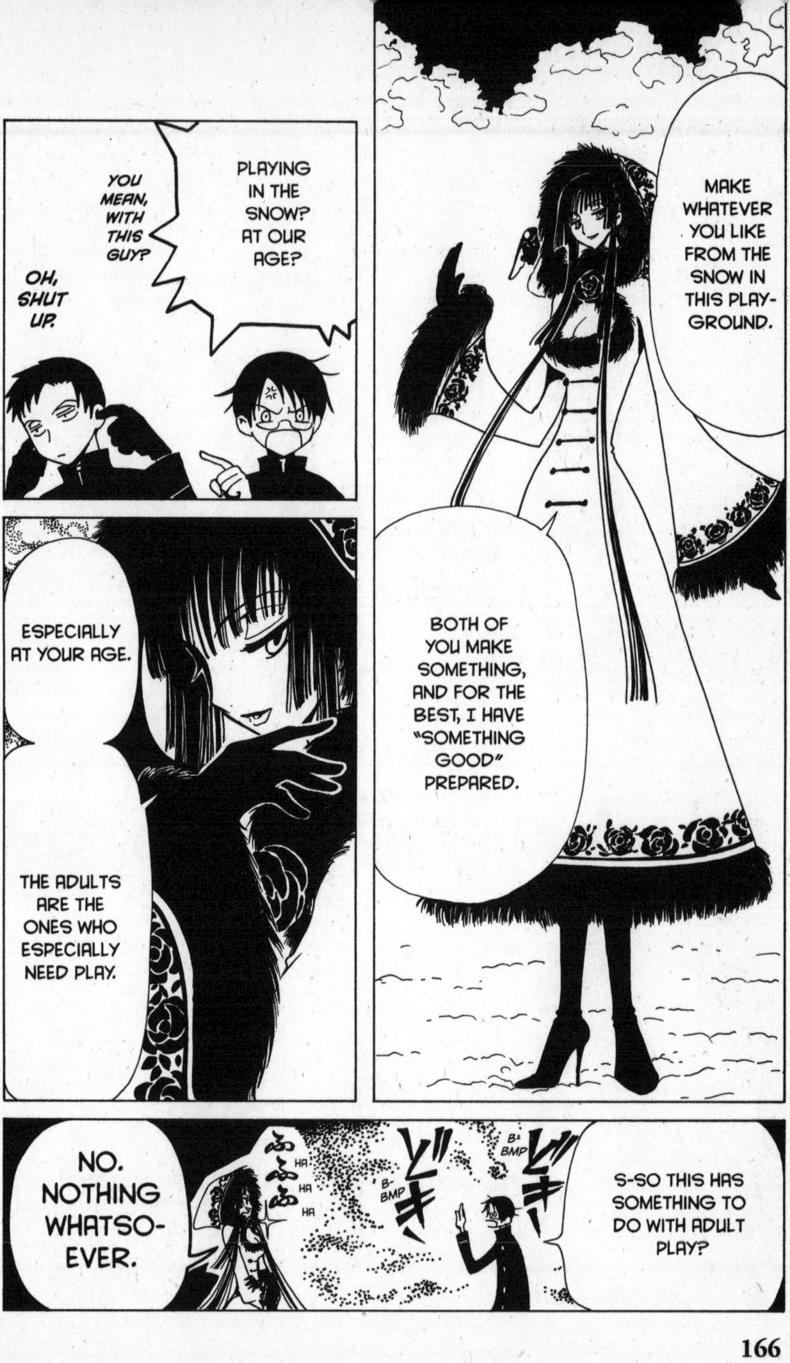
MAKE WHATEVER YOU LIKE FROM THE SNOW IN THIS PLAY-GROUND.
BOTH OF YOU MAKE SOMETHING, AND FOR THE BEST, I HAVE "SOMETHING GOOD" PREPARED.
PLAYING IN THE SNOW? AT OUR AGE?
YOU MEAN, WITH THIS GUY?
OH, SHUT UP.
ESPECIALLY AT YOUR AGE.
THE ADULTS ARE THE ONES WHO ESPECIALLY NEED PLAY.
S-SO THIS HAS SOMETHING TO DO WITH ADULT PLAY?
B-BMP
B-BMP
ふふふ
HA HA HA
NO. NOTHING WHATSO-EVER.

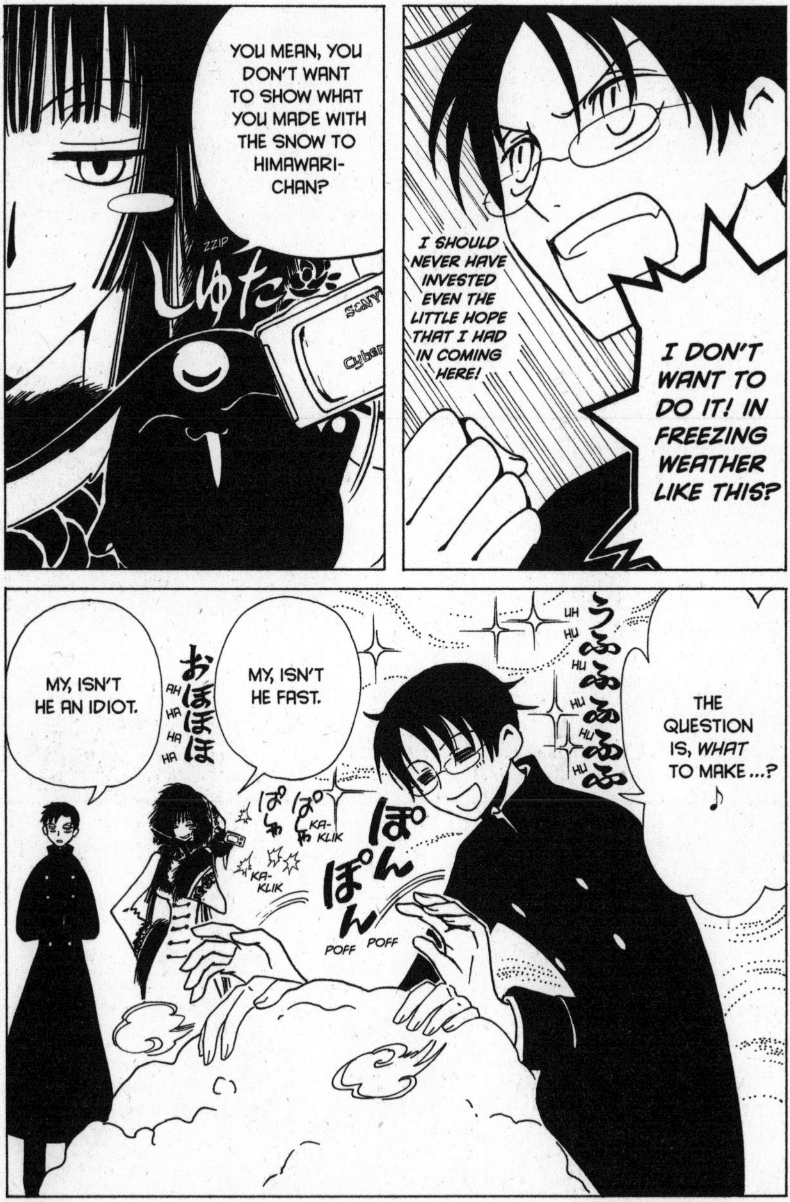
I DON'T WANT TO DO IT! IN FREEZING WEATHER LIKE THIS?
I SHOULD NEVER HAVE INVESTED EVEN THE LITTLE HOPE THAT I HAD IN COMING HERE!
YOU MEAN, YOU DON'T WANT TO SHOW WHAT YOU MADE WITH THE SNOW TO HIMAWARI-CHAN?
しゅた
ZZIP
THE QUESTION IS, WHAT TO MAKE...? ♪
うふふふふふ
UH HU HU HU HU HU
MY, ISN'T HE FAST.
おほほほ
AH HA HA HA HA
MY, ISN'T HE AN IDIOT.
ぱしゃ ぱしゃ
KA-KLIK
KA-KLIK
ぽんぽん
POFF POFF

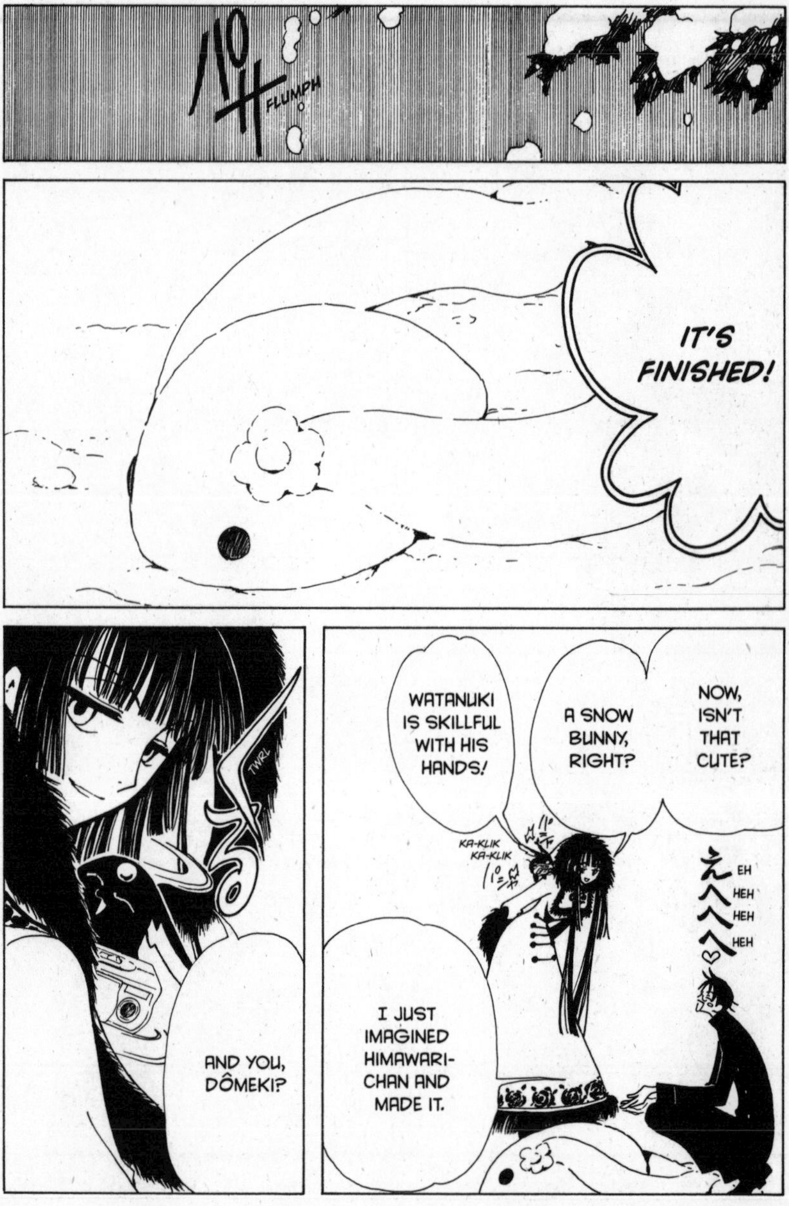
FLUMPH
IT'S FINISHED!
NOW, ISN'T THAT CUTE?
A SNOW BUNNY, RIGHT?
WATANUKI IS SKILLFUL WITH HIS HANDS!
えへへへ
EH HEH HEH HEH
KA-KLIK KA-KLIK
I JUST IMAGINED HIMAWARI-CHAN AND MADE IT.
TWRL
AND YOU, DÔMEKI?

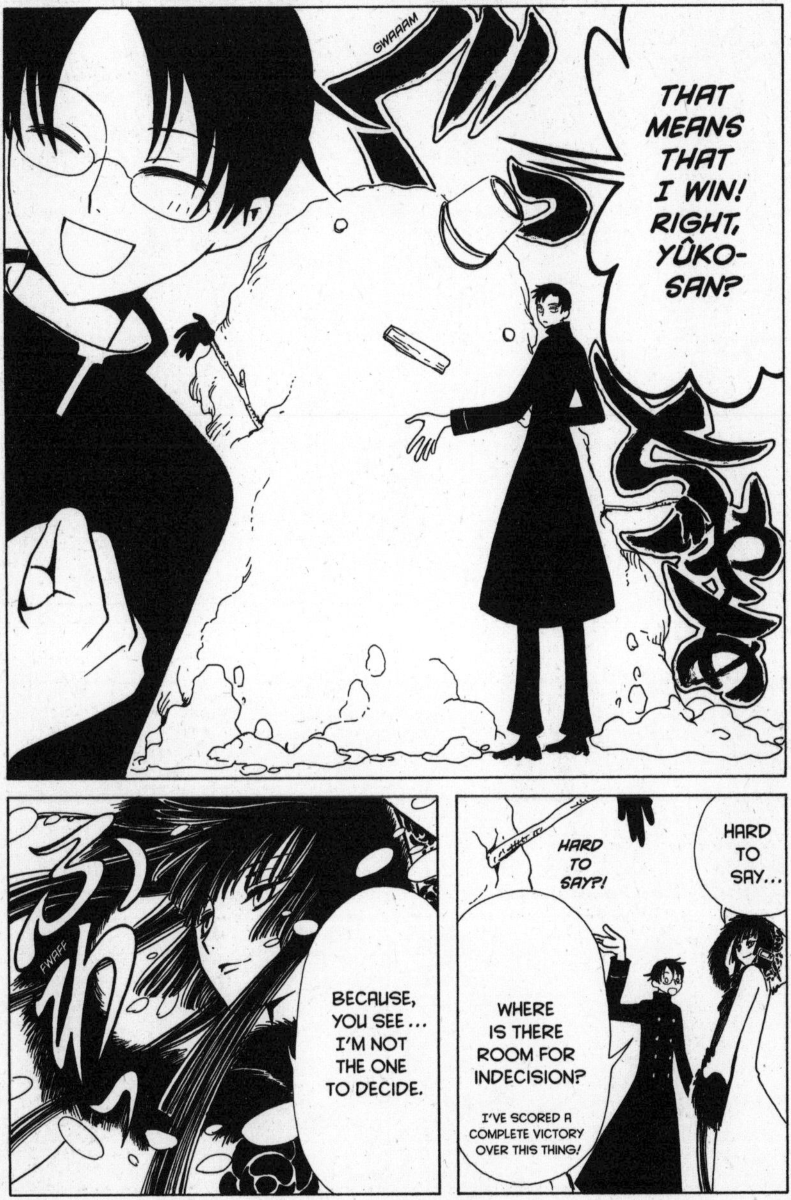
GWAAAM
THAT MEANS THAT I WIN! RIGHT, YÛKO-SAN?
HARD TO SAY...
HARD TO SAY?!
WHERE IS THERE ROOM FOR INDECISION?
I'VE SCORED A COMPLETE VICTORY OVER THIS THING!
FWAFF
BECAUSE, YOU SEE... I'M NOT THE ONE TO DECIDE.

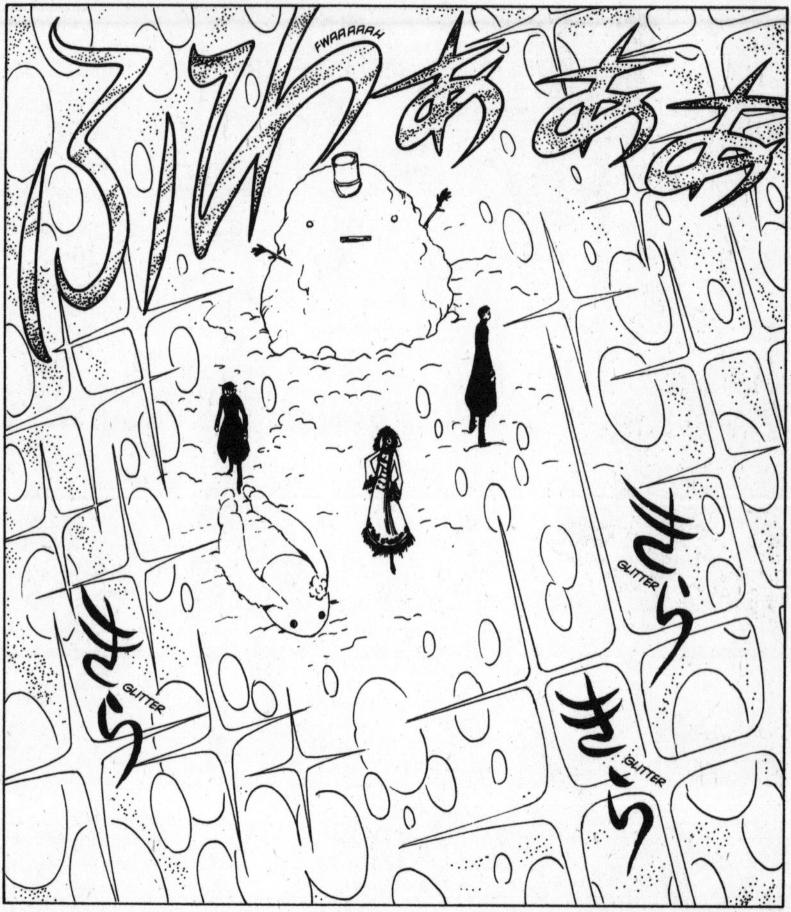
ふわあああ
FWAAAAAH
きら
GLITTER
きら
GLITTER
きら
GLITTER
きら

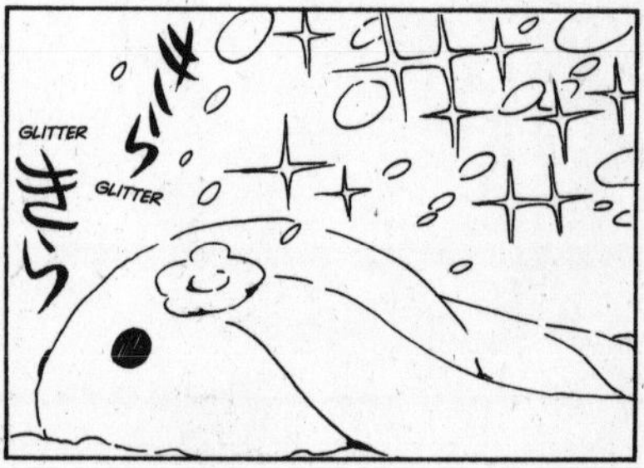
きら
GLITTER
きら
GLITTER

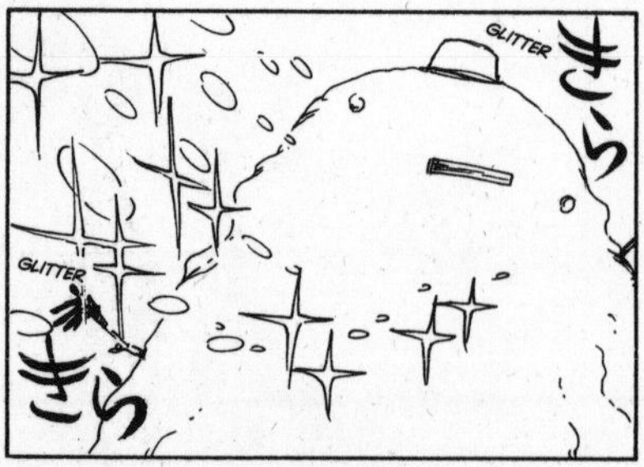
GLITTER
きら
GLITTER
きら

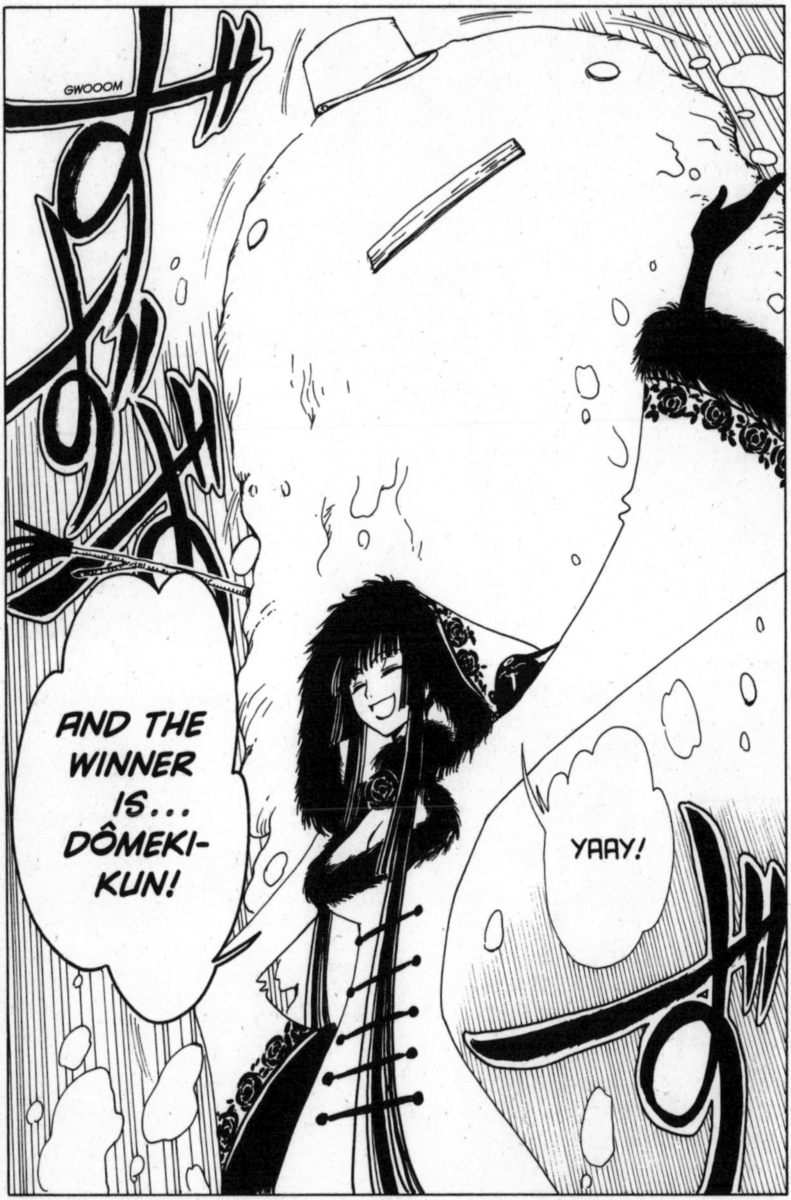
GWOOOM
AND THE WINNER IS... DÔMEKI-KUN!
YAAY!

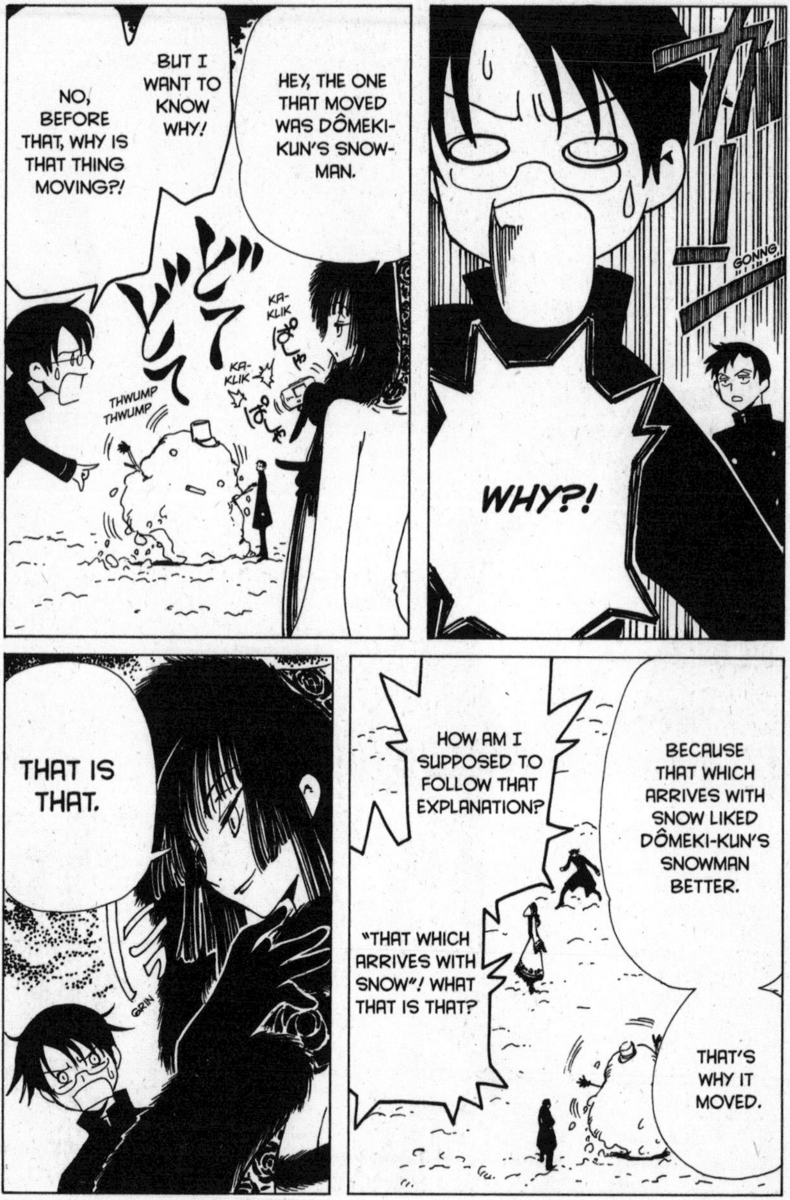
GONNG
WHY?!
HEY, THE ONE THAT MOVED WAS DÔMEKI-KUN'S SNOW-MAN.
BUT I WANT TO KNOW WHY!
NO, BEFORE THAT, WHY IS THAT THING MOVING?!
KA-KLIK
KA-KLIK
THWUMP THWUMP
BECAUSE THAT WHICH ARRIVES WITH SNOW LIKED DÔMEKI-KUN'S SNOWMAN BETTER.
THAT'S WHY IT MOVED.
HOW AM I SUPPOSED TO FOLLOW THAT EXPLANATION?
"THAT WHICH ARRIVES WITH SNOW"! WHAT THAT IS THAT?
THAT IS THAT.
GRIN

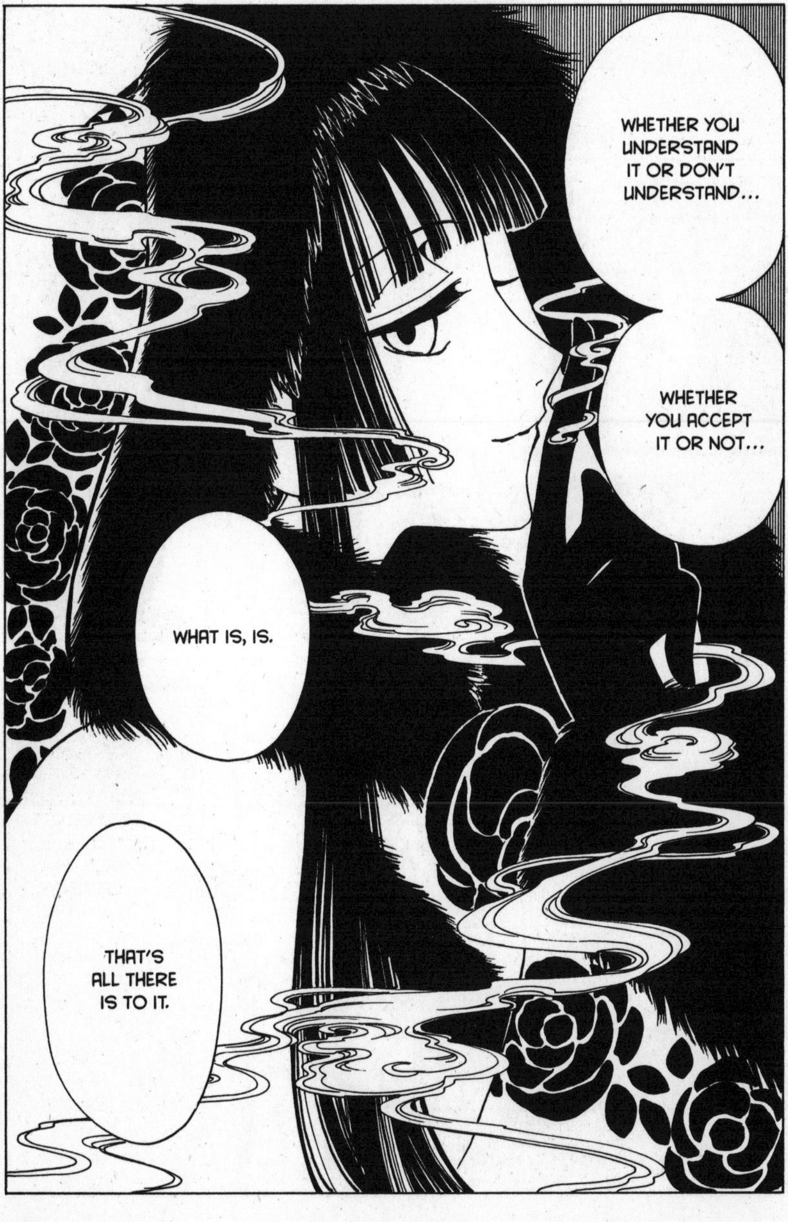
WHETHER YOU UNDERSTAND IT OR DON'T UNDERSTAND...
WHETHER YOU ACCEPT IT OR NOT...
WHAT IS, IS.
THAT'S ALL THERE IS TO IT.

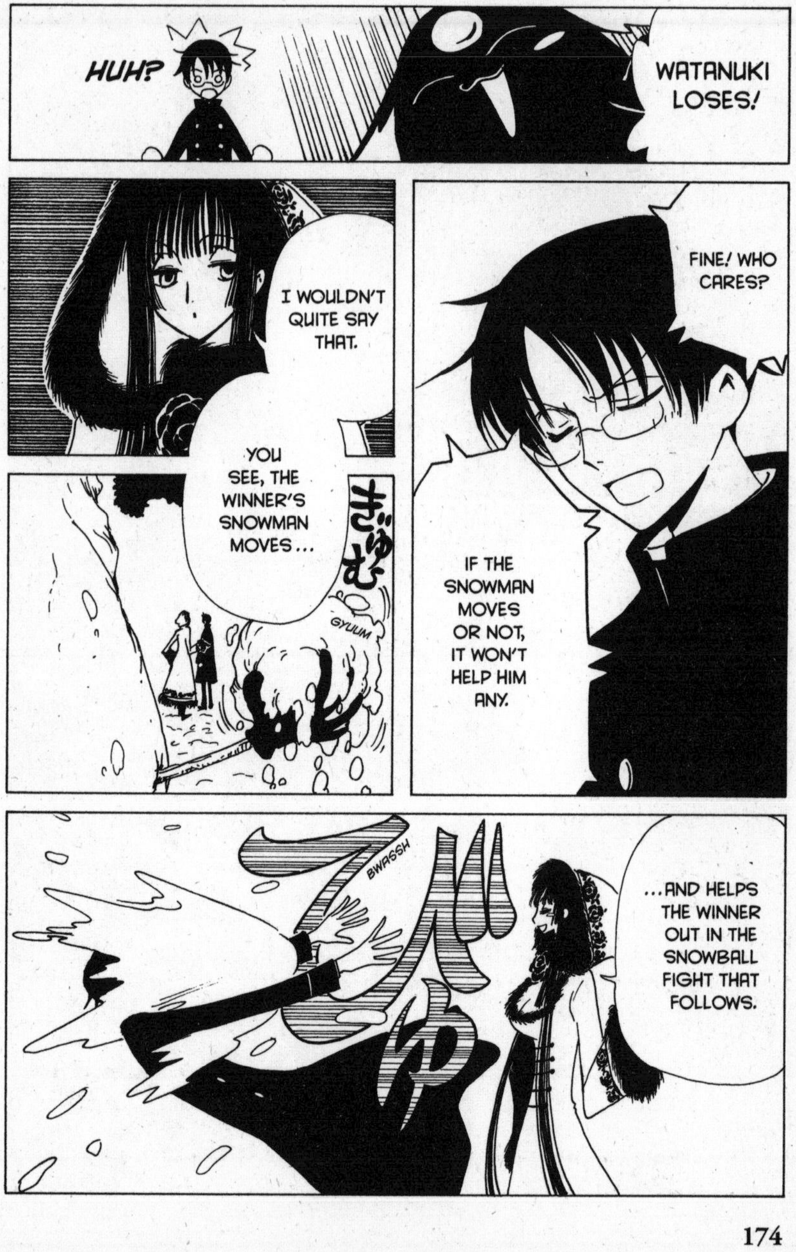
WATANUKI LOSES!
HUH?
FINE! WHO CARES?
IF THE SNOWMAN MOVES OR NOT, IT WON'T HELP HIM ANY.
I WOULDN'T QUITE SAY THAT.
YOU SEE, THE WINNER'S SNOWMAN MOVES...
ぎゅむ
GYUUM
...AND HELPS THE WINNER OUT IN THE SNOWBALL FIGHT THAT FOLLOWS.
BWASSH

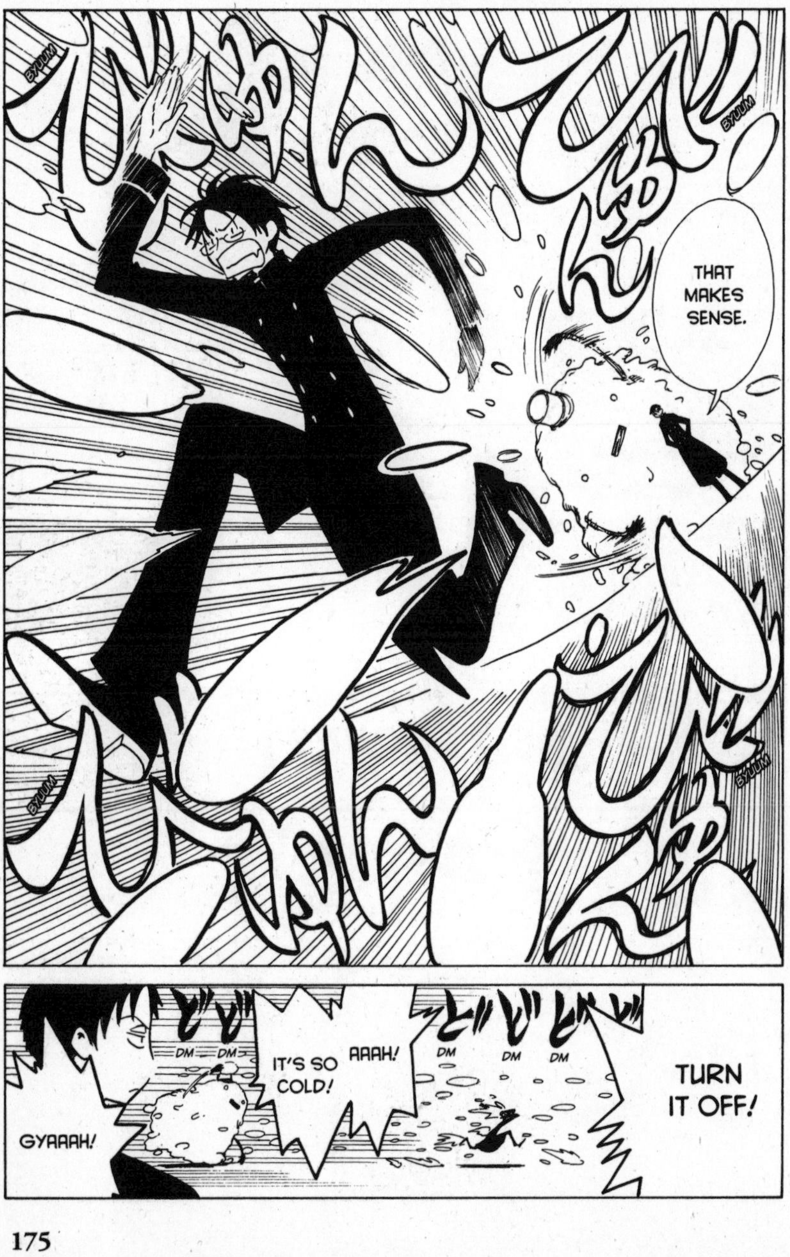
BYUUM
BYUUM
THAT MAKES SENSE.
BYUUM
BYUUM
TURN IT OFF!
DM DM DM
AAAH!
IT'S SO COLD!
DM DM
GYAAAH!

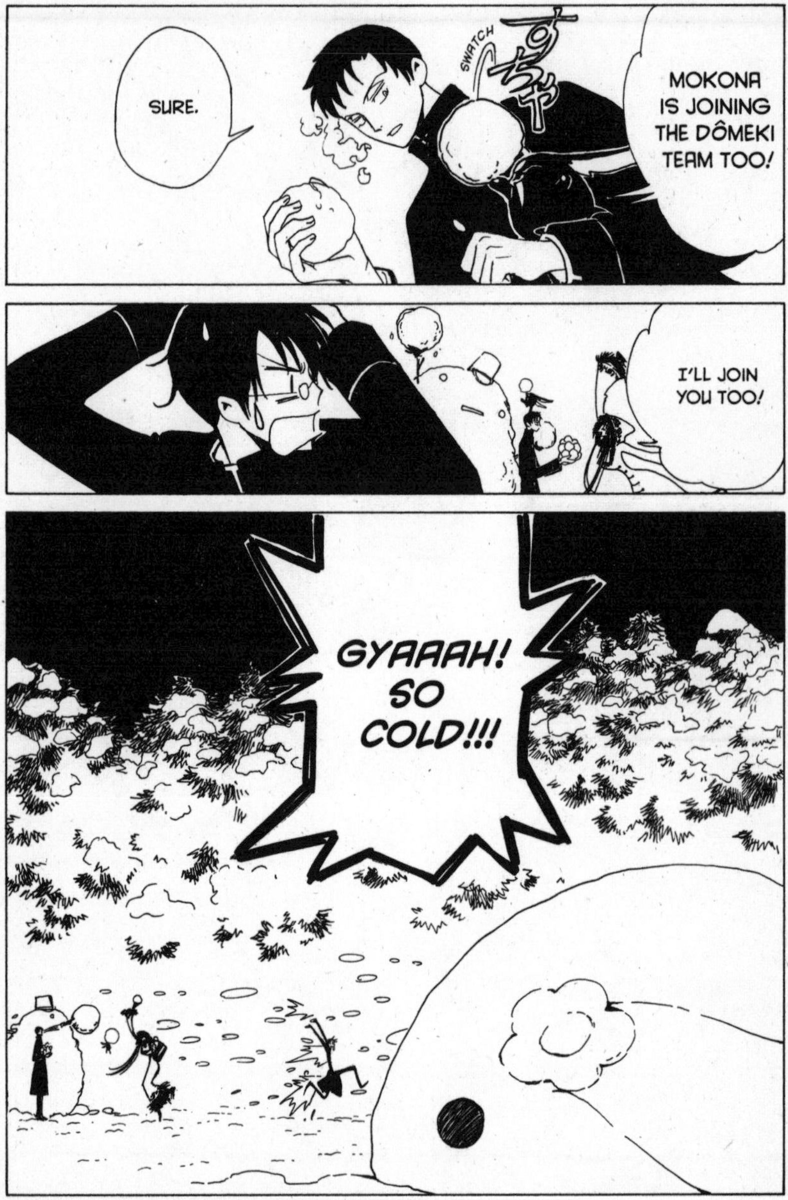
MOKONA IS JOINING THE DÔMEKI TEAM TOO!
SWATCH
SURE.
I'LL JOIN YOU TOO!
GYAAAH! SO COLD!!!

~≈ Continued ≈~

in *xxxHOLiC* Volume 9

About the Creators

CLAMP is a group of four women who have become the most popular manga artists in America—Satsuki Igarashi, Tsubaki Nekoi, Mokona, and Ageha Ohkawa. They started out as *doujinshi* (fan comics) creators, but their skill and craft brought them to the attention of publishers very quickly. Their first work from a major publisher was *RG Veda,* but their first mass success was with *Magic Knight Rayearth*. From there, they went on to write many series, including Cardcaptor Sakura and Chobits, two of the most popular manga in the United States. Like many Japanese manga artists, they prefer to avoid the spotlight, and little is known about them personally.

CLAMP is currently publishing three series in Japan: Tsubasa and xxxHOLiC with Kodansha and *Gohou Drug* with Kadokawa.

Translation Notes

For your edification and reading pleasure, here are notes to help you understand some of the cultural and story references from our translation of xxxHOLiC.

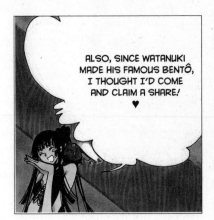

ALSO, SINCE WATANUKI MADE HIS FAMOUS BENTÔ, I THOUGHT I'D COME AND CLAIM A SHARE! ♥

Page 1, Bentô

The traditional boxed lunch of Japan usually features a main course on a bed of rice and includes pickled veggies, salad, cooked egg, and other foods along with sweet beans for dessert. But the term *bentô* has been expanded to mean just about any meal that can be taken from place to place.

Page 4, Flowing Somen

Chilled noodles sent down a bamboo chute. (See a more detailed explanation in the notes for volume 7.)

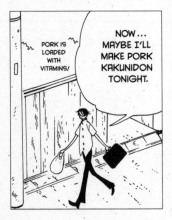

NOW... MAYBE I'LL MAKE PORK KAKUNIDON TONIGHT.
PORK IS LOADED WITH VITAMINS!

Page 10, Pork Kakunidon

Pork that is cubed and boiled to make a topping for a ricebowl-style meal.

Page 17, *Neko-Musume*

Unlike the modern *Neko-Musume* (cat girl) that's popularly depicted in anime, the traditional *Neko-Musume* is a cat that can transform into the shape of a young girl. Sometimes her catlike attributes stay in place (ears, eyes, tail, etc.) and sometimes they don't. As a

Neko-Musume gets older, it may become a *Nekomata* and gain additional odd powers.

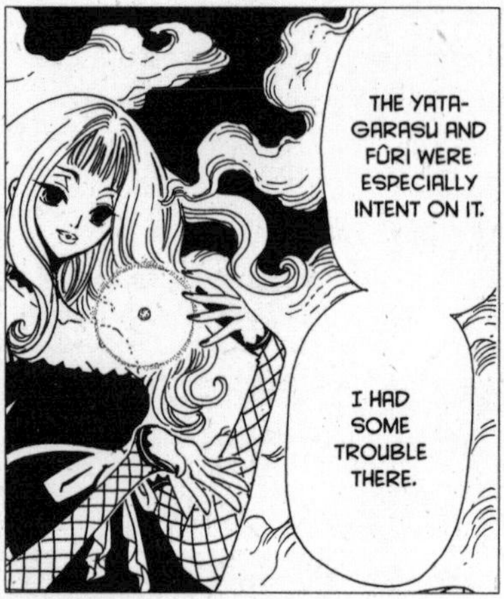
THE YATA-GARASU AND FÛRI WERE ESPECIALLY INTENT ON IT.
I HAD SOME TROUBLE THERE.

Page 67, Yata-garasu

A bird that both inhabits and represents the sun exists throughout East Asian mythology. In Japan it is the bird of Amaterasu, the sun goddess—a raven called Yata-garasu.

Page 67, Fûri

The name includes the characters for wind and *tanuki* (the badger spirit), and as the characters imply, it's a storm *tanuki* with great magical powers.

Page 69, Jorô-Gumo

Literally it means the Prostitute Spider. The Jorô-Gumo as it exists today is an orb spider with the Latin name *Nephila clavata*. There are tales of a mystical Jorô-Gumo from the Izu peninsula that depict her as the beautiful mistress of a waterfall who tries to ensnare a man in her webs and plunge him to his death. In another story, she takes fatal revenge for a broken promise.

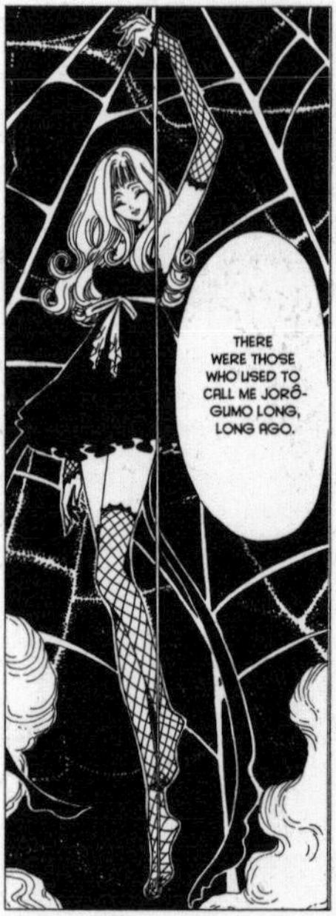
THERE WERE THOSE WHO USED TO CALL ME JORÔ-GUMO LONG, LONG AGO.

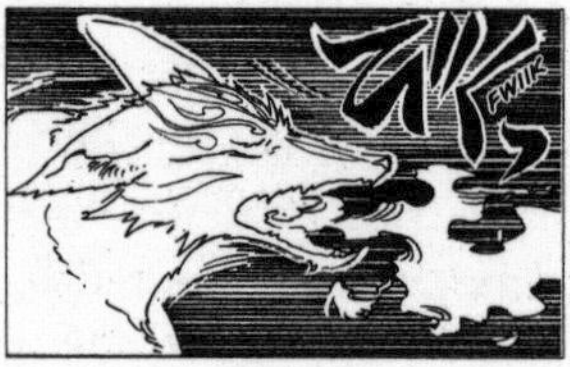
FWIIK

Page 72, Fox-Fire

The Japanese is *kitsunebi*, which translates directly to Fox-Fire.

THANK YOU FOR PROVIDING THE MEAL.

Page 90, Thank You for the Meal (*Gochisô-sama*)

Many standard set phrases are used in daily life in Japan. When finishing a meal, one says what the Jorô-Gumo said: *Gochisô-sama*, which means, "You have provided a feast." (See a more detailed explanation in the notes for volume 7.)

Page 99, Welcome Home (*Okaerinasai*)

Another standard phrase in Japanese is used when one comes back to a place where one belongs (usually home, but it can also refer to one's workplace or a frequently visited restaurant, etc.). Those already there greet the returnee with *okaerinasai*, which can be translated as "welcome home." The returnee usually says *tadaima*, which means "just now" but can be translated to "I'm home!"

WELCOME HOME.

I'M A LIGHTNING MANIPULATOR

OVER THE YEARS PEOPLE'VE CALLED ME RAIJÛ, AMONG OTHER NAMES.

Page 116, Watanuki-sama

One does not usually refer to oneself with an honorific. But in this case, Kimihiro is trying to point out that he did something selfless and deserves respect for it.

Page 137, Raijû

The name Raijû is made up of the kanji for "thunder" and "beast." In Japanese mythology, it usually appears in the form of living creatures such as cats or monkeys, but there are cases of it taking flight as a ball of lightning or fire. Raijû is the companion of Raiden, the Shinto god of lightning. Marks of lightning on a tree are said to be made by Raijû's claws.

Page 139, *Darling* and *cha*

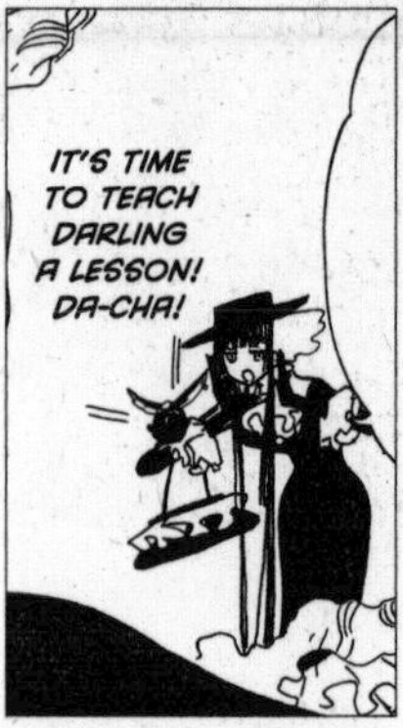
IT'S TIME TO TEACH DARLING A LESSON! DA-CHA!

Devotees of old-school otaku obsessions would recognize this as a standard line from the Rumiko Takahashi classic manga and anime, *Urusei Yatsura*. For those who don't recognize it, the story features Lum, a cute oni-like (Japanese ogre) alien with the power to emit electric shocks. She winds up engaged to her "darling," a high-school boy, Ataru, who is the world's biggest skirt-chaser. When he shows interest in anyone other than Lum, she punishes him with electric shocks. She ends nearly all of her dialogue with the relatively meaningless but very cute *-cha* or *da-cha* sentence-ending particle.

Page 160, Tsukudani

A mixture of sweet beans, seaweed, fish, and meat that is preserved by boiling it down in soy with some *mirin* (Japanese sweet wine) added. These are usually served as a side dish or as a topping for rice.

Page 164, Collect

The word Yûko used and then defined was *shûgô*, and the second dictionary meaning of the word was to put numbers together in mathematic sets, to which Kimihiro replied that math has nothing to do with the situation. Unfortunately, we couldn't find an official mathematic translation for "collect" (there probably is one, but we didn't find it), so we went with the accounting meaning of the English word. A more natural word would have been "gather," however the word Mokona was defining in the same panel was the related word "collective noun" (*shûgô-meishi* in Japanese), and so to stay with the closest possible translation, we stuck with the word "collect."

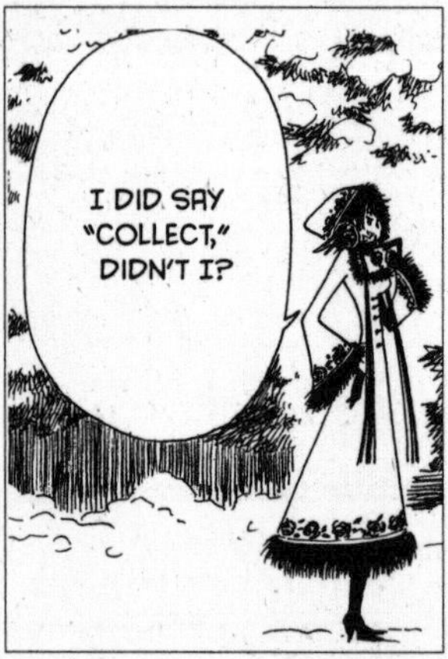
I DID SAY "COLLECT," DIDN'T I?

Sugar Sugar Rune

BY MOYOCO ANNO

QUEEN OF HEARTS

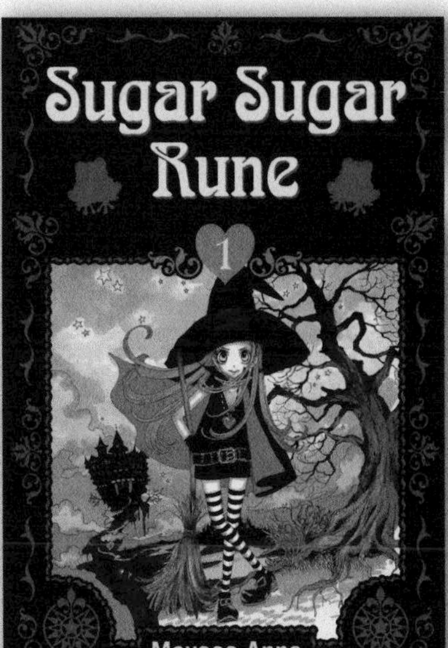

Sugar Sugar Rune
1
Moyoco Anno

Chocolat and Vanilla are young witch princesses from a magical land. They've come to Earth to compete in a contest—whichever girl captures the most hearts will become queen! While living in a boarding school, they must make as many boys fall in love with them as possible if they want to achieve their goal. Standing against them are a pair of rival princes looking to capture their hearts because they want to be king!

There's danger for the witch-girls, though: If they give their hearts to a human, they may never return to the Magical World....

Ages: 10 +

Special extras in each volume! Read them all!

DEL REY

VISIT WWW.DELREYMANGA.COM TO:

- **View release date calendars for upcoming volumes**
- **Sign up for Del Rey's free manga e-newsletter**
- **Find out the latest about new Del Rey Manga series**

BY JIN KOBAYASHI

SUBTLETY IS FOR WIMPS!

She . . . is a second-year high school student with a single all-consuming question: Will the boy she likes ever really notice her?

He . . . is the school's most notorious juvenile delinquent, and he's suddenly come to a shocking realization: He's got a huge crush, and now he must tell her how he feels.

Life-changing obsessions, colossal foul-ups, grand schemes, deep-seated anxieties, and raging hormones—School Rumble portrays high school as it really is: over-the-top comedy!

Ages: 16 +

Special extras in each volume! Read them all!

GHOST HUNT

MANGA BY SHIHO INADA
STORY BY FUYUMI ONO

The decrepit building was con-demned long ago, but every time the owners try to tear it down, "acci-dents" start to happen—people get hurt, sometimes even killed. Mai Taniyama and her classmates have heard the rumors that the creepy old high school is haunted. So, one rainy day they gather to tell ghost stories, hoping to attract one of the suspected spirits. No ghosts materialize, but they do meet Kazuya Shibuya, the handsome young owner of Shibuya Psychic Research, hired to investigate paranormal activity at the school. Also brought to the scene are an exorcist, a Buddhist monk, a woman who can speak with the dead, and an outspoken Shinto priestess. Surely one of them will have the talents to solve this mystery. . . .

Ages: 13+

Special extras in each volume! Read them all!

VISIT WWW.DELREYMANGA.COM TO:
- Read sample pages
- View release date calendars for upcoming volumes
- Sign up for Del Rey's free manga e-newsletter

TOMARE!

[STOP!]

You're going the wrong way!

Manga is a completely different type of reading experience.

To start at the *beginning*, go to the *end*!

That's right! Authentic manga is read the traditional Japanese way—from right to left. Exactly the *opposite* of how American books are read. It's easy to follow: Just go to the other end of the book, and read each page—and each panel—from right side to left side, starting at the top right. Now you're experiencing manga as it was meant to be!